RAINBOWS IN THE MUD
INSIDE THE INTOXICATING WORLD OF CYCLOCROSS

PAUL MAUNDER

BLOOMSBURY
LONDON · OXFORD · NEW YORK · NEW DELHI · SYDNEY

Bloomsbury Sport
An imprint of Bloomsbury Publishing Plc

50 Bedford Square	1385 Broadway
London	New York
WC1B 3DP	NY 10018
UK	USA

www.bloomsbury.com

BLOOMSBURY and the Diana logo are trademarks of Bloomsbury Publishing Plc

First published 2017

© Paul Maunder 2017

Paul Maunder has asserted his right under the Copyright, Designs and Patents Act, 1988, to be identified as Author of this work.

All rights reserved. No part of this publication may be reproduced or transmitted in any form or by any means, electronic or mechanical, including photocopying, recording, or any information storage or retrieval system, without prior permission in writing from the publishers.

No responsibility for loss caused to any individual or organization acting on or refraining from action as a result of the material in this publication can be accepted by Bloomsbury or the author.

British Library Cataloguing-in-Publication Data
A catalogue record for this book is available from the British Library.

Library of Congress Cataloguing-in-Publication data has been applied for.

ISBN: TPB: 978-1-4729-2595-4
ePub: 978-1-4729-2596-1

2 4 6 8 10 9 7 5 3 1

Typeset in Adobe Garamond Pro by Deanta Global Publishing Services, Chennai, India
Printed and bound in Great Britain by CPI Group (UK) Ltd, Croydon CR0 4YY

To find out more about our authors and books visit www.bloomsbury.com. Here you will find extracts, author interviews, details of forthcoming events and the option to sign up for our newsletters.

For Lesley, Anya, Oscar and Amelia

Contents

Prologue: Into the Forest — vii

1. Summer Rain — 1
2. Cross is Coming — 9
3. The Drop of Death — 29
4. Edgelands — 33
5. Punks and Sharks — 40
6. Under the Rainbow — 60
7. The Flemish Fairground — 70
8. An Education — 86
9. Into the Dunes — 94
10. The Method of Torture — 115
11. Live Transmission — 137
12. Storming the Citadel — 158
13. Midwinter — 179
14. The Deep South — 190
15. Climbing the Mountain — 214
16. If the Shoes Fit — 223
17. A Lifetime — 262

Acknowledgements — 269
Index — 270

Prologue
Into the Forest

Everyone remembers their first bike race. Mine was a cyclocross race around a scrap of farmland near Oxford. November 1985, by my reckoning. I was 11 years old, and about to fall in love.

I had no idea what a cyclocross race was, but my dad must have done some research because he'd procured for me a pair of hockey boots with studded soles. We did a pre-race lap of the circuit and discussed where to ride and where to push. I was astonished. They expected us to ride our bikes through these thickets, up this steep muddy path and back down this precipitous drop? Were they insane?

There were three of us on the start line. One of my rivals had a better bike than me, and proper cyclocross shoes, but was only nine years old. The other kid wore wellies. Alongside our three dads there were two race officials. No spectators, although the cows in an adjacent shed did look mildly interested. The flag dropped. I moved into an early lead and never relinquished it. I'd won my first race. My prize for victory? Three Mars Bars. The road to a professional contract with a European team unfurled before me. Going to school the next day seemed pretty pointless. This muddy patch of Oxfordshire countryside was the scene of something significant.

After our Under-12s race, the seniors took to the mud. Their race was on a bigger loop taking in a ploughed field and some rather spectacular drop-offs. After the race some of the hardier souls washed themselves using water from a cattle-drinking trough. My dad and I watched in awe and fascination. What was this crazy sport we'd stumbled into?

Cyclocross has always been present in my life. It's how I started racing, and though I loved it then, it always seemed only to be a gateway drug. You moved on to road racing in your mid-teenage years, because that was where fame and glory awaited. For many years in my twenties and thirties life diverted me from cyclocross. It was only when I had children that the fire was rekindled. For a year my daughter had a habit of bouncing out of bed at five o'clock, and my wife and I took turns to be dragged downstairs with her. One dark November morning I was sitting at the kitchen table, precious mug of tea in hand, brain fuddled, browsing cycling websites when I came across a link to a cyclocross video. Beside me my daughter was tucking into toast and jam and watching *Sesame Street* videos on her iPad. When you have children you rediscover all the things you responded to when you were young, like Lego and remote-control monster trucks. Perhaps cyclocross fitted into that category of memories being dredged. Anyway, I clicked. Sporza's Belgian commentators began a heroic competition with Elmo and the rest of the *Sesame Street* crew.

My recollection of seeing cyclocross on television during the late eighties – a rare event – was of a grimly muddy, foggy and confusing affair. Quintessentially British, in other words. Yet here were pin-sharp images of brightly clad riders charging around a

Belgian field, huge digital screens in the background, thick crowds and riotous advertising banners everywhere. This was something I could get into.

Soon a Sunday afternoon ritual developed. While a chicken roasted in the oven and rain trickled down the windows, Anya and I would sit together and watch the live feed from whichever Superprestige, Bpost bank trophy or World Cup race was on. I joked to friends that she was the only three-year-old in south-east London who could speak Dutch. They looked back at me with a mixture of scepticism and pity.

My daughter soon got bored, but for me the love affair took hold. I consumed everything I could find about the sport. My knowledge grew. I went to races at home and abroad, got to know people involved in the sport, began to write about it.

*

Thirty years after that first race near Oxford and I'm standing on another patch of mud watching a cyclocross race, my wife and two young children are with me, and this time we're in Milton Keynes, a mere 30 miles from the scene of my first race. Around us are ten thousand fans, all ringing cowbells and yelling and pumping air-horns. Ten thousand fans at a cyclocross race in Britain. It's a UCI World Cup race, the highest level of the sport, and despite the name it's the first time a World Cup round has been held outside mainland Europe. Next to the coffee and doughnuts van there is a smart marquee, with diners inside enjoying lunch on pristine white tablecloths. A security man is stationed at the entrance, and a corporate banner flutters in the wind. A corporate tent. At a cyclocross race in Britain. I shake my head in disbelief.

On the faces of the crowd are expressions of delight, excitement, admiration. And some, those of a certain age, just look pleasantly stunned. Their sport – and cyclocross does inspire passionate feelings of kinship – has gone from the periphery to the mainstream. It's like your team being promoted from League Two to the Premiership overnight.

And the expansion hasn't only occurred in Britain. In America cyclocross is the fastest-growing discipline within cycling. The growth has been organic, built on the hard work of enthusiasts who organise and ride events across the country. A vibrant community has developed around the scene. As with all cult sports, cyclocross in America has its own identity, distinct from its European heritage. It has a party atmosphere, particularly on the West Coast, with beer hand-ups to racers, heckling and dodgy costumes. But underneath, the race meets have a sense of genuine camaraderie, a feeling of family. Basically, it's great fun.

In Europe all paths lead to Belgium, the heart and soul of cyclocross. Here the sport is as popular as soccer. Professional races attract huge paying crowds and are shown live on television. The stars of Belgian cyclocross earn big salaries and are celebrities, their efforts followed by adoring fanclubs. And whereas watching road racing generally involves a long trek to a good spot, an equally lengthy wait, then a few moments of exhilarating whiz and swish, cyclocross is the perfect spectator sport. The circuits are short and accessible, there are several races on each day, and a plentiful supply of beer and *friets* is always on hand. The sport is expanding, changing. Once niche, it's now becoming increasingly mainstream. Its heartland may be the woods and fields of Flanders, but across the world people are taking to the mud and letting their back wheel slide.

My own racing career didn't amount to much, but what it gave me is far more valuable. Ever since that cold day in 1985 I've loved cyclocross but only now do I feel I've come to fully understand it. It's the most demanding, intriguing, beautiful and dramatic sport. It makes the winter fun. It makes Christmas bearable. It's what bikes were invented for.

In the winter of 2015 I immersed myself in this world. I wanted to better understand the sport, its connections, its history, and its stories. The journey would take me to Belgian cow pastures, Air Force bases, a hippy town in North Carolina and many more strange places. I would meet riders, organisers and fans. Perhaps I was naïve, or overly optimistic, but the sport I uncovered was a much more complicated and, at times, darker world than I expected. I was exhilarated, troubled, fascinated, and moved. But, as with anything worthwhile, light and shade are two sides of the same coin.

Author's Note

First a declaration. Cyclocross is full of geeks, but I'm not one. Riders, coaches, fans are obsessed with tyre choices, gear set-ups, types of brakes . . . the list is endless. I could have devoted a whole chapter to tyre pressure. But while I understand and respect this aspect of the sport – technical improvements make a rider go faster – it leaves me cold. I'm more interested in the culture of the sport than I am in tread patterns. So if you're looking for technical geekery, this isn't the place. There are plenty of websites catering for your very specific needs.

Secondly, cyclocross is a relatively young sport, and there have only been a handful of books written on the subject in English. It's tempting then for a writer to attempt a full history of the sport – an encyclocrosspaedia, so to speak. I have resisted this temptation, principally because such a book would have bored me rigid. Given the choice, I prefer insight over information. Naturally there will be people, places, stories that I have not been able to include, either deliberately or through my own ignorance. I can only say that I have followed my nose; not necessarily the most trustworthy pilot, but it's all I have.

Lastly, I have tried where possible to verify facts, and to credit sources. If I've missed anything or anyone, I can only offer my sincere apologies. I'll be more than happy to compensate with a plastic glass of Jupiter and a polystyrene tray of chips smothered in mayonnaise.

1

Summer Rain

Paris in July. The final day of the Tour de France used to be a celebration of cycle sport, a sunny procession along beautiful boulevards, with the world's media marvelling at the drama and elegance of our sport. But in 2015, standing just off the Champs-Élysées, I can only feel a sense of melancholy around the proceedings. Rain beats down on the slick cobbles. The atmosphere around the race has been soured by murmurings of doping by the winner, Chris Froome. Nothing has been proven, and the sniping from the French media (in itself depressing) has fuelled aggression towards Froome. Fans on the roadside have spat on the yellow jersey. As the peloton rattles past for another lap, I feel unsettled. My love for cycling has been, for thirty years, solid. It's been a constant in my life. Now, though, I just feel exhausted, and maybe – whisper it – just a bit bored. I watch the race finish but instead of hanging around for the speeches and yellow jersey ceremony I slip away, up the rue Royale.

It's a relief to get away from the incessant noise of the Tour; the announcer with his false drama, over a Europop background that is fun for a while, but wears thin pretty quickly. Even with an event as big as the Tour, it doesn't take long to get back to the normal world, just another Sunday afternoon in Paris. Most of the shops are shut, the traffic is light, dog-walkers are venturing out during a break in the rain. I walk briskly. The sport I love feels battered, formulaic. It has become too professional, too scientific. The riders are increasingly aloof. I think of an interview I read with a Spanish rider a few years earlier when he said, 'Yes, of course, I only ride for the money. I don't enjoy racing my bike.' At the time that sentiment – or lack of it – shocked me. Now it seems to be common currency in the professional peloton. There has always been cynicism in the sport but now it feels endemic.

Paris, unlike most cities, is beautiful in the rain. With time to kill before my train back to London, I keep walking, heading north. Crossing the Boulevard de Clichy near the Pigalle Metro station, the roads narrow and begin to rise. Though impossible to see it from the city's trench-like roads, I'm climbing towards Montmartre. And as the sweat rises between my shoulder-blades (waterproof jackets are never a good idea in summer, even when it's raining) I remember seeing an archive film clip about a cyclocross race on these very streets. It seems so preposterous that I stop and look it up on my phone. No, my memory hasn't failed me. Standing there on a street corner outside a *tabac*, with chains of German tourists nudging past me, I watch the crackly black and white footage of the Cyclocross de Montmartre.

The course was a simple combination of city streets, dirt paths around the windmill on top of the hill, and leg-busting flights of stone stairs (280 steps on each lap according to one source). A criterium mashed up with stair climbing. Many of the heroes of road racing took part in the race, which was held every February between 1942 and 1948. The winner in that last year was the diminutive Frenchman Jean Robic, Tour de France champion the summer before.

And the crowds were enormous: an estimated 100,000 spectators spilled out from the city pavements, lining the hillside in a deep bank of dark overcoats and warm hats. During the war, Parisians went through a difficult and ultimately humiliating process of attempting to go on with their lives under Nazi rule. The city was held up by its conquerors as a model of freedom and co-operation, but the reality was much more ambiguous. If Paris was more free and more relaxed than the rest of occupied France, a legacy of intense guilt was being created.

But even on the newsreel footage one can see the pure joy of the crowds watching this cyclocross race. The fifty-strong peloton charges through the streets, and the spectators – unrestrained by barriers – jump and wave with delight at being so close to their heroes. This is the sense of belonging that cycling, and cyclocross specifically, can inspire.

Pressing on towards the Sacré-Cœur I come to the bottom of one of those flights of stairs. I try to imagine approaching on a bike, leaping off, shouldering the bike and running up the stairs – in stiff leather shoes with metal cleats. Madness, but fun.

At the top, surrounded by pigeons and tourists, I turn to admire the view and to catch my breath. Down in the city the Tour de France circus is preparing to disperse. Money, bitterness and insinuation will follow it. But I feel exhilarated. If road cycling has lost something of its soul, perhaps in those grainy black and white images I might find some redemption.

Travelling back from Paris that wet July day a question began revolving in my mind, gaining a little more shape as the kilometres sped by the train window. If road racing bored and disappointed me, why did cyclocross so thrill me? Me, and those 100,000 Parisians – and the thousands of Belgians who stand in dark forests throughout the winter. The answer – my answer, at least, having now spent a season immersed in the sport – turned out to be more complex and more moving than I'd expected.

*

Following professional cyclocross riders on social media can be an envy-inducing affair. There is a recurring theme, particularly among those based in America, of posting a certain kind of photo. This photo features a stunning remote landscape, a trail snaking away into the vast beautiful emptiness, and overhead a bright blue sky. Sometimes a pristine, latest-technology bike will make it into the shot. For anyone based in northern Europe, stuck all day at a desk, seeing shots like these is both inspiring and thoroughly demoralising. One of the biggest culprits of this phenomenon – we might call it freedom porn – is a certain Katie Compton. Not that one can really blame her. If I lived in Colorado and had all summer to explore its trails, I'd want to show off too.

In road racing the off-season – traditionally a period of relaxation, family and allowing a few extra pounds to pile on – has in recent years been squeezed by a race calendar that now runs from January to late October. Riders on professional road teams get barely a month of time to themselves before they're back on the hamster wheel of training camps, testing, measuring. In cyclocross the race calendar runs from September to February, so the off-season is a full six months. And because cyclocross has a culture of independence and individuality, most riders are free to use the off-season as they wish. Some travel abroad, some explore the wild regions of their country, some use the time to focus on other kinds of work. This can make professional cross riders hard to track down during their off-season, unlike European-based road professionals, who in the winter will either be in Majorca or the Canary Islands. Every cyclocross rider continues riding their bike through the summer. For the vast majority, even the professionals, the idea that they are riding for financial gain is preposterous. They love cycling, and during spring and summer are free to ride without the stress that goes with racing. Only in July and August do the heavy-duty training plans start, and with them a chance to do some road racing to sharpen the legs and the wits.

In early June 2015 Katie Compton travels from her home in Boulder, Colorado, to Iceland to compete in the Blue Lagoon Challenge, a mountain bike race through the spectacular black volcanic rock of Reykjanes. Compton, formerly a tandem pilot in the Paralympics, is by far the most successful American cyclocross racer of all time, male or female. At the time of writing, she has won the overall World Cup twice, 22 World Cup races and 12 US national championships. In total she has won over a hundred UCI ranked races. Though she has chosen cyclocross over mountain biking as her primary focus, Compton still races her mountain bike at a high level throughout the summer. It's good for maintaining base fitness, conquering the potential boredom of the off-season, and being part of a lively social scene. In the Venn diagram of cyclocross and mountain biking, Katie is firmly in the middle. The Iceland race is intended to be just for fun, to be combined with a vacation, but it ends badly. A recurring saddle sore turns into an antibiotic-resistant staph infection, swelling up and forcing her to ride most of the race out of the saddle. Most people would have dropped out at this point, but that's not really Katie's style. Back in the United States, her husband Mark drives Katie straight from the airport to hospital in Denver, where the cyst is removed. The resulting wound is very sensitive and has to be given time to heal. Katie is unable to ride her bike for three months.

For someone who loves wilderness and sunshine and snow, being housebound is difficult to accept. And for Katie this latest problem has come on the back of many years battling mysterious leg pains and exercise-induced asthma. Injury and illness are anathema to any elite athlete, but for Katie it feels like she has had more than her fair share – much more. What makes it doubly hard is that she cannot see a way out. Her asthma can be treated and kept under control, but the legs pains, which began in her teenage years and can severely hamper her racing, are unexplained. As the cyclocross season approaches, Katie is still not training, and has slipped into a bout of depression.

In Europe, the sport's top riders have more obligations. With great sponsorship, comes great responsibility, to paraphrase Spiderman. European riders, like Americans, are able to go on holiday and forget about racing during the spring. But sponsors want their logos on show as much as possible, so all top-level cyclocross teams also double up as second division road teams, and have a full calendar of one-day races and short stage races. The big stars get to select a programme of summer road racing that builds their form towards the autumn; those further down the hierarchy have to grunt their way around the lanes of Belgium as often as the team management dictates. For Belgian fans, watching their local *kermesse* on a Sunday afternoon in July, seeing their cyclocross heroes spinning around on their road bikes, adds a certain frisson. It's a reminder that the cross season is approaching, and it elevates their local race.

In the Flemish town of Izegem, bathed in late summer sunshine, crowds gather on a Sunday afternoon to watch Izegem Koers, a second division one-day road race. The beer tent and the bars throughout the centre of town are doing a brisk trade, VIPs shuffle along the buffet table, families wander around the team cars, trying to spot a famous rider. This is just one of dozens of road races that populate the summer weekends throughout Flanders. For most of the riders freewheeling their way to the start line these races are a serious business – this is how they earn their salary and advance their career. But within the race there is a group for whom such races are merely training, and some of these riders are much bigger stars than any of their road colleagues.

As the field lines up in the town's main shopping street, between two banks of crowds in short sleeves and sunglasses, with many faces already reddened by beer and sun, the most famous names are called to the front line for photo opportunities and hand-shaking with local dignitaries. The town crier – a man of suitably generous proportions, wearing a magnificent black cape, white ruffled collar and black hat with white plumage – poses with bell aloft. The rider he is standing so proudly beside is Sven Nys, the greatest cyclocross racer of all time; the Pelé of cyclocross. Nys is here for training, but there is something poignant here too. Nys's impending retirement at the end of the cyclocross season means that this is his last road race as a professional. This is the last time his adoring public will be able to watch him whiz around their streets, smile and sign autographs after the race, chat to friends and would-be friends. The season ahead will be his valediction. He's relaxed, he looks tanned and fit, though those close to him will know the pressure he is putting himself under to perform. There will be no going through the motions. A year ago he was going through a much-publicised divorce, his psychological equilibrium was disrupted, he over-trained, and consequently had a disastrous season. Above all, Sven wants to win, to go out on top.

Still, for now, the world of cyclocross is transplanted from the field to suburban roads, with no expectations. The cyclocross riders are relaxed because they're on safe ground – at most they will have a job to do for their road-focused colleagues. Road racing is training, and although the freezing depths of January may seem a long way off, their first big test of the season is a lot nearer to hand. And it will be in the most unlikely environment of all.

2
Cross is Coming

Those of us who live and work in cities are somewhat inured to the passing of the seasons. Weather is just something we experience in the dash between subway station, coffee shop and office door. For many, the easiest way to gauge the season is by the Starbucks menu.

Cyclists, and anyone else who undertakes an outdoor pursuit, are well placed to pick up the signals of a changing season. My daily commute in London takes me through the finery of Greenwich Park, the trendy former industrial buildings of Deptford and New Cross, then into Southwark and Lambeth. From my suburban starting point, I ride on cycle paths and through housing estates, and the city gradually crowds in around me, growing taller as I slide between red buses and black cabs. In the first days of September the weather, not surprisingly, isn't very different from the last days of August. Yet in my mind, we have moved into autumn. And because we are now in autumn, I'm alert to any sign of it. The air is sharper, cleaner. The summer colours are in abeyance. There is more knitwear to be seen on the streets of the capital. I like knitwear.

One thing is demonstrably different – the football season has started. Like most British children, I was brought up with football. As a young man growing up in London my father went to games every Saturday afternoon. Brentford, the Bees, were his team. They still are. He and his mates would cycle down to the ground and roar themselves hoarse in the stands, along with 20,000 other likely lads. When he moved out of London – first to rural Kent, then Oxfordshire – the physical tie was snapped. He was no longer part of the community in which he spent his early years, deliberately so, for he wanted to better himself intellectually and materially. Going to Brentford games was no longer viable, particularly once I'd come along, and switching allegiance to another team felt disloyal. So his football consumption became focused on the television, specifically the venerable BBC programme *Match of the Day*. One of the abiding memories of my childhood is his Saturday-night ritual of pouring himself a beer into a silver tankard specially reserved for the occasion, and sitting down to watch *Match of the Day*. When I became old enough to stay up with him, I would watch and absorb his body language, and the comments directed at the television. He would sit a little forward on the sofa, tankard in hand, watching the game closely. At a moment of drama he would shuffle forward to the edge of the seat, as if ready to leap into the air, mimicking the tense movement one sees at football grounds as fans rise and fall according to the action. And when he bemoaned the referee's visual impairment, or the cynicism of the Arsenal back four, was the London twang in his accent a little stronger? Whatever he might have said about his childhood – the poverty, the lack of ambition of his family – this made me think that he still responded to this aspect of working-class London life, even had some affection for it.

Without the loyalties engendered by class and community, my own interest in football soon evaporated. Cycling became my all-consuming passion. But the correlation of football to cyclocross is an important one. In Belgium and Holland cyclocross ranks second to football in terms of popularity, and like football it is at heart a blue-collar sport. Its foundation is family, community and class, in that order.

In London we tend to think of football now as being a middle-class game, at least that is how the media portray the Premiership – an economic model that has spiralled up into the stratosphere. So it was a timely reminder of the roots of the game when I cycled, oblivious, into a crowd making their way to Millwall's first home match of the season. The Den, Millwall's ground, is infamous for the greeting it gives visiting fans. This is largely a legacy of the seventies and eighties, when Millwall fans were among the most terrifyingly violent in the country. The Den is an intimidating place for visitors because it's surrounded by housing estates. If you're from, say, Cardiff, and you're getting into a spot of bother near the ground, you could run off into the estates, but that might not prove to be a wise decision. There's no way to get to the ground without running the gauntlet of the local boys.

As I cycled past the gaggle of (mostly) men walking to the ground, supervised by a very visible police presence, I thought about how we still want to belong. Even in this atomised and corporatised age, the desire to belong still exists. That is why the people of Bermondsey and Southwark stick with Millwall, whatever the team's league position. That is why my father sits watching *Match of the Day* with a beer, and that is why people go to cyclocross races.

As the football season bursts to life, the road cycling season ends with a slow fade. After the Tour de France, the professional road racing season goes into a kind of stasis. For cycling fans, August is a dull time of year. There are good historical reasons for this. Traditionally after the Tour, riders embarked on a petrol-draining odyssey around Europe, riding well-paying criteriums. Those who had been successful in the Tour could cash in by driving from race to race, hoovering up the start money. Post-Tour criteriums still exist but the circuit has diminished in recent years. The need for riders to recover, physically and mentally, remains. The UCI has attempted to fill this dry period with new races, such as the Eneco Tour. But cycling is a sport that thrives on history, and new races don't often capture the imagination. For cycling fans, if a race hasn't been on the calendar for fifty years, and hasn't been won by Eddy Merckx, it doesn't matter.

In September the road season moves into its final phase with the Vuelta a España, the World Championships and the autumn Classics. Here there is romance and history and beauty – the last chance of glory for those riders whose season has disappointed; for fans, another chance to see races that mean something. But there is also the sadness of encroaching autumn. Weariness too: of formulaic racing and incomplete start lists, of new events created in the Middle East for purely financial reasons – not to mention the weariness of sitting in front of the television for hours on end waiting for a sprint finish. Fortunately something far more exciting is on the horizon. Something punchy, intriguing, dirty and full of personality. September means only one thing. Cross is coming.

*

At this point, before we get too far into the mud, it seems apt to explain the basic format of a cyclocross race. We'll go with the contemporary rules to keep things simple.

A cyclocross race takes place on a closed circuit of between 2.5 kilometres and 3.5 kilometres. The course, according to the UCI rulebook, 'shall include road, country and forest paths and meadowland alternating in such a way as to ensure changes in the pace of the race and allowing riders to recuperate after difficult sections'. Races for senior men are one hour plus a lap; for women forty minutes plus a lap; for Under-23s fifty minutes plus a lap; and for juniors forty minutes plus a lap. All categories ride the same course. The UCI rulebook on bikes is extensive, but the summary is that all machines in a UCI event must have dropped handlebars, rubber tyres no wider than 33mm, and no studs or spikes are permitted on tyres. Like Formula One, every race has a pit area, where teams can hand up fresh bikes to their riders. Also like in Formula One, in cyclocross the start is so important that riders are gridded. A rider's position on the grid is based on UCI points from previous races, rather than any kind of timed qualifying session. The rules of the race itself are very similar to road racing. First rider over the line wins. Anyone lapped is pulled out. Dangerous riding is forbidden. The interpretation of these last two is anything but consistent. Those are the facts. As with most things in life, you'll find the best explanation on YouTube.

*

A fit-looking fifty-something with a suitably American perma-tan and a ready grin, Brook Watts's influence in the cyclocross world goes far beyond his role as a race organiser. Not that his creation – the unique CrossVegas – isn't hugely influential in itself. From the moment you meet him, with his soft warm handshake, you are disarmed. He is more of an impresario than an organiser, and like all great impresarios he's a great salesman too. He'll sell his race, given half a chance, but the product he's really peddling is cyclocross. He loves it, and he wants you to love it too. As a student at the University of Texas in 1978 Watts organised one of the first US national championships. The roster was eighteen riders, with one woman. A student of advertising, Watts had been targeting a career in corporate marketing, but when a friend said to him, 'I'm starting an international stage race, wanna help?' Watts's future took a very different direction. He helped to stage the Tour of Texas, was involved with the 1984 Los Angeles Olympics, ran a recreational cycling programme for 7-Eleven and was part of the team who organised the Tour de Trump and Tour DuPont. When the economic bubble supporting the boom in American racing burst in the early nineties, Watts moved into the corporate marketing world he had originally wanted to join, and there he learned about event marketing, sponsorship deals and promotions.

CrossVegas, though, didn't come about as part of a corporate marketing strategy, or even as a philanthropic urge to boost the fledgling American cyclocross scene. It was a dare. Every September the bike industry gathers in Las Vegas for Interbike, a trade show based at the gargantuan Mandalay Bay Convention Center in Paradise, Nevada. Retailers, media, professional riders and sundry cycling types fill the aisles for three days, placing orders, shaking hands and ogling shiny new bits of kit. And in the evenings they enjoy all the temptations that Vegas has to offer.

But Brook, and his friend Chris Grealish, also a long-time cross promoter, weren't tempted by drinking, strip bars or Céline Dion shows. There was nothing for them to do. So they dared each other to organise a cross race. An outlandish idea, but an inspired one. From the start, the event was a success. With Interbike in town, CrossVegas had a ready-made crowd. Sponsorship deals were likewise easy to attract, and many of the big brands had their top riders in town anyway to promote their latest products. In sporting terms, the timing was good too: because the European cross season doesn't get underway until early October, those riders who made the long trip from Belgium or Holland could use CrossVegas as a fun warm-up race. A distraction, a change of scene, and a couple of training days lost to jet lag in late September wouldn't be critical.

Since its first outing in 2007 CrossVegas has grown in stature: more top European riders made the trip, more spectators turned out, more media coverage was generated. This is the virtuous circle all promoters are chasing. CrossVegas worked as a pre-season race because it was as much about putting on a show as putting on a serious bike race. There were Elvis impersonators singing the national anthem, promotional girls in bikinis, and dollar-grabbing – a uniquely American aspect of the sport, where spectators hold out dollar notes for riders to grab as they shoot past.

'I'm all about the show,' Brook tells me, with a conspiratorial wink. 'Show first, bike race second.'

Of course, it's Vegas. But the professionalism of the organisation, together with the UCI's wish to globalise the sport, got the race bumped up to World Cup status. It was a move that surprised many, and doubtless there were some traditionalists who groaned, but for the UCI it made perfect sense. They got to stretch the geographical reach of their flagship World Cup competition, and they could do so without threatening any of the Classic European races staged between October and February. Most of the big teams were already used to the logistical challenge of transporting bikes, wheels, rollers and supporting kit to Vegas. And the UCI could be confident that Brook's team would rise to the challenge of their higher status.

For the European riders, however, the proposition is a little more vexing. In the days when CrossVegas was only a race you did for fun, or for your sponsors, there was no pressure. By mid-September most top riders were not on top form, but they were fast enough to compete with a bunch of American riders who'd been training for Vegas like it was the World Championships. The Belgians could hold their own, have fun and go home.

But now, with the race a World Cup, anyone who wants to be in with a chance of overall World Cup honours has to ride to get some points. Every team wants their full squad on the start line, and wants that squad to be competitive. The start of the season has suddenly been moved forward a month. It's like the UCI moving Paris–Nice into early February. Added to which is the jet lag, a problem many European riders have never had to deal with because if you live in Flanders all the other big races are within a two-hour drive.

For 2015, this inaugural year of CrossVegas being a World Cup race, approaches to this confusing situation vary. Some riders, like Wout van Aert, fly in, race, then fly out again. The Telenet–Fidea team make the trip longer by building in a pre-race training camp in Colorado. Lars van der Haar, the Dutch star, builds probably the most elaborate programme around Vegas. Because he rides for a top-flight road team, Van der Haar is able to select a programme of summer road racing to develop his form, and also to put him in the right continent. In early September he rides the Tour of Alberta, Canada's biggest stage race, then begins a slow migration south, taking in Portland, Oregon, on the way, where he competes in a local cross race in Vancouver Lake Park. By the time he gets to the start line in Vegas the hope is that Van der Haar will be fully acclimatised, benefiting from the road speed in his legs, and familiarised with riding his cross bike in anger.

On a normal summer's evening the Desert Breeze Park Soccer Complex, on the western edge of Las Vegas, will be dotted with runners, dog-walkers, perhaps a couple of teams having a game. There are skate parks and picnic tables. In the distance loom the peaks of the Red Rock Canyon Conservation Area. The eponymous breeze drifts in from the west, bringing with it sand, rain and cowboys.

On this night in September, though, the atmosphere is much more lively. The first ever World Cup on American soil is in full swing. Its showtime. The music is pumping. The announcer's voice reverberates around the grassy bowl on which the event is based. Smoke rises from the food concession vans into the clear night sky. The beer is flowing, but there isn't the kind of catastrophic drunkenness one sees at a Belgian race; here the alcohol seems just to heighten the mood and the volume of the spectators. Beyond the arc-lights blink the hotels and casinos of the Strip, but everyone's eyes are on the slim, snaking track around which the world's best riders are about to race.

At her team truck, Katie Compton is making her last preparations. She has won here twice before, in 2008 and 2009, but this year is altogether different. After the health issues that curtailed her summer training, Katie is struggling to find fitness. She has only been back on the bike for eleven days, nowhere near long enough to get race-fit. But there is some positive news: being unable to train meant that she could spend time researching her ailments, and after listening to a podcast about thyroid issues, Katie began to investigate the root cause of her problems. She discovered that she has a genetic defect, causing her body to not tolerate folic acid. Blood tests confirmed her self-diagnosis, and with a fairly straightforward change in diet to control her folic acid intake, her problems were solved. No more leg pains, and no more asthma, because the asthma was also a symptom of the genetic defect. For twenty years Compton has been fighting her own body. Now she understands how to sidestep her enemy. But at this relatively late stage of her career, will the missed base training prove the undoing of her whole season? She's about to submit herself to the first test.

On stationary rollers she goes through her warm-up routine, sprinting then spinning. She sips regularly at a bottle of energy drink. Sweat drips from her nose. This is not cyclocross weather, it's around 90 degrees. After her warm-up she zips up her skinsuit, puts her sunglasses and helmet on, and rolls away through the car park. Mark, her husband and mechanic, shoulders her spare bike and begins the hike to the pits. There are shouts of 'Go Katie' as she weaves through the crowd towards the starting grid. The riders gather behind a barrier, 50 metres behind the grid. Some chat, laugh, catch up with friendly rivals they haven't seen since last season. Others stay silent, stare into the middle distance. Then the call-up begins. One by one the racers are called up by the announcer, introduced to the crowd and asked to come forward into their starting position. When your name is called you head to the barrier, get the width of your tyres checked by a UCI commissaire, then pedal forward into your row. When everyone is in position and the television cameras begin their slow sweep across the front row, the mood grows more serious. The riders have one last drink before tossing their bottle to a helper, the announcer attempts to bring the crowd down to a nervous hush. He calls out, 'THIRTY SECONDS TO GO!'

All eyes fall upon the red lights. Total focus. When the lights turn green, the sprint is on.

In cyclocross the sprint is at the start of the race, not the end. The principal objective is to get to the first obstacle, usually a tight corner, in one of the leading positions. This dramatically reduces your chance of being baulked by riders ahead. Some commentators make a great deal out of this race to what they call the 'holeshot', as if leading into the first corner is almost as impressive as leading into the final corner. In reality, most elite riders aren't too bothered about leading here. A position in the top five is usually good enough to keep you out of trouble.

The CrossVegas course is unique in cyclocross in being almost totally on grass. And that should make it a fast course, even more so given the hot, dry conditions. But Vegas grass is not Belgian grass. Vegas grass is deep and spongy and energy-sapping. What looks, on television at least, to be an easy course is anything but. The course may not have much elevation change compared to the Classic European races, but the surface means that the strongest rider will win. It is – in the delightfully silly phrase used by television commentators – a 'pedaller's course'.

'No Belgian rider has ever told me, "Brook, your course is too easy,"' says Brook Watts.

And in the women's race, the Belgian and Dutch stars have to cling onto a trio of mountain bikers, who dominate the early laps. Coming off the end of their summer season, the mountain bikers, including Italian Eva Lechner, Canadian Catharine Pendrel and Czech Kateřina Nash, are in strong form. There isn't much pressure for them – cross being their off-season fun – and the course suits their ability to turn out consistently high levels of power.

With two laps to go, Belgian champion Sanne Cant is following the three mountain bikers, with a chasing group being led by Katie Compton and fellow Colorado resident Georgia Gould. Katie and Gould drive hard to get across to the leading group, but go deep into oxygen debt to do so, and when Nash nudges the pace up just a little, they slip backwards again. For Katie, twice a winner of the overall World Cup, it's a frustrating situation to be in. Her form is much further behind where she would usually expect to be at this time of year, after her illness-induced three months off. Before CrossVegas she only got in ten days of meaningful training, so it's remarkable that she is anywhere near the top ten.

Having tested her rivals with a small acceleration, Nash turns up the power gradually and pulls out a convincing gap. Cant, with little racing in her legs, is unable to close her down, and the race is won. Nash goes through the bell with a 26-second lead. She looks smooth, with a high cadence, fluid dismounts and remounts – an impressive display from the 38-year-old Olympian who has competed at the highest level in mountain biking, cyclocross and cross-country skiing. At the finishing line she shows her mountain biking roots by veering over to the barriers and high-fiving the crowd's outstretched hands.

Fifteen seconds later Lechner leads in Cant for the other podium spots. Katie, having eased back in the last lap, comes in fifteenth.

The women finish and the fans make a dive for the beers. Last year there was controversy when several of the riders complained that they were being sprayed full in the face with beer, and that full beer cans were being lobbed onto the course. Lars van der Haar said that he wouldn't come back if it happened to him again. So far there has been no repeat of 'beergate', as the American cycling media dubbed the incident, but there is still an hour of racing to go.

On the start-line of the men's race, there is only one rider the dignitaries want to have their photo taken with – Sven Nys.

Among those hanging, grinning, off Sven's shoulder is Elvis Presley. Having just belted out his rendition of 'Viva CrossVegas' Elvis recognises a fellow rock 'n' roll star in Sven, and seems a little awestruck.

Despite all the exceptional factors – the time of year, the heat, the jet lag, the distinctly American style of course – the race follows a fairly predictable pattern. The talented young Belgian Michael Vanthourenhout opens an early gap, then is joined by Sven and Wout van Aert, the heir apparent to Sven's throne. Van Aert celebrated his 21st birthday the day before the race, but clearly wasn't tempted by any of Las Vegas's more sordid attractions. On the toughest climb of the circuit he powers away from Sven and rides to victory.

The previous season ended disappointingly for Van Aert, with his Dutch rival Mathieu van der Poel winning the World Championship many had predicted would go to Van Aert. But with Van der Poel out of action, recovering from a serious knee injury, Van Aert is able to stamp his authority on this first World Cup of the season.

In sixth place, less than a minute down on Van Aert, is US national champion Jeremy Powers. Something of a poster-boy for American cyclocross, Powers is undisputedly the best American rider. He throws a huge amount of energy into the sport he loves. He helps to run a programme for developing riders in Massachusetts, does coaching clinics, gives talks and a whole range of other promotional activities for his sponsor. He even has his own superhero nickname, 'JPows', and if you happen to be passing his campervan before a race you might just get a free water bottle emblazoned with a Lichtensteinesque JPows! logo. I suspect there is a level of irony at play here – I certainly hope so. Jeremy certainly gives good brand, as the marketing people say. Yet underneath the brash self-promotion there is a serious athlete. Powers has built his life around performance on the bike, and his commitment has yielded dozens of victories at America's biggest races. But for any ambitious American rider, Europe is the benchmark for all things cycling. Just as the American road racers of the eighties travelled to the Tour de France with 7-Eleven, to be followed by Greg LeMond, George Hincapie and Lance Armstrong, so American cyclocross racers – if they are serious about their sport – have to race in Belgium. Belgian cyclocross is the siren song, tempting American racers across the Atlantic with the promise of great riches, and the danger of sharp rocks. Over the years Powers has raced in Europe in the World Cups, the Superprestige and GVA Trofee races, and has occasionally broken into the top ten. Tonight is a big opportunity for him. He's on home grass, on a course that suits his fast riding style.

Sixth place, at the back of a group of top Belgian and Dutch riders, is a good result. But Powers has mixed feelings. Having led a chasing trio for much of the race, then been outsprinted by the well-travelled Van der Haar and Belgian enigma Kevin Pauwels, it's hard for Powers to reconcile sixth with the third place he was chasing so hard.

Van der Haar, author of those extensive preparations, finishes fourth. Van Aert took a different approach. He flew into Vegas a couple of days before the race, and afterwards drove straight to the airport. His training? 'Nothing special,' his team's press officer says. 'Just the usual early season training. It's the first World Cup, you have to be fit.'

Like, duh.

You can almost hear the clicking sound of Belgian brains being recalibrated as they fly back over the Atlantic. While there is much public positivity from the European riders about CrossVegas becoming a World Cup, one wonders what they privately think of it. There is the sense, in the weeks that follow, of a return to the normal rhythms of the season. While the Europeans shake off their unaccustomed jet lag, the American cross community travels 3000 miles east, to a very different venue. One that is more redolent of Moby-Dick than Elvis Presley.

*

I once had a boss I didn't much care for. We've all been there. On the day I left the job, I was in the shared office kitchen, making a last cup of tea, when my eyes fell upon his mug. It was a mug I had admired for some time, an American diner mug he must have picked up from a trip to New York. On one side it had the name Edward Hopper, on the other side it had a sketch detail from Hopper's most famous painting *Nighthawks*. With shameful deftness I appropriated the mug for someone who clearly loved it more than its owner. Me. And for almost twenty years I've drunk coffee out of that mug, while beavering away at writing stories.

Nighthawks is an atmospheric urban landscape, but Hopper's early breakthrough came from a set of watercolour depictions of houses in Gloucester, Massachusetts. Though visually bright, with the sun bouncing off the houses' walls, the paintings were provocative because the houses that were their subject were considered then, in 1923, to be vulgar and in poor taste. The Brooklyn Museum bought six, the critics wrote good things, and Hopper's career prospects began to improve. He and his wife Josephine spent a great deal of time in Gloucester and Cape Cod throughout the rest of their married life.

Gloucester is a fishing town, curled around a natural harbour on Cape Ann, Essex County. Its historic streets, art galleries, museums and the surrounding rocky coastline are a draw for tourists in summer. And all year round the trawlers and lobster boats head out into the Atlantic from the safety of Gloucester harbour. Over the course of the town's 350-year history more than 10,000 Gloucester fishermen have been lost to the sea; a mural in the City Hall building records their names. Hollywood saw the potential here; the film *The Perfect Storm*, based on Sebastian Junger's book, and starring George Clooney as the captain of the doomed fishing boat *Andrea Gail*, was filmed here. *Moby-Dick*, the literary classic of the seas, is set a few miles down the coast from Gloucester. On one side of Gloucester harbour is Stage Fort Park, a pleasant landscaped green space dominated by a huge boulder, sixty feet high and two hundred wide. The rock has a rather enigmatic air. Embedded into one of its sides is a plaque which reads, 'On this site in 1623 a company of farmers and fishermen from Dorchester, England, under the direction of Rev. John White, founded the Massachusetts Bay Colony.'

One wonders what the Rev. John White and his merry crew would make of the scene on this sunny weekend in late September, as men and women rattle and skid their way around Stage Fort Park on cyclocross bikes. The Gran Prix of Gloucester is one of the oldest and most prestigious races on the American calendar. Cyclocross is a young sport in America, so 1999 – the year of the inaugural event – qualifies as ancient history. And while the race hasn't had the meteoric rise of CrossVegas, Gloucester has become something of a self-styled Classic. The cream of American cross comes here looking for UCI ranking points, prizes and perhaps a lobster dinner. And because it's only a week after Vegas, some of the more forward-thinking European riders also come here to compete in a fun, low-pressure event.

The field hurtles down through a set of S-bends and onto the sandy trails that make up most of the circuit. Being dry, flat and without many technical sections, the course is fast. A dirt race. Dust flies up from the leading women's tyres and chokes those further back. Everyone is wearing sunglasses to protect their eyes. Katie Compton gets an OK start and begins hunting down the riders in front of her.

Cyclocross is unique within cycle sport, perhaps within sport in general, for the combination of abilities it asks of its competitors. In modern sports science there is something called your Functional Threshold. This is essentially the maximum level of exertion you can maintain for an hour. Most riders base their training around this level. Exceeding it will put you into the red; which means it will hurt. The deeper you go into the red, the more you hurt; and the more often you go into the red, the quicker fatigue will build up. In a typical cyclocross race riders can expect to go into the red up to thirty times per lap. At every climb, every sprint after a sharp turn, every run-up. Being able to go hard, then recover quickly, is critically important. At the same time, each feature of the course has the potential to send you sliding to the floor, or at least to slow your progress. Riders speak of riding a clean race, which simply means making no mistakes. This is a Zen state, unattainable for all but a handful of riders. For most, a more realistic objective is about minimising the damage of your mistakes, getting back in there and exploiting any opportunities afforded by others' errors. Cyclocross is far more combative than road racing in this sense. If your opponent crashes, attack. If she punctures, attack. If she has a bobble (the delightful word used to describe an untimely slowing caused by an error), attack. Because wind doesn't often play a significant role, team tactics are negligible. You don't need a team to protect you from the wind, to bring you bottles, food and clothing as road *domestiques* do. And you don't need a team to chase down early breakaways by riders who haven't got a hope of winning, because such breakaways rarely happen. In a cyclocross race there is no benefit to being in a team; the principal reason that teams exist is to give a sponsor more exposure by having several riders in the same race. Those riders don't need to help each other, and may even compete against each other. Cross is simply an intense hour of racing, from the moment that traffic light turns green. It is a war of attrition, and at any second one mistake can heap success or disaster on a rider. That's why the fans love it so much, and that's why it's such a uniquely demanding sport. You cannot enter into an arena like that without total mental focus.

In Gloucester, as she moves into a race-winning lead, Katie Compton is displaying that kind of mental focus. Even via a shaky internet feed, I can see it in her eyes. Lap after lap, past the Happy Taco food stand, the Atomic boutique coffee roasters, the crowds enjoying the sun and yelling super-positivity into the riders' ears, she looks fast and smooth, but it's in her unwavering stare that you see why she's been so successful over the years.

Cyclocross is visceral, physical, brutal. But so is cage-fighting. What sets cyclocross above sheer brutality is its intellectual aspect. It exercises the grey matter. A rider must always be thinking, plotting, calculating. Staying upright is to a large degree a matter of instinct and learned skill. Going fast, while staying upright, is a much more complicated proposition. Which line to take? When to dismount and remount? Which gear to use? Which tyres and at what pressure? Stay in the group or push on alone? The questions are endless. Perhaps that's why there are so many people riding cyclocross well into their sixties and seventies, because it's forever challenging them, a puzzle that is never finished.

For Katie, once she puts her nose into the lead, her opponents have little chance of coming back into contention. Winning is a habit for her, it feels natural. Though she's still some way off her top physical condition, her technique and mental focus are unwavering. As she rides up the hill to the finishing line, her arms aloft and a big smile on her face, the announcer tells the crowd, 'This is a *huuuuge* win for Katie Compton.' In the context of her career to date, this is something of an exaggeration, but after a summer beset with bad health the victory must indeed feel like an important step.

3

The Drop of Death

I've never been a fan of track and field athletics. It has always seemed so simple. Boringly simple. Compared to the labyrinthine politics of cycling, a running race is brain-numbingly straightforward. There is, however, one event that has always intrigued me, more for its symbolism than its technical challenges – the steeplechase. The modern version of the event is 3000 metres long and includes twenty-eight barriers to jump over, and seven water jumps. There is something strange and wonderful about seeing a pack of runners leaping into a pit filled with water, then scramble out to continue running, their spikes leaving a trail of damp patches on the track. Like many modern athletics events, steeplechase was first created at the University of Oxford in the mid-nineteenth century. It was an imitation of the horseracing steeplechase, which originated in Ireland a hundred years earlier. As typified by the Grand National, these races now take place on purpose-built courses, but originally it was a race from village to village, across fields and hedges and gates and streams, with church steeples as the focal points in each village.

Cyclocross also began life as a form of steeplechase. There is no definitive version of how cyclocross started, but the generally received story is that towards the end of the nineteenth century, a soldier in the French army, Daniel Gousseau, came up with the idea of riding his bicycle cross-country in order to keep up with the horse-bound general he was supposed to be looking after. Gousseau must have been successful in his off-road ventures because, soon after, whole battalions of French troops were being trained to ride bicycles between engagements. And Gousseau must have enjoyed riding off-road for, so the story goes, he and his friends began having informal races between villages, riding as the crow flies and dealing with whatever obstacles came their way. The pastime soon became popular for road riders seeking to keep fit, and mentally fresh, during the winter. It wasn't long before the racing became formalised; Gousseau wrote to the French Cycling Union in 1901 to introduce his concept of cross-country racing, then called *cyclo-pédestre*. He wanted official approval for a French championship, arguing that such an event would promote a sport that supported the military in keeping fit. The officials bought it and in 1902 the first French cyclocross championships took place, a year before the first Tour de France. The first Belgian championship was held in 1910, and other European nations followed in subsequent years.

Those first events replicated the steeplechase format, with competitors riding from point-to-point and crossing natural obstacles en route. Unsurprisingly no footage exists of these early races, but we can imagine them as slogs across the French landscape, the foolhardy racers being watched by thickets of incredulous country folk. In 1907 the event was won by Octave Lapize, who went on to win the 1910 Tour de France. Alongside his Tour victory Lapize became famous for the accusation he shouted at Tour officials as he struggled up the Col du Tourmalet on a monster 326 kilometre stage with seven mountain passes: 'You are murderers, yes murderers.' But Lapize, who died during the First World War when his fighter plane was shot down, also has a claim to cyclocross fame, because he was the first man to shoulder his bike and run with it. Fellow Tour de France rider Eugène Christophe used the new technique to great effect, winning seven French championships between 1909 and 1921. It also came in handy when his forks broke on the descent of the Tourmalet in the 1913 Tour de France. Christophe, who was riding towards the yellow jersey, wept with frustration as his rivals swooped past where he stood, helpless, at the side of the road. When he regained his composure he set off in search of a village where he might mend his forks. He walked for ten kilometres with his bike on his shoulder, and when he arrived at Sainte-Marie-de-Campan a young girl showed him to the blacksmith's forge which has now gone down in Tour legend. The blacksmith offered to mend Christophe's forks, but a race official and rival team managers reminded him of the rule that riders must undertake their own repairs without assistance, so Christophe spent the next three hours labouring to weld his own forks back together.

In Britain cyclocross was beginning to capture the imagination of the more hardy cycling folk. *Cycling Weekly* carried occasional pictures of French cross-country races, with captions that hailed the toughness of those taking part. Perhaps it was the old cross-Channel rivalry that encouraged the creation of events such as the Catford Paperchase and the Bagshot Scramble. Invariably these events were run over point-to-point courses, or on big loops, and many were team competitions. Most competitors rode fixed wheel bikes, and although some races had fields of a hundred or more, including the fastest roadmen of the day, the cycling press was pretty sniffy. This sort of racing was neither licensed nor controlled, and in the way the riders scrambled from field to field, crossing whatever road or stream or hedge got in their way, it must have seemed rather chaotic.

Alongside the national championships another major event developed in France, with the snappy title of Le Critérium International de Cross-Country Cyclo-Pédestre. This race, held in a forest in a western suburb of Paris, began in 1924 and became the unofficial World Championship. Its history boasts such famous riders as Francis Pélissier and Jean Robic. Huge crowds flocked to the course and they particularly congregated at the renowned *trou du diable,* or 'drop of death', a vertiginous descent that only the most skilled could ride. One of the dominant riders of the time was Robert Oubron, who won four times between 1937 and 1942. Oubron, from Versaille, developed a new technique for running with the bike, involving taking very small quick steps, and holding the handlebars close to his chest. It's a technique which became the foundation of running in modern cyclocross.

Over time the success of the Critérium International persuaded other organisers to put on races, and the courses became shorter and more urban, to make them more appealing to spectators. The Cyclocross Montmartre, which ran between 1942 and 1948, was the logical endpoint of this development. With over 100,000 spectators, the best riders in France, and a spectacular urban setting, this was a show that couldn't be ignored. Brook Watts would have been proud. The UCI realised that it was time to make cyclocross official.

4

Edgelands

Close to where I live there is a park called Maryon Wilson Park. It's a hilly, wooded site, surrounded by housing estates. At its centre is a rather shabby petting zoo, with doleful deer and forlorn sheep. It's a site of special scientific interest, and a site of special cyclocross interest too, for this park was a regular fixture on the London Cross Leagues of the eighties and nineties. Cyclocross riders are much more connected to their courses than roadies, so when a course is no longer used it becomes 'lost'. Spend long enough on social media forums and you can find that cyclocross course that your memory has grassed over, a picture of that infamous ditch that caught you out on every lap.

Courses can reflect the preferences of their designers. No surprise there. But they can also have a personality; indeed the iconic courses of our sport have charisma, even a sense of humour. None more so than the Koppenbergcross. In theory this is a race which pays homage to the revered cobbled climb, but in reality the race turns off the climb before its steepest sections, and the road section rarely makes an impact on the result. The off-camber climbs and descents which follow are much more significant. It's like the cyclocross world is having a little joke at the expense of the roadies – your infamous climb is so easy that we turn off it and climb the cow pasture next to it. The Koppenbergcross has a distinctly pastoral feel to the scene. It embodies all that is traditional in cyclocross – it's in the heart of Flanders, it's centred on a small village not a faceless motor racing circuit, and it doesn't contain any contrived artificial features. It's as though the organisers are so confident in the attractiveness of their race that they don't need to resort to bridges and rollers and sandpits.

Such features are principally for the television coverage. The rollers at Loenhout, for example, have no impact on the race, but look spectacular from a head-on camera, the riders bobbing up and down as they pump their bikes with their arms. A bridge is a more useful weapon in the designer's armoury because it can create figure-of-eight shapes or create crossing points. For me, the most interesting features are those that seem to symbolise something deeper, a connection to the landscape, be it farmland, industrial or suburban. At the Jaarmarktcross in Niel the course snakes through the yard of the Coeck concrete factory and instead of conventional barriers the road is lined with stacked bags of concrete. At Hasselt the parkland around which the course loops is bordered by an expansive building site, so this year riders were sent into the site and over a huge mound of earth.

This is a sport born in the fields – *veldrijden* (the Dutch word for cyclocross) means field-driving – but cyclocross can colonise any landscape. Many races – Ruddervoorde, Overijse – take place in and around a village, and the normally quiet streets are transformed into a festive riot of noise and colour. Some lucky householder might find a team warming up outside their property.

And here lies the unique beauty of cyclocross. It is thoroughly embedded in the landscape, both physical and social, but it doesn't try to peddle some nostalgic vision of a pastoral past. In his book *Landmarks*, the nature writer Robert Macfarlane has used the term 'edgelands' to denote the mixed up, suburban landscape in which many of us live. The edgelands are neither urban nor countryside, but the frayed boundary between the two. Describing the London suburb where another nature writer, Richard Jefferies, lived, Macfarlane focuses on the pathways between town and country: 'Fields began where suburban streets ran to their end; footpaths led quickly into copses and woodlands; streams and rivers ran under stone bridges and between houses. Nevertheless it was still recognisably a marginal zone, intersected by roads and railways, and travelled through by Londoners both escaping the city and by itinerant workers seeking it out.'

The edgelands are the spiritual home of cyclocross. It is not a wilderness sport; we don't expect to see races on the side of a mountain, or in a desert. Like punk rock, our sport is thoroughly suburban.

I am a child of the edgelands. The village in which I grew up felt like a rural idyll when I was six years old, but in reality it was well within London's orbit, and I have lived in similar places all my life. There is very little true wilderness left in England. My parents – Londoners who escaped the capital and found the countryside more to their liking – settled in the Chiltern Hills, the long curving ridge that sits between the spires of Oxford and the industrial estates of Reading. But this landscape – pretty and comforting, but rather tame – wasn't enough for them. For holidays they would take us to the Lake District or Cornwall or Snowdonia. Our surname perfectly fits my father; as a verb 'maunder' means to talk in a rambling manner. Talking was his profession (he was a lecturer), and talking was his leisure. The principal difference being that in his leisure time he was usually leading a group of walkers up a mountain as he talked. My mother and I come from the less chatty side of the family. But we're fine stout walkers. Tagging along at the back of the group, or sometimes striding away off the front, I was able to tune out the chatter and absorb the landscape. I developed a profound love for these places, the fells and tarns, the exposed moorland and limitless skies. Those walks taught me about the wind and the rain, and the power of nature – and the joy of pulling some Kendal Mint Cake out of your rucksack at the top of a stiff climb.

As an adult, I've somehow lost touch with that landscape. I always think of myself as a country boy at heart, but the truth is that I've never lived anywhere remote, and the chances to escape out onto the hills are few. London has sucked me back into its vortex, and while I thrive on its energy, often I long for open space and solitude.

Today, the last Sunday in September, I will get plenty of both. I've driven up from London to Yorkshire to watch an utterly unique cyclocross race. It's an event that takes riders out into the wilderness, gives them a good smack round the face and sends them home tired, elated, wanting to do it all over again. And it inspires such devotion from those who have ridden it that I almost feel nervous going to see it, in case I don't comprehend what they see in it.

Usually when going to a bike race I would go to the start area, get a coffee and mill about looking at bikes and riders and generally soaking up the atmosphere. Today I have a different plan.

The Three Peaks Cyclocross race started in September 1959 when a grammar school boy called Kevin Watson, a strong distance runner and keen cyclist, had the bright idea of taking his bicycle over the well-established Three Peaks walking route based around Horton-in-Ribblesdale. Watson, who was 14 years old at the time, rode and pushed his bike over the 30-mile course, taking in the summits of Whernside, Ingleborough and Pen-y-ghent, each of which is over 2000 feet. The paths to the top of these three fells are steep and rocky, but Watson was able to ride his bike for the majority of the course, only shouldering it on the most difficult sections. His feat caught the imagination of a team of cyclocross riders from Bradford, who attacked the course the following year. In 1961 the first official Three Peaks race took place.

Not everyone was supportive. The founder of the Rough-Stuff Fellowship, a group of likeminded cyclists who took their touring bikes off-road, wrote to a cycling magazine deploring the creation of a bike race in an area of natural wilderness, using footpaths (which were otherwise illegal to cycle on). The organiser John Rawnsley responded by restricting the race to forty riders, insuring them against any damage to property or animals, and extending a warm welcome to the complainant. The Three Peaks went ahead, and the toughest cyclocross race in the world was born.

In almost sixty years, the race has changed little. It has grown – there are now 600 riders – but the essence of the event is still the same. The course hasn't changed, indeed cannot change significantly without completely undermining the identity of the race. Rawnsley's rule that you must ride a cyclocross bike has been stuck to steadfastly, and adds to the sense of English eccentricity. Much of the course, particularly the descending, is ideal for a mountain bike. One would think that adapting the rules accordingly would be common sense. No, the organisers know this would make the Three Peaks into just another mountain bike race.

I park my car at the foot of Whernside, lace up my walking boots, check my rucksack has got sufficient quantity of Kendal Mint Cake, and set out towards the famous, stunning Ribblehead Viaduct. Today is clear, bright and warm. A thin mist hangs over the hills, and the sunshine is hazy, bringing a strange intensity to the colours of the moors, the purples, greens and browns. The wind has a chill edge to it, but for these parts it is barely a breeze. Talk to any regular entrant and you will hear about the wind and rain of such and such a year, when you could barely stand on the summits and the weather closed in so fast you couldn't work out which way to get down the mountain. 'Don't forget,' they'll tell you, 'this is the only cyclocross race in which it's mandatory to carry a survival blanket and a whistle.' The curlews are singing as the path takes me up the climb.

The line of riders stretches across the corrugations of the hillside. The gradient makes this impossible to ride, so the riders have to carry their bikes, their shoes clattering on the limestone slabs, wheels slowly spinning, a constant discordant rhythm of heavy breathing. There are many club jerseys on display, together with a few eccentric outfits. Some riders carry food and drink in a backpack, knowing they could be out on the hills for over four hours. There are all ages too, from teenagers to pensioners.

The Three Peaks is only really a race for a few riders, and those riders are a special breed. They are generally cyclocross riders from the north of England, who are familiar with the terrain, but above all very, very fit. Eleven times winner Rob Jebb is a fell runner and skyrunner (long distance off-road running races at altitude) and for many years he was untouchable in the Three Peaks because he was the only person to run up the hills, with the bike on his shoulder. For everyone else it is a personal challenge, though I hesitate to compare it to a sportive because its course is punishingly hard, and its ethos is much more tough and stripped down. Part of the appeal is in pitting yourself against the landscape and the weather, not something most of us get to do very often. Another part of the appeal lies in its spirit of the scramble. It is both old-fashioned and pioneering. It places no importance on aesthetics, tactics, money or sponsorship, because it is simple and brutal. 'Come and survive me,' it says.

Pained faces continue to come past where I'm sitting, legs trudging. The world of the spectator, detached, judging, analysing, is very different from the world of the competitor. I am only a visitor, whereas they are engaged with the rocks and mud, they are fighting the slopes. I still do not really understand this race, and why so many adore it. I think the only way for me to understand it would be to do something I am never going to do – ride it.

Why climb a mountain? To get to the top. Why climb a mountain carrying a cyclocross bike? Because it makes it easier to break your neck on the way down.

5
Punks and Sharks

After the surreal opening skirmish in the Nevada desert heat, the European cyclocross season begins to find its normal rhythm in October. Though the weather, this year, is unseasonably warm, the colourful circus that makes up the top tier of the sport begins its annual round of visits to familiar, loved venues. Although the epicentre of the professional cyclocross world is Belgium and Holland, the afterglow spreads as far as France, Luxembourg and Switzerland. These countries, and many more as far afield as Australia and Japan, have their own calendars of races.

Besides the World Cup, there are two other series that run for the duration of the season. Of the two, the Superprestige – as the name cleverly implies – is the more prestigious. It's been running since 1982, and for the cyclocross traditionalist this is the heart and soul of the season. Many of the Classic races are part of the Superprestige series, and its brand value has been protected over the years by a clear strategy of not letting sponsors take over the identity. Its founder and president is Etienne Gevaert. Now in his seventies, Gevaert is one of most influential men in Belgian cyclocross. He lost his sight when he was 13 and went on to become *soigneur* to the De Vlaeminck brothers, Roger and Erik. In 1981, a group of

Belgian cyclocross organisers had the idea to create a season-long competition, and on a train journey back from the 1981 World Championships in Spain the group had a meeting with the Belgian Cycling Union to thrash out the details. Initially there were events in France, Holland, Switzerland and Czechoslovakia, but gradually the other countries lost interest and the series became focused on Belgium and Holland. The modern competition includes eight rounds, of which only one is outside Belgium – the opening round in Gieten, a small town in the far north of the Netherlands. Recently though, as if to counter claims of Belgian cyclocross being parochial, the organisers have taken the bold step of staging a round in Wallonia, the French-speaking region of Belgium, at the motor-racing circuit at Spa-Francorchamps. Some of the younger Flandrian riders thought they had to take their passport.

Whereas the Superprestige has firmly planted its identity in the minds of the viewing public, its rival series has fallen into the trap of taking its name from its title sponsor. Variously called the GVA Trofee, the Bpost Bank Trofee and the DVV Trofee, this second series also has eight rounds, and its geographical reach is even less impressive than its older rival. All eight rounds are in Flanders. The principal difference between the two competitions is that the DVV Trofee works on the basis of aggregated time, whereas the Superprestige uses a points system.

The concept of season-long competitions never really came to life in road racing. There was the World Cup of the 1990s, itself a rejuvenation of the Superprestige Pernod International, which ran between 1959 and 1987. Sponsors and governing bodies, desperately trying to wrest some power away from race organisers, tried their hardest to make these competitions valued, but they were always an afterthought. No rider set out to win a season-long road competition. The events were too diverse and the timescale too stretched. In cyclocross these series work because the same small group of elite racers contest races week in, week out, between October and February. The public can see the narrative unfolding before them.

This season the Superprestige and Bpost Bank Trofee series kick off with races at Gieten (Netherlands) and Ronse (Belgium), respectively. Ronse, also known as the GP Mario de Clercq in honour of the former World champion who is involved in organising the race, is notable this year for making a small but not insignificant piece of history. It will be the first time a full women's race has been broadcast live on television. Up to now, the women have been edited into highlights. This year Sporza, the principal Belgian broadcaster, have committed to show all the top women's races live. Many of those campaigning behind the scenes – including Helen Wyman and Sven Nys – for more equality, have pointed out to the media, organisers and governing bodies that there are sound commercial reasons for showing women's racing. Sound moral reasons too, of course, but in any professional sport money is more articulate. Given that the demand for cyclocross on television is almost insatiable in Belgium, showing a forty-minute women's race, in which Belgian hero Sanne Cant is pretty likely to emerge victorious, is a safe bet in terms of viewer numbers. And strong viewing numbers increases advertising revenue. The women's sponsors get more exposure, ratcheting up their own return on investment, and everyone benefits.

The scene, this second Sunday in October, is pastoral and relaxed. The course climbs and descends a steep hill, close to the Hotondberg, one of the Tour of Flanders' many bergs. The land is mainly meadow, dotted with oak trees, some low brick farm buildings in the distance. On top of the hill is a white windmill, the Hotondmolen, on which is stretched a banner saying, 'Welcome to the Hotond Arena'. The hill not only makes the course physically testing, it also creates a natural amphitheatre from which fans can see most of the course. With no need to run about or crowd at the barriers, many are taking the opportunity to perch on the grassy slope and have a picnic lunch. The weather is warm and sunny, though a stiff breeze makes it feel cool. It's the kind of weather that confuses: some wear T-shirts, some wear winter coats and scarves.

The first televised women's race doesn't go to script. Sanne Cant has a rare off day and finishes fourth. The winner, Czech Pavla Havlíková, is an experienced racer, but something of a surprise, having not competed the previous week in Gieten, nor at CrossVegas. The men's race is won by Wout van Aert, extending a winning streak to five races out of five, with compatriot Kevin Pauwels in second and Lars van der Haar in third. After the finish Van Aert collapses from his bike and sprawls on the tarmac, panting and grimacing. The win is convincing but the effort to secure it was immense. Naturally the television cameras are there to capture his heaving chest and his impressively voluminous hair. 'Only twenty-one years old, only twenty-one,' says Sporza's commentator, softly. It's in moments like this that the sport's heroes are forged. Van Aert's race was controlled, technically consummate, and ruthless in its tactical execution. On the bike his facial expression rarely changes. Emotion doesn't play on his face as it does with other riders, and rarely does the effort show as pain. So for television viewers, lounging at home on the sofa, to see him throw off his sunglasses and helmet and portray the sheer intensity of physical and emotional effort he had to go through, that's what will make Van Aert their hero. Sporting heroes are made through deeds, but also through their personalities. As Sporza's commentator and man on the ground Renaat Schotte says to me, 'Van Aert can be as big as Sven, but he needs to develop his personality.' Not his legs, or his VO_2 max, but his personality. This is the symbiotic relationship between sports stars and the media. They need each other, and there is always a push–pull tension between each other.

At the start of the Ronse race, as the elite men line up, the camera works its way across the front row of the grid. It takes in each rider's face, for long enough to give the commentator a chance to introduce them, then moves on. For selected riders the camera angles down from their face to their front tyre. The commentator then indulges the tyre-geeks with that particular rider's choice. From seasons past, the cameraman knows he has to get Sven's tyre. Sven is the big star. Today he shows Sven's tyre, but lingers longer on Wout van Aert's. It's in everyone's interests for Van Aert to be seen as the heir apparent to Nys.

Renaat played an incidental role in the development of Nys from blandly successful youngster into the charismatic and popular figure we know today. In the 2003–04 season Nys won the first three rounds of the World Cup, in Italy, Germany and

Switzerland. Coming into the final round at Pijnacker in the Netherlands he was still wearing the overall leader's white skinsuit but, with double points on offer, his overall victory was not assured. The Dutch rider Richard Groenendaal, a teammate of Nys's on the Dutch Rabobank team, had not won a round of the series all season but had scored consistently enough to be in with a theoretical chance of winning. When he slipped away from Nys and a group full of Belgians it was not a huge concern to Nys because as long as he finished in the top five he would win the World Cup.

Groenendaal won, but behind him there was treachery afoot. Nys controlled the chasing group and was in a good position for the final sprint to the line. The Belgian team all knew that he had to finish at least fifth, but four of them outsprinted Nys, together with a Swiss rider, pushing him down to seventh. The World Cup went to a pleasantly surprised Groenendaal. Watching back the video of that final sprint, the fourth Belgian to outsprint Nys, Wesley van der Linden, does so in a desperate lunge for the line. He clearly wanted to relegate his teammate. That the Belgians were all racing in their national colours that day made the betrayal even more sharp.

Nys was stunned, then furious. As he walked through the area around the podium, Renaat caught him and asked him what he thought of what had just happened. Nys looked back at Renaat and said one line, a Flemish expression which translates (roughly) as, 'They can all go to the trees.'

That evening Nys swore to himself, and to the media, never again to concern himself with team loyalties, be they trade or national. He wanted to win everything, to utterly destroy his opposition. He became the cannibal of Baal, and whereas formerly he used to be quiet and timid, with nothing to say in interviews, he became gradually more animated and entertaining. The Belgian public saw him winning, and then they saw he had his own personality. The cult of Sven began to build. Writing about winter sports, the American essayist Adam Gopnik has illustrated how in the early part of the twentieth century people reverted to the idea that winter sports were not a social affair (as ice skating had been until then) but an opportunity for individuals to show courage in the face of adversity. Ernest Hemingway, writing for the *Toronto Star*, wrote about this 'cult of the lonely individual' in relation to the luge and sledding events of the Winter Olympics. Sven Nys's popularity has been founded on an exceptional record of performance, but also because he demands respect, doesn't take any shit, and isn't afraid to forge his own path.

Interestingly, the career of Wesley van der Linden never really progressed after 2004. The previous season he finished second in the Under-23 World Championship and had looked set for a stellar career. The world of Belgian cyclocross is small and ruthless – it pays to be careful with your loyalties.

*

Personality has played a big part in Katie Compton's success too, though her story is very different from Sven's. Originally from Delaware, now settled in Colorado, Katie has ploughed a determined, independent and very successful furrow throughout her career. If you meet her off the bike, you'll probably be struck by how different she looks from how she does on the bike. Petite, with a long cascade of blonde hair, and a face with the healthy glow of someone who loves outdoor sports, she is reserved, self-contained but always approachable. Her smile is disarming, and she's professional to the point of meticulous, even when things aren't going her way. Dealing with the media, thanking fans and officials, representing her sponsor – it's all part of the game. Unlike some racers, who take their self-promotion as seriously as their training, she is humble. And it's this humility that has so endeared her to the American cross community. Her style, her demeanour, is genuine. She's managed to pull off the difficult trick of being a hero to seven-year-old girls and urban hipsters. She's an all-American girl, with just a hint of counterculture about her.

Check out her Twitter account and you'll see that her handle is Katie 'Fn' Compton. The abbreviation is for the sake of politeness, because the 'Fn' stands for 'Fuckin'. The story goes that one weekend, after she had started winning regularly, one of her friends phoned a mutual friend and asked who'd won the race that day. 'Katie Fuckin' Compton,' the friend replied. 'Who'd ya think?' The name became abbreviated to KFC, and because it seemed to perfectly encapsulate her tenacity and strong-mindedness, it stuck.

Her modesty has meant that over the years she has rarely complained about the crippling health conditions she's had to contend with. The exercise-induced asthma, serious allergies to pollen and bees, and intense pains in her legs have all hit her during races, and made for a *palmarès* that looks erratic, until you know the context. The one race that has eluded her is the most prestigious, the World Championship. Every season, by the weekend of the Worlds, in late January or early February, either her form or her health or just her luck has waned.

Coming into this season, after a summer beset with severe health issues, Katie's form is well behind where she usually is. But could that be a blessing in disguise? A slow start to the season often means a rider comes into January feeling fresher. With seven-time World champion Marianne Vos not riding cyclocross this season as she recovers from a knee injury, could this be Katie's year to grab the rainbow jersey of World champion?

Valkenburg, in the Limburg region of the Netherlands, close to the Belgian border, nestles in a valley in the hills known as the Dutch Alps. It has quaint castles, parks, restaurants, cafés and watermills. A spa and wellness resort reinforces the feeling of being in a place where the pre-war bourgeoisie might have come to take the water. These days Valkenburg is famous for its cycling connections. It is home to the spring Classic, the Amstel Gold Race, and has also hosted the World Road Championships five times. The focal point of all these events has been the Cauberg, an unremarkable stretch of road that climbs out of town, made famous because the finish line of all these grand races has been at its summit.

My father and I went to the 1998 Worlds in Valkenburg and stood on the Cauberg in the cold autumnal rain, waiting for the peloton to come round for another lap. The following cars and phalanx of motorbikes all had their headlights blazing yellow through the gloom as the riders, covered in road-grime, teeth gritted and eyes focused on the damned objective of a rainbow jersey, stomped up the hill. By the final lap we were chilled to the bone and full of the coffee and hotdogs we'd been consuming all day, but the sheer nervous excitement of the huge crowd filling Valkenburg's streets was utterly exhilarating.

As if to keep the cycling connection alive through the dark winter months, the locals organise a cyclocross race every October. Held in the grounds of the casino, the Caubergcross has become a permanent fixture of the World Cup. Using the same hillside that the famed Cauberg road climbs, the course is a mixture of fast forest trails, grassy off-cambers and short punchy climbs. This year a spell of rain has softened the ground, and after the junior and Under-23 races many sections are heavily rutted. It's a course that requires power – the ability to hit those climbs hard then recover quick enough to maintain a gap on the faster sections. Grip and control are needed too; if misjudged just one of those ruts can end your race. It's very different from the CrossVegas course, and American courses in general, something not lost on the large American contingent that has travelled to race here. In the days before the race, with the course open for training, there are many photos posted on social media of specific features. One of the most dangerous is a precipitous and slippery drop with a 90-degree turn at the bottom. There are crash barriers to catch the riders who get their line wrong. One amusing video clip posted on Instagram shows a group of Belgian elite men standing at the top of the descent during an official training session, discussing lines and strategies. Then Amanda Miller, perhaps better known for her road racing than her cyclocross, pedals along and confidently rolls down the drop, her bike slithering under her. Sometimes it's better not to overanalyse things.

For Katie Compton, Valkenburg is a short drive from her European base in Kalmthout, a small town just north of Antwerp. Travel on race day itself might be brief, but to get to Europe usually means at least fourteen hours in the air, with all the interminable airport transfers and waiting around that go with flying. After Vegas and Gloucester, Katie's had a block of quality training at home in Colorado Springs, but she comes into the race with relatively low expectations. It takes time to build form.

Last year Katie won this race. Despite a mechanical issue that meant she had to change bikes on the first lap, she rode a controlled, calculating race, picking off riders ahead of her and then going clear. The weather then was warm and sunny, much like in Ronse last weekend, but today in Valkenburg it's cold and overcast if dry. For the first time this season the crowd are all wrapped up. By lunchtime they are well-lubricated with beer – Amstel, of course. In the men's race Lars van der Haar has a good record here. It's a course that suits him, and he's on home turf. This year is no exception; Van der Haar runs out a clear winner, ahead of Van Aert and Nys. After the dominance of Van Aert in the opening races of the season, this is an important victory for Van der Haar. While he's been at the top of sport for several years, there is a sense that his career has been eclipsed by the more flashy talents of Mathieu van der Poel and Wout van Aert. Most riders follow a progression over the years, building strength and experience, and in their late twenties can expect to be at the height of their powers. Van der Haar, still only 24, seems to be following this path, and with Sven Nys due to retire in 2016, his future looks bright. As Van der Haar rolls across the finishing line and punches the air, there is an expression of redemptive anger on his face. I'm still here, it seems to say.

The women's race, won by Eva Lechner, whose form has carried through from Vegas, is notable for the strong performances of several American women. Katie Antonneau, whose nickname is *la petite blaireau* (little badger, not because she's related to Tour de France winner Bernard Hinault but because she's small and fierce on the bike), finishes second, a breakthrough performance for her on the biggest stage. In fifth is Amanda Miller, she of the impressive descending skills. For her too this is a great result in her first World Cup outside America. Crystal Anthony finishes twelfth and one place behind her comes Katie Compton.

'It started off bad and got worse,' she tells a reporter from *VeloNews* after the race, then modifies her statement in case her self-deprecating irony didn't translate well. 'It's fine. I rode OK. I just don't have any power.'

There is time yet for her form to build, but one senses the anxiety. January, and the World Championships, is not so far away.

*

I would usually resist the kind of generalisations created in trying to define a 'national character'. There is a risk of stereotyping, and of defining a country by a hopelessly outdated set of characteristics. Much of the conversation about the English character feels like it's based on what the country was like in the 1950s. Or our perception of what it was like in the 1950s. Having said all that, my time in Belgium has affirmed many of the received wisdoms about the Belgian character. The Flemish people – Walloons are a rarity in cyclocross – are reserved, understated, modest and humble. They tend to value hard work and loyalty. The Flemish identity is important to them, but equally important is their region, their village. People don't move from their village. The next village is another world, Brussels is another universe. So local community is the bedrock of their lifestyle and identity.

The writer Richard Hill, who has lived in Belgium for many years, has described (in his book *The Art of Being Belgian*) the country's bunker mentality. History has taught Belgians that other countries will fight their wars on Belgium's fields, and will march through Belgium's cities and towns to get to the country they want to invade. Today Belgium is a cockpit, Hill says, in the sense of being the control centre for the European Union, but in the past it was a theatre of war. The Belgian people have a healthy scepticism, plus a tendency to batten down the hatches at the slightest sign of trouble. He goes on to give the example of the opening days of the Gulf War when many Belgians reverted to their 'bunker mentality', going out to strip the shop shelves of essential items, as if they were expecting to see the whole thing out from their living rooms. In societies that appear staid, respectable and quiet, there is always something going on under the surface.

As I watch the Superprestige at Zonhoven, I find myself drawn to the colours of the race, rather than the racing itself. It's a gloomy day, with overcast skies. And the race is set in a forest. Other than the usual raucous advertising panels, the backdrop is dark. On the more remote parts of the course there is only grey sky, a black tree-line and thousands of spectators in dark rain jackets. Along the sandy forest paths the heroes of Belgian and Dutch cyclocross come charging, lit up by their fluorescent clothing.

While road racing has had a crisis of confidence about its long love of garish design, cyclocross hasn't been bitten by the tasteful bug. Take Wout van Aert's kit – black shorts with fluorescent orange side panels; a black, gold and fluo orange jersey; fluo orange socks, gloves and helmet. All, naturally, emblazoned with a dozen logos. Truly a horrible design that even Van Aert struggles to pull off.

The irony is that when an element of hipster style infiltrates this world, it is usually derided. The Canadian Mark McConnell rides regularly in Belgium, and is jeered and cheered in equal measure, principally because he has a thick bushy beard. He's a competent rider who takes his sport seriously, but the beard doesn't fit with what the average working-class Belgian thinks a professional cyclist should look like. His popularity is growing, because year after year he comes back for more, and the crowds see that he loves this sport (which they consider *their* sport), he respects the sport, and maybe there is a bit of room for a few oddballs. The Belgian bunker mentality can translate into a suspicion of foreigners. You have to prove yourself before admittance into the inner circle of Belgian life, and even then you will still feel very much the outsider.

Especially if you are American. Richard Hill makes the point that because the Belgians tend to be introverted and reserved, it can take time to get to know them. Their friendship, once won, is warm and genuine but will require an investment of time and energy, and, for an American, this is a major cultural shift with which to grapple. In their own way the Dutch are also very different from the Belgians, hence the intense flag-waving rivalry that manifests itself at cyclocross races.

The principal feature at Zonhoven is a huge sandpit in a clearing in the forest that forms a natural amphitheatre. The racers plunge down it twice and clamber up again twice. The sand is deep and unforgiving – in every race several riders crash spectacularly on the descents. A front wheel getting stuck in a rut is a common problem. And for every wobble, there are ten thousand fans there to give you their opinion. As I watch Lars van der Haar leading the Zonhoven race, I realise that I've missed the point. The fans *want* their riders to stand out, to be pricks of colour against a muted winter palette. Winter sports give us a vibrant aesthetic because we need that injection of colour in our lives. Downhill ski racing has an aesthetic of contrast – strong colours against the white-out backdrop. Cyclocross has a different backdrop – dark forests, mud, overcast skies, but the same principle applies. The heroes are luminous, literally. They represent a rebellion against the drudgery of everyday life. It may not be large-scale rebellion, but it's enough to sustain you through the long dark winter.

*

A transatlantic hop takes us from the deep dark forest of Zonhoven to the rather more sunny climes of Santa Cruz, California, where we can see a different side to this strange sport. In the grounds of the Harbor High School there are many peculiar creatures aboard bicycles. A shark, Darth Vader, a headless horseman, Captain Hook and Tinkerbell on a tandem, a man wrapped in bubble wrap, and a provocatively dressed flight attendant – all competitors in the annual Surf City All-Hallows Costume Cyclocross. Costume cross races have become very popular in the United States, and are a perfect expression of the fun side of the sport. The Surf City series has four events through the autumn, all in the Santa Cruz area, with around twenty-five races at each meeting. Everyone is catered for, from children on their first pedal bikes to the over-65s. Many of the racers who have dressed up today are serious about their racing, but clearly cannot resist a chance to demonstrate their ability to ride fast dressed up as a shark. After the costume race, the Lycra-based racing resumes, building up to the elite races. The men's race is won by a 21-year-old Californian called Tobin Ortenblad. Ever ready with a pearly white grin, and sporting an Errol Flynn-style moustache, Ortenblad is a dashing feature on the American circuit.

Here is the beauty of the American take on cyclocross. In the same race meeting, riding on the same course, signing on in the same little tent, are young children focused on racing towards a sugar-based treat reward, grown men worrying about whether they're going to overheat in their Wookie outfit, and elite athletes plotting their path to the highest level of the sport. Cyclocross is fun. Just riding your bike over some challenging terrain is fun, irrespective of whether you're racing or not. And it's accessible. Race organisers make sure to keep the 'barriers to entry' low. In most races you can ride a mountain bike. Sponsorship subsidises low entry fees. And, most importantly, in cyclocross there is no sense of failure. You simply go round and round, doing your laps, fighting the course and perhaps a few other racers, but no one really knows where you are in the race, and no one really cares. You're out there getting muddy, that's all that matters.

There is a DIY, independent ethos to the sport in America. You can race alone, you don't need much of a budget, and you can take it as seriously as you want to. Because cyclocross training is generally short and very intense, it's easier to combine with a full-time job than road racing is, which demands long endurance rides. So the sport seems to attract those with an independent spirit. Riders like Cam Dodge, who can compete with the best in the country and yet turns down offers from professional teams because he likes to do his own thing, riding alone (generally at the front) in his all-black skinsuit. Riders like Dan Chabanov, who used to be cycle messengers and came to the sport through the fixie culture and alleycat racing in New York.

Molly Hurford, a journalist, cyclocross rider and fan, has seen the sport evolve in the United States: 'When I got into it I was super into punk rock, mohawks and all that. Cyclocross was the punk rock of racing. There are all the crazy elements – the beer hand-ups and the heckling. But most of all it's fun and easy to get into. Road racing is conformist and you need to be on a team. And mountain biking is just intimidating. Even quite recently, the top guys in America didn't really take it [cyclocross] very seriously. There was no money in it, and the courses were just in someone's backyard.'

The roots of cyclocross in America can be traced back to the sixties, but if we're looking for a definitive start point, let's take the first national championships in 1974. Throughout the seventies, cross in America grew organically, in regional pockets. Invariably in each region there were a handful of passionate riders who became organisers. It's a minor quirk of cycling history that cross in America was born at almost exactly the same time as mountain biking, yet the two grew up very separately – twins separated at birth, we might say. Mountain biking started in the mid-seventies in California, where a group of pioneers created the now legendary Repack downhill race. The riders and their modified beach cruiser bikes were loaded onto the back of pick-up trucks and driven as far as the tarmac would take them. When the road ran out they unloaded their bikes and rode or pushed them to the top. The course was 2.1 miles long and had an elevation loss of 1300 feet. Most of the bikes had old-fashioned hub brakes which got so hot from the heavy braking that their grease vaporised, requiring the hub be frequently repacked – hence the race's name. The race ran between 1976 and 1979, but in a sense the race itself was the least important thing. At race meetings the riders compared bikes, technical innovations and riding techniques. This renegade group of friends, operating outside the cycling establishment, created the germ of modern mountain biking, and many went on to fuel the growth of mountain biking.

During the 1980s, mountain bike racing spread across the United States, with the governing body NORBA running annual series of cross-country and downhill races. At a time when the denizens of European road racing were embracing the United States, with the Coors Classic attracting top European riders, and the World Road Championships taking place in Colorado in 1986, the UCI ignored mountain biking. Possibly they thought it too similar to cyclocross and not worthy of recognition in its own category, but as the decade went on it was impossible to deny the rapid growth of mountain biking, and that it was developing an identity quite distinct from cyclocross. In 1990 the UCI officially recognised mountain biking as a branch of the sport, and sanctioned the first World Championships in Durango, Colorado. The following year the Grundig World Cup series began, with events in Europe and America. In 1996 mountain biking was incorporated into the Olympic Games in Atlanta, and its swift rise to maturity was complete.

Being much more robust and stable than road bikes, and with an adventurous 'go anywhere' vibe, mountain bikes quickly became a commercial success, selling in huge numbers in America then Europe. And because they were a young technology there was plenty of room for technical innovations such as front and rear suspension systems. This commercial success supported the growth of the sport, and brought money into it through sponsorship. Bike manufacturers have always been the principal sponsors in mountain biking.

Perhaps because bike manufacturers and the media saw such potential in mountain biking, cyclocross in America has had to find its own path, with much less investment. Throughout the eighties and nineties the only national event was the national championships. Otherwise racers only competed in their local races and hungrily consumed news of European cyclocross. In the late nineties a national elite series called the SuperCup was organised, and the best riders had a chance to compete against each other more than once a year.

In the last ten to fifteen years, the growth of mountain biking has slowed, and that of cyclocross has sped up. Recognising that cyclocross is a fun and safe entry point to bike racing, USA Cycling has thrown its weight behind growing the sport. Inevitably this will mean cyclocross in America will continue to become more professional and more structured. And as this process takes place, both in the United States and in Britain, a subversive element is creeping back in. Unsanctioned racing, like the Incredibly Cross series in London, has seen rapid growth, its racers attracted to the ever so slightly anarchic concept of attending a semi-secret race with the minimum of organisation. Because the races take place on common land, like local parks, but without permission from the authorities, and without the government of British Cycling, the locations are kept secret until a day or two before the race then circulated via social media. It's like the illegal raves in the dying days of acid house, when you had to call a phone number to hear a recorded message tell you where to drive to meet up with a convoy of cars that would lead you to the rave. The illegal rave scene was partly in response to the way the music industry had become corporate and heavily policed. Whenever something grows organically, and then is subsumed into a corporate structure, someone will seek to get back to its essence. For cyclocross this means a group of middle-aged Londoners doing what Daniel Gousseau and his friends did more than a hundred years ago – creating a course and racing, nothing more than that.

6

Under the Rainbow

Most of today's classic cross races are youngsters compared to road racing's iconic events. The Koppenbergcross, for example, began in 1988. The longest-running single event is the World Championships, which take place in late January, and are the climax of the season.

With the international growth of cyclocross, and events like the Cyclocross Montmartre in the late 1940s, the UCI saw that cyclocross deserved recognition as a discipline in its own right. The first official World Cyclocross Championships took place in 1950 in the Bois de Vincennes, an expansive public park on the eastern fringe of Paris. Yet this milestone in the development of the sport was something of a last-minute decision by the UCI; it was only two days before the race that they awarded an already planned event the status of World Championship. Its winner was Jean Robic, the tiny Breton who'd won the Tour de France in 1947 with a brazen attack on the final day. Robic was a hugely popular figure in France, despite his rather sullen and spiteful attitude. *L'Équipe* journalist Pierre Chany said, 'He had a face that was speckled like a bitter apple, large ears and a little nervous and muscular body. At the same time proud and stubborn, he detested all those whom nature had made better proportioned and those whom nature had given what he considered a more handsome body.'

Because the sport was – officially, at least – new, the UCI shared the World Championships around Europe. For its first ten years the event took place in seven different countries. It even has the historical honour of being staged in a country which only existed for eight years: the Saar Protectorate, a tiny but wealthy piece of land in West Germany, was annexed by France after the Second World War then returned to West Germany in 1956.

Those early years of the World Championships were dominated by France. After Robic, the rainbow jersey went three times to Roger Rondeaux, but it was André Dufraisse who can legitimately claim (at the time of writing, in the summer of 2016, he has just celebrated his 90th birthday) to be one of the all-time greats. Dufraisse, from Limousin, finished second behind Rondeaux in 1951 and 1952. Then in Crenna, Italy, in 1954 he won the first of five consecutive rainbow jerseys. In a rather poetic loop of fate, his final victory was in the city of Limoges, France, where he had taken part in the first ever cyclocross race in 1949. Even after he acceded to stronger opponents towards the end of his career, he was still able to take three bronze medals between 1961 and 1963. Dufraisse's nickname was 'Coppi of the Fields'.

While French riders were winning the first cyclocross rainbow jerseys, the British cyclocross community was still at an early stage of its evolution. The first British participation in the World Championships was in 1953, at San Sebastián in Spain. A team of five riders made the trip, and though they suffered a variety of misfortunes, including foot blisters, crashes and mechanical failures, the team and by extension the British cycling establishment now started to understand the seriousness of the European scene. Hampered by political bickering between different governing bodies, the British cyclocross calendar was still very much based on fun events such as scrambles and team relays. In their book *Mud, Sweat and Gears* Ken and Maureen Nichols give us a delightful description of what a British cross racer in the early fifties would wear to race: 'The jerseys were made of wool, often with two pockets across the chest and three at the back. These were fine until it rained, when the two pockets would catch the water and expand like small breasts, leaving the rider to squeeze out the water whilst still racing. Woollen or leather gloves, cotton undervests, a racing jersey topped up with perhaps a woollen jumper were the training gear of choice. Below the waist it would be "plus twos" fitting to just below the knee (closer tailored than plus-fours). Long woollen socks, gaily patterned and in bright colours would add a bit of flair. Shoes would be black leather lace-up (polished to a mirror shine) fitted with shoe-plates screwed to their soles for grip . . . All this was topped off with a zip-up cotton jacket and woolly bobble hat.'

A cool outfit, and one that will appeal to today's hipsters, but horribly impractical for the task at hand. It's tempting to think of the pioneers of the sport in Britain as a bunch of cheerful eccentrics in brightly patterned socks – and no doubt the farmers and publicans who came across them in the fields and villages thought as much – but the British cyclocross community quickly became serious about its sport, both in athletic and organisational terms. The many thousands of spectators at the World Championships (there were reportedly 20,000 at Crenna in 1954) demonstrated just how big the sport could become.

In the autumn of 1954 a group of Britain's more serious riders and coaches began to coalesce around the idea of a British Cyclocross Association. Once established the BCCA governed the sport all the way through until 2001, when cyclocross was taken on by British Cycling. In February 1955 the first national championship was held in a gravel pit near Welwyn Garden City. The base of the pit was deep mud, the slopes were covered in snow, and a freezing wind bit into the competitors and spectators. The winner, Alan Jackson, crashed twice on his way to victory, and everything was captured by BBC television cameras around the course. A summary of the race was shown that evening on the news.

Back in continental Europe, following the Dufraisse era, the sport saw an enthralling duel between Italy's Renato Longo and Germany's Rolf Wolfshohl. In 1959, in Geneva, the pair fought a close battle for the World Championship, with the long-legged Italian, who had switched from motor-paced racing the previous year, coming out on top. Wolfshohl took the next two titles, though something of a shadow hangs over his win in Hanover in 1961. When they undertook their pre-race course inspection the UCI were dismayed to find the course had been designed specifically for local boy Wolfshohl, who was strong technically but often lost time to Longo on climbing and running. They asked the organisers to toughen the course, but in the event

Wolfshohl was on such imperious form that he rode most of the race alone in front anyway.

In 1962 the German was sick, allowing Longo to even up the score. Then the following year, on a frozen course in Calais, northern France, Wolfshohl used his technical abilities to win again. After that he focused on road racing, only riding cyclocross as winter preparation, giving Longo free rein to take three more World titles.

Any rider who felt frustrated by their performance in the World Championships had a chance of revenge at a glamorous-sounding event called the Martini International, which took place near Paris after the Worlds. By the late 1950s the top British riders were respected enough to be invited to ride, even though they were usually the only amateurs on the start list. After riding the race in 1959, Paddy Hoban wrote a report to the BCCA confirming that Martini had paid for all the team's expenses, and that after the race they presented themselves to a cocktail party at Martini & Rossi's penthouse on the Champs-Élysées.

At this time many top road riders also rode cyclocross during the winter, for training and mental diversion. In the sixties, road racing became more specialised and some of those aiming for Tour de France success preferred to spend their winters in the south of France. But some remained, including Charly Gaul, the Luxembourger climber who later became a recluse, and Raphaël Géminiani, the quick-tempered Frenchman who knocked five of a spectator's teeth out with his pump in a rage on the 1957 Giro d'Italia. The French connection to cyclocross is so deep-rooted that the tradition of road riders competing on the mud has continued to this day. Bernard Hinault rode cyclocross events in his native Brittany, as did Marc Madiot, and in recent years the climber John Gadret has also represented France at the World Championships. It's an honourable tradition but possibly has held France's development back. While French professionals were playing at cyclocross, other countries began to take it very seriously indeed.

If the fifties belonged to the French, and the first half of the sixties to Longo and Wolfshohl, 1966 marked the beginning of a new era in cyclocross. In the small town of Beasain, in the Basque Country, a young Belgian called Erik de Vlaeminck surprised the cyclocross world by storming to the World title.

De Vlaeminck dominated cyclocross between 1966 and 1973, winning the World Championship seven times and the Belgian championship four times. He is the Eddy Merckx of cyclocross, and though Sven Nys has since surpassed his overall record, De Vlaeminck's achievement in the World Championships alone has assured his place in the cyclocross hall of fame.

De Vlaeminck was born in March 1945 in Eeklo, a market town in East Flanders. His family were travelling clothiers, and his early years were spent in a trailer – younger brother Roger was later known by the nickname 'the Gypsy'. Though his father loved cycling, Erik initially pursued gymnastics, but a fractured hand prevented any possibility of future success, so Erik turned to cycling. Rather than head out onto the road, Eric instead disappeared into the woods behind his trailer, riding his bike, running with it, developing the foundations of his future skills. Perhaps it was the gymnastics training, but he was a natural on a bike. He had an extraordinary sense of balance and poise, and when combined with power and a distinctly Flandrian attitude to adverse conditions, De Vlaeminck was unbeatable.

He made his debut in 1962 and quickly established his reputation as a rising star. In 1966, at the age of just 20, he won his first World Championship on the tough course in Beasain. De Vlaeminck had only just made his professional debut, but was already clearly better than the preceding master, Longo. After De Vlaeminck's first title, Longo would get another chance in 1967 in Zürich when De Vlaeminck's bike disintegrated. Thereafter the Belgian's domination was total. Once it got beyond two hundred career victories, De Vlaeminck's record gets a bit hazy, as if no one could be bothered to keep counting. In the 1970–71 season, De Vlaeminck won thirty-two out of thirty-four races. The two he lost went one apiece to his brother Roger and Erik's arch-rival Albert van Damme.

In 1970 Erik won his only rainbow jersey on home soil, at the motor racing circuit at Zolder. On the day of the race, the course was soaked from two days of heavy rain, but De Vlaeminck was undaunted by any type of condition. Behind him, in seventh place was Britain's John Atkins, a performance that still stands as the best by a British rider in the male professional World Championship.

De Vlaeminck's final rainbow jersey was won in 1973, in London's Crystal Palace Park. Thousands of costume-clad Belgians and cowbell-swinging Swiss fans made the trip to the first ever World Cyclocross Championships to be staged on British soil. In fact so many spectators arrived at the entrance to the park that huge queues ensued, and the police told the organisers to open the gates and let everyone in for free. Amazingly the event still made a profit. Erik de Vlaeminck came to London supposedly out of shape, but once the race started the British fans were treated to the sort of virtuoso display the Belgians and Swiss took for granted. On the steepest climb of the course, De Vlaeminck was the only rider to stay on his bike. The race for the bronze medal was much more exciting than De Vlaeminck's procession to gold. Rolf Wolfshohl made a late charge to catch and pass two riders on the final lap, earning him a record twelfth medal at the World Championships.

Before the advent of season-long competitions such as the Superprestige and World Cup, the European cyclocross circuit was much less structured, but with no fewer races. There were Classics such as the Druivencross, which survives to this day, but there were also dozens of smaller races in Flemish towns, villages and parks. The national championships were, for many Belgians, the climax of the season. There were so many strong Belgian riders in the sixties and seventies that the national championship was often a harder, more intense race than the World Championships.

De Vlaeminck's experience of competing for the black, yellow and red jersey of Belgian champion was not as straightforward as for the rainbow jersey. Albert van Damme specialised in the national championship and won the title six times between 1963 and 1973; De Vlaeminck won four times. Van Damme, known as 'the Lion of Laarne', and a florist by trade, racked up over four hundred victories during his career, but he was always best known as Eric de Vlaeminck's nearest rival. The Belgian public loved to watch close battles between the two, so organisers were keen to secure Van Damme's presence at their races.

Van Damme was a big, rugged rider who took training and preparation very seriously. In 1974 he travelled to Spain for the World Championships in a Belgian team that did not contain Eric de Vlaeminck. Van Damme was 33 and nearing the end of his career, but he saw his opportunity. On the day before the race, with rain pouring out of a grey January sky, Van Damme was the only Belgian rider to ride around the course. The others stayed in the hotel. The next day Van Damme won his only World title, beating Roger de Vlaeminck and Peter Frischknecht.

Where was Eric on that day in 1974? He was back in Belgium, in prison.

Having stopped racing in 1973, De Vlaeminck had slipped further into the alcohol and amphetamine addictions that had troubled him for years. Convicted of falsifying a doctor's prescription, and involvement in a hit-and-run accident, De Vlaeminck was sentenced to a short prison sentence. The fame and fortune that came with success had been too much for him. De Vlaeminck had burst onto the Belgian cyclocross scene just after it had become a televised sport. His exploits were watched in households across the country – live television coverage made him the sport's first superstar. For seven years he rode the crest of that wave, but – unlike Sven Nys – he didn't have the psychological capability to remain at the top for longer.

After nineteen months out of racing, De Vlaeminck returned to the sport. The spell in prison seemed to have shocked him into conquering his demons, but his fluidity was gone. Though his status as folk hero with the people of Flanders was undiminished, De Vlaeminck now had a degree of notoriety too. He was closely watched by the police and by his team. Legend has it that the Belgian cycling federation were so worried about his potential for misbehaviour they would only issue him a racing licence one day at a time. He won no further major trophies.

In the years after his retirement the people of Eeklo would have become familiar with the sight of their most famous son driving dump-trucks for the municipal authorities. He also worked for a while as a builder. It's tempting to slot this image in with the Flandrian tradition of the working man, and a continued penitence for his sins, but in reality De Vlaeminck's career choice was probably out of financial necessity. He'd spent all his salary and winnings on amphetamines. Hell-raising is expensive.

7
The Flemish Fairground

We respond to Flemish races because something resonates in the way they look. Cobbled spring Classics such as the Tour of Flanders and Gent–Wevelgem have developed their own aesthetic, their own icons and legends. The cobbles themselves, of course, are evocative. But so is the low-slung horizon, and the ditches and dykes, the freezing rain – cyclocross races fit neatly into this aesthetic. Modern photographers are adept at creating images to perpetuate these legends. And we can trace this aesthetic back much further, to the art of the Northern Renaissance – in particular the 'peasant' art of Pieter Bruegel the Elder. Think of *Hunters in the Snow* (1565), one of the classic pre-modern depictions of winter. The snowbound Flemish landscape with its steep bergs is harsh and unforgiving but the village towards which the hunters trudge does at least look warm and inviting. Human life here may be hard but it endures.

The modern landscape of Flanders is, on the face of it, pretty unremarkable. A lattice of fields and woods, dotted with modest villages and light industrial estates. For much of the year the light is low and watery. In spring the air is thick with foul-smelling fertiliser. And whatever silvery sunlight appears between the clouds is usually short-lived. Against this gloomy backdrop a bike race is a vibrant thing, full of colour and noise and life. A road race slips through the lanes and is gone in a few moments, but as any cycling fan knows, the riders are only part of a bike race. Watch the Tour of Flanders and you'll see every village on the route in celebration mood. This is why Flanders is the beating heart of road racing – because the racing is so firmly embedded, not only in the landscape but in the people. There are roadside food stalls, beer tents in fields, banners, costumes, decorated villages and above it all the incessant buzz of the television helicopters. Through this the tough men of cycling come charging.

To win at Flanders takes a special sort of rider. Over the years it has been dominated by local men. Men like Briek Schotte who rode in twenty consecutive editions, winning twice, in 1942 and 1948. Men like Walter Godefroot who, as a teenager, worked ten hours a day as a carpenter, and then went out on his bike because cycling was the only way to get himself out of the working class. The typical Flandrian is characterised as a man of fighting spirit, a man prepared to defend his battle-scarred land, a man of the people.

Karel van Wijnendaele, the father of the Tour of Flanders, had a vision to create a vehicle to promote not only his *Sportwereld* newspaper but also cycling and the Dutch language. Since the establishment of modern Belgium in 1830, Flemish culture and language had been suffocated by the French-speaking Walloons. There was resistance, much of it focused on works of literature such as Hendrik Conscience's *De Leeuw van Vlaanderen*. Correspondingly Flemish nationalism adopted the Lion of Flanders as its emblem. Van Wijnendaele wanted to emancipate the Flemish community by providing it with its own sporting heroes. The vision of a Flandrian war hero, portrayed by Conscience, was of a hard-working man, tough, with immense willpower, humble, proud of his family and community. Van Wijnendaele saw the opportunity to translate this vision into a cycling hero.

Crucially it was agreed that the race should start and finish in Ghent. At the time a French-speaking elite held power in this quintessentially Flandrian city. Van Wijnendaele wanted to get ordinary Flemish people out onto the streets, cheering on their own riders, in their own language, sponsored by their own newspaper, as a political nose-thumbing to the Walloon interlopers.

Though cyclocross was invented around the same time as the Tour of Flanders was first conceived, it has only been since the middle of the twentieth century that Flanders took cyclocross to its heart. Perhaps that's because the Tour of Flanders virtually was a cyclocross race in those early years, so diabolical were the state of the region's roads. Now, cyclocross sits comfortably alongside the Tour of Flanders, culturally and aesthetically. It celebrates the same things, in a slightly different way. The sport embraces the land but, most of all, it celebrates the working man.

In Bruegel's time Flemish society not only endured, it prospered. During the sixteenth century in towns like Ghent the weaving trade supported the growth of an affluent and sophisticated middle class. This in turn supported the development of art and architecture that still influences artists and designers today. The Northern Renaissance, centred in Antwerp, might have been a response to the Italian renaissance but it was equally innovative.

Bruegel and his peers, for instance, were among the first Western artists to paint landscapes.

There is another Bruegel painting that better illustrates why events like the Tour of Flanders and cyclocross are so meaningful to Flemish society. *The Fight Between Carnival and Lent*, painted in 1559, was one of many works examining the life of peasants, their weddings, dances, festivals and rituals. Currently residing in the Kunsthistorisches Museum in Vienna, the painting is set in the market square of an unnamed Flemish town and shows the transition between Carnival, the last winter feast, and Lent. Half of the painting is taken up with the debauchery and indulgence of the peasants celebrating Carnival. There is drinking and dancing, and in the foreground a fool rides a beer barrel with a pork chop attached to the front. There are beggars and bonfires and women carrying waffles. The hilarity and excess of Carnival is contrasted with the other half of the painting, in which we see the self-denial and sobriety of Lent. The churchgoers bear ash-marks on their foreheads as signs of their penitence.

Debauchery and indulgence contrasting with sobriety and penitence? That sounds like a Belgian bike race. The fans get drunk and eat *friets* and waffles, while the sober and tortured riders pass by in a procession, their faces smeared with ash and mud. Is this stretching the symbolism a little too far? Perhaps. But if Breugel were alive today I like to think he'd be out there on the Koppenberg, watching the fans, absorbing the atmosphere.

Manfred Sellink, director of the Royal Museum of Fine Arts in Antwerp and a renowned expert in Bruegel, agrees but offers a deeper analysis: 'Bruegel might certainly have been interested in these aspects of a cycle race. But Bruegel would as always add layers, providing more questions than answers. Are the riders really sober and penitent? Is it vanity which pushes them to aim for eternal glory? Some might even sell their soul to the (doping) devil to secure their place in eternity.' Carnival, according to Sellink, was a short period when the common people were allowed to let themselves go, when anything seemed possible, including turning over the hierarchy of power. Of course that never happened. After Carnival the same power structures were present, solid as ever. Isn't that just like a modern sporting event, where for one day we're all equal, then on Monday morning we face the reality that nothing has really changed?

These connections — between riders and their fans, between debauchery and sobriety — are in my thoughts as I travel through sleepy northern French villages on the first Sunday in November, past military cemeteries at Ypres and Poperinge, with the sun beginning to burn off an early fog. I'm heading for the Koppenbergcross, the first Belgian Classic of the cyclocross season, and travelling in good company. Beside me is Balint Hamvas, one of the most respected photographers on the circuit. Having covered this race five times, Balint knows these roads well. 'You get to know all the petrol stations of Belgium,' he tells me. Ah, the romantic life of a freelance photographer.

As we approach Oudenaarde, a nondescript little town made famous by its cycling connections, Balint tells me about a month-long trip around the United States he undertook recently. Along with wheat intolerance, thick beards and a disdain for organised religion, Balint and I also share a fondness for all things

American. I listen with a tinge of envy as he recounts his journey. I tell myself that my own journey into the heart of the Belgian winter will be just as epic. Probably.

*

All sports have their iconic arenas. In cycling these are usually mountain passes, finishing straights in grand cities, and cobbled farm tracks. Falling firmly into the last category is the Koppenberg. Situated to the south of the town of Oudenaarde, the Koppenberg is a narrow country lane that climbs over a berg, a small Flandrian hill. From an aerial view the road would be barely visible, tucked into a gully of steep banks lined with trees. And the hill itself doesn't look remarkable, just another undulation in this rolling green landscape. It's only when one approaches the Koppenberg by road, on a bicycle, that one appreciates why riders refer to it as 'the witches' wall'. It is steep – 20 per cent near the top. Narrow – only two can safely ride abreast. Cobbled – though not as bad as in the past, the cobbles today are still unforgiving. And slippery – if the cobbles are wet, getting traction means staying in the saddle. Each of these things on a hill in a major bike race is challenging. When combined, they are treacherous. The Koppenberg is the centrepiece of the Tour of Flanders. And though the race is rarely decided there, it is where the race often comes alive. Live television coverage usually starts just before the peloton hits the climb.

The Koppenbergcross, part of the Bpost Bank Trofee series, is the much younger, cheeky cousin of the Tour of Flanders. Though it has only been around since 1988, the Koppenbergcross has established itself as one of the highlights of the cross season. For some, it is the perfect embodiment of Belgian cyclocross. It's a race that sits comfortably in the landscape, pays reference to road racing, but has its own identity. Helen Wyman, who has won the race three times, calls it 'the most iconic cross race in the world, simply because of its value to any Belgian'. The Koppenbergcross is a beautiful race. It weaves through fields, meadows, copses of trees and clusters of country cottages. On a sunny day there is a distinctly pastoral feel to the scene. It's an example of just how embedded into the landscape cyclocross is.

Balint, having secured the precious red bib that shows he's an officially approved photographer, disappears into the press centre to set up his kit. I take a walk down to the start–finish straight, which is on a section of closed main road, to watch the end of the juniors' race. Near the podium and the ticket booth the Koppenberg bar is doing a brisk trade, brisk for eleven o'clock in the morning anyway. Beyond the course, still on the closed main road, the teams have parked their vehicles. As with any bike race, a wander around the team vehicles is always fun: pretty bikes to gawp at, stern mechanics to watch, and if you're lucky your favourite rider will come swishing past.

My objective today is to find an American rider called BrittLee Bowman, who bizarrely is racing here by virtue of winning a raffle, but I'm soon distracted by the row of Telenet–Fidea motorhomes, nine of them in all. Each of the big riders has their own, emblazoned in the team blue and yellow colours, liberally awash with sponsor logos, and with a rather camp smiling photo of said superstar. Unfortunately the images are sized and positioned so that one has to make a conscious effort to look up at the rider's cheerful expression; what's in line of sight is their bottom. The riders themselves are nowhere to be seen. But the team helpers are busy setting up bike stands, pulling wheels from storage compartments, and handing round trays of pastries. The hierarchy of Belgian cyclocross is expressed through its parking structure. The biggest teams get the best spots, everyone else has to hope that they can sweet-talk the parking attendant (a job to be prized among the ranks of volunteers who make these events happen). I'm not sure who BrittLee has travelled here with, but I suspect she'll be parked at the wrong end of the road.

A crowd has gathered around one truck, black and green and advertising a co-operative bank called Crelan. Indeed there are crowd-control barriers around the truck and its counterpart, a Crelan-branded motorhome. Beyond the barriers a PR man is giving out leaflets, a television camera crew is waiting, and several middle-aged men and women are looking self-consciously pleased with themselves to be behind the barriers. This, of course, is the set-up for Sven Nys. The man himself is presumably still inside the motorhome with his feet up, perhaps having a pre-race snack. The crowd outside gazes expectantly at the closed door of the motorhome while a mechanic lines up five fluorescent yellow Trek bikes.

A little further down the road is an anonymous white van, with a lonely but distinctive blue bike parked outside. Two men in matching jackets are sitting talking across the bike. One is BrittLee's host, the owner of the ChainStay cycling house, an operation that offers American riders a home from home; the other the mechanic. BrittLee is out warming up, they say, and they seem surprised I've come looking for her.

'How's she feeling? Nervous?' I ask. In an email to me a week earlier BrittLee had expressed doubts about even finishing the race.

Her host, Gregg replies, 'She's fine. It's all in her head. She's good enough to hold her own.'

The story behind BrittLee's trip to Europe – her first – demonstrates the endearing, community-focused side of the cyclocross clan. But its context demonstrates a troubling undercurrent.

In 2014 the women's race at Koppenbergcross was renamed the GP Twenty20. More importantly it became the first European UCI Category 1 race to offer the same prize money for the women as for the men. While one might think the organisers are taking either moral leadership, or perhaps engaging in a more cynical public relations exercise, the truth is altogether more strange. Twenty20 is a bike shop in Baltimore, and its owner, Kris Auer, organises the Charm City Cross in the Maryland city, a UCI ranked event in early October. How did a bike shop owner from Baltimore come to stump up the prize money for a top Belgian race? The connection is Helen Wyman, multiple British champion and Koppenbergcross winner. A passionate and effective campaigner for equal rights for women in cyclocross, Wyman knew Auer from her early season American trips, and she connected him with the Koppenbergcross organisers. They were only too happy to take his money and garner the extra publicity, but one wonders whether they didn't also feel a little embarrassed.

If it takes the generosity of a bike shop owner from another continent to give Belgian promoters a kick in the proverbial, what does that say about their own ambition for positive change?

This year, the second of a two-year contract between the Koppenbergcross and Twenty20, Auer offered several prizes at a raffle to be drawn at the Charm City Cross. First prize is an all-expenses-paid VIP trip to the race in Belgium. The winner did something rather unexpected, but very much in keeping with the spirit of equal opportunities and generosity, and immediately offered it to a young upcoming American female rider: BrittLee. Out of the blue, she signed up for the one of the most famous European bike races, and packed her bags.

An elite racer for the House Industries–Richard Sachs team, BrittLee lives in New York City but spends much of her time in Easthampton, Massachusetts, where she trains and races with her boyfriend Stephen Hyde, an elite racer and product of Jeremy Powers's development programme. BrittLee is an example of the kind of independent, entrepreneurial spirit that the sport attracts. A native New Yorker and daughter of a photographer and an art director, she rides elite cross during the winter and manages a domestic road racing team during the summer. Because neither pays the rent, she works as a freelance designer. And being a designer, BrittLee understands the power of visual symbols. Her bike, a pale blue steel-framed custom build by Richard Sachs, legendary New York frame-builder, is a thing of beauty to anyone who remembers the steel racing bikes of the eighties. Less subtle, but more social media friendly, are her glasses. While most riders wear the ubiquitous Oakleys, or something similar, BrittLee sports a pair of oversized spectacles with bright green frames. She's a ball of energy, always talking, always laughing. She takes her sport seriously, but you get the impression that it's in the mix-up of racing, managing, designing and socialising that she gets her kicks. If BrittLee dedicated herself entirely to riding a bike faster she could be a slightly better rider, but she'd be a lot more bored.

Wherever the funding is coming from, the GP Twenty20 has quickly accrued a high profile. Positive media coverage for the event is healthy for the sport, and the field of fifty-one riders is testament to how strong women's cyclocross has become in a relatively short period of time.

After a 200-metre sprint up the main road towards Oudenaarde, the women turn sharp left and dive down a ramp into a meadow. With the ground hard and dry the pace remains high and the riders bounce back onto tarmac, snaking through the village streets, past a TV camera position and a *friets* van and they're rattling across the cobbles of the Koppenberg itself. All the major players are at the front – Belgian champion Sanne Cant, Britons Nikki Harris and Helen Wyman, young Dutch star Thalita de Jong and Telenet–Fidea teammates Ellen van Looy and Jolien Verschueren. Yet as the gradient begins to bite and the racers click down through their gears, it's the young Belgian Femke van den Driessche who accelerates, with apparent ease, away from her more accomplished rivals. No one panics. It's only the first lap. But it's surprising. Van den Driessche is a promising talent, but she's only 19, and has never ridden this well before.

Back in the race, and Jolien Verschueren is proving the woman to beat. The 25-year-old kindergarten teacher from nearby

Kortrijk isn't very stylish on the bike – all knees and elbows – but has strong technique and a killer attack on a steep climb. Early in the race it looks as though Van den Driessche, Harris and Wyman will be able to forge a decisive lead group with Verschueren, but the diminutive Belgian has other ideas and rides clear on the toughest part of the course. Weighing less than 50 kilograms, she's built for climbing. After that, she's gone. An impressive win, especially considering Verschueren has a full-time job.

BrittLee Bowman finishes in twenty-first place, roughly halfway down the field. 'That was hard, but fun,' she says, breathlessly, when I catch her after the finish. 'The climbs were super-hard and I was losing ground there on the girls I was with, but then I'd catch them again on the descents. Those S-bends coming down the hill were really slippery – like riding on cowshit and banana skin. I had no traction, and I went with really low pressure in my tyres, so going through the corners in the village I was just feeling my tyres folding underneath me.

'The whole trip's been awesome. Gregg's made it so easy for me. He picked me up at the airport, went out and bought all the food I like. There's a great service course at the house so I can build my bike up. There are other riders like Helen Wyman who I can go out for a ride with. It's just so well organised here. I'd love to come back.'

For BrittLee it's a perfect, if exceptional, way to start her career of racing cross in Europe. For most American riders, managing the logistics of a European campaign can be a stressful and time-consuming exercise. With all the organisation done for her, including the funding, she's able to focus entirely on the racing.

Together we watch the elite men thunder away from their start line, down the finishing straight and into a tight muddy left turn, then BrittLee heads off for a recovery drink and some warm clothes. I begin following the hordes trudging up the hill, hoping to find a good spot where the racing is visible, the sun is unobstructed and the beer is close to hand.

The gaps between races allow the crowds to refresh their beer, *friets* and *frikandel* supplies or move to a different part of the course. There are many small children here. Some entertain themselves by running or rolling full pelt down the hillside, with their parents risking ligament damage to keep up. Others prefer to throw themselves at the huge inflatable grinning man advertising the *Het Nieuwsblad* newspaper.

By the time the elite men's race is underway the beer stalls are starting to claim some casualties. While Sven, Wout and the others slide past through the S-bends, a group of young men are running at each other, pint glasses in hand and crashing to the floor. There they start wrestling. Fingers are hooked through belt loops, palms shoved into faces, beer spilt on jackets. The wrestlers grunt and laugh, their friends cheer. A family beside me pulls their little girl out of the way. Slightly unnerved by this display of mock violence I move to a different part of the course and find a narrow space at the barriers. The woman I'm standing next to looks me and up and down over the top of her sunglasses. Her bloodshot eyes land on my press pass, hanging around my neck. She takes it between her fingers and turns it over.

'Press. *Pers*,' I say. 'Journalist.'

She doesn't seem impressed.

A few feet further down the same section of barriers a man has passed out in the mud. He lies prone on his back, his face calm, his hands by his side. His friends are taking photos of him on their phones.

The result of the 2014 Koppenbergcross is symbolic of the Shakespearean battle of the generations that the Belgian media love to whip up. By the end of the hour's racing Sven Nys and Wout van Aert approached the finish together. Van Aert led Nys across the last section of mud, past the pits and towards the VIP beer tent. Only a small ramp remained before a sharp left turn into the tarmac finishing straight.

The acceleration out of that final turn was going to be critical. Across the course, in living rooms across Belgium, everyone held their breath. Could the old master show the young pretender that he was still boss? The fingers of Belgian journalists hovered over their laptops. Then Jan Denuwelaere came into shot. Denuwelaere, a teammate of Van Aert's, was a lap down and rolling along quite casually, apparently unaware of the duo coming up to his back wheel. Van Aert caught Denuwelaere in the turn itself, coming round the outside, and opened his sprint. Denuwelaere moved over to give Nys room to pass, but paused before doing so. Nys got past him but Van Aert couldn't be caught. Furious, Nys sat up and made some fairly unambiguous gestures at Denuwelaere, who crossed the line then immediately turned around and pedalled back down the finishing straight towards his camper, rather than face getting a punch from Sven. Sven's righteous anger continued well into the post-race interviews, where he accused Denuwelaere of deliberately blocking him to help his teammate. Denuwelaere, naturally, denied such a claim.

But if you watch the replay a couple of times, the evidence is damning. On an earlier stretch of the course, as the camera focused on Van Aert and Nys, it caught another rider briefly – Denuwelaere – and that rider was looking backwards. He saw his teammate approaching, and the next time you saw Denuwelaere he was riding faster, to stay ahead of the duo, and still looking backwards. He knew that as a rider about to be lapped he should pull over to the side of the course. And he knew, being one of the most experienced riders on the scene, where he could make a difference. Blocking Sven's sprint out of that final turn would give his teammate victory. The next day in the race at Zonhoven, 50,000 fans boo Denuwelaere.

Cyclocross is not an intrinsically dirty sport (at least, only in the muddy sense), but at this level it is a professional sport with significant amounts of money flowing between riders, managers and promoters. It's possible that Denuwelaere made a calculation that his manoeuvre might help secure his future with Van Aert's team, and that any sanction from the race officials would be puny by comparison. In the event he got neither – no punishment from the commissaires and no contract for the following season.

Back at the team trucks there is a cheerful, workmanlike atmosphere: the drone of pressure washers as mechanics clean bikes, sending mists of spray into the air; the smell of lubricant being applied to transmission systems. As the mechanics work the team helpers chat and laugh, hand round trays of pastries and keep a watchful eye on the younger riders. It's easy to spot those not happy with their race; 19-year-olds don't hide their emotions well. Men who were gods of the field half an hour ago are now unmasked as boys, skinny and baby-faced, yet they are learning how to strike the poses of a professional cyclist.

I'm struck by how relaxed and cheerful everyone seems. Compared to the stressed, often exhausted faces one sees at a professional road race, this is more like a cycling club outing, or an extended family celebration.

Bikes are loaded back into trucks, spare wheels zipped into their cosy bags, and the spectators stroll – or stagger – back towards their cars and minibuses. I head off to the press centre, walking back through the finishing line as a gang of men get to work dismantling the gantry, the camera positions and the podium. Beyond the barriers the Koppenberg bar is still pumping out Europop, its crowd leaning on tables, walls and each other, red-faced and bleary-eyed.

From behind me comes the unmistakable quick whir of a freewheel. It's Jan Denuwelaere, the villain of last year's race. In his iconic red, yellow and black jersey of national champion (in the category of elite racers without a contract) he comes spinning past, then turns right into a side street that leads out into the countryside. He lives 70 kilometres away, so why not ride home? For Denuwelaere his bike is his weapon, his office, and his transport home. Belgian children are brought up with bicycles in their lives, not only as machines to race, but as machines for living, a utility technology.

8

An Education

Two weeks after Koppenbergcross, a group of skinny American kids, weary from transatlantic flights, arrive in the small town of Sittard, in the Limburg region of the Netherlands. These are the most talented young American cyclocross riders, and they are here for the second of four blocks of racing and training, under the auspices of the USA Cycling Cyclocross Development Race Camp. The third block will be over Christmas and the New Year, the fourth will be in late January, building up to the World Championships.

For the governing bodies of English-speaking nations, the idea of a European mainland base for its young riders has been around since the early nineties, when Australia created a development camp in Italy. Part of the success of British Cycling was its ability – through better funding – to establish a base in Tuscany, where elite riders of all categories could live, train and race. USA Cycling's European operations were, for many years, scattered across several locations – men's endurance in Izegem, Belgium; women's endurance in Lucca, Italy; and mountain biking in Freiburg, Germany. In 2013 these different programmes were centralised to one location – Sittard, a town intent on developing a reputation as a centre for elite sports. In the grounds of a former Catholic monastery (which looks both pretty and forbidding, in a horror film kind of way) there is a series of modern residential buildings, designed in dormitory style. There is also a large semi-industrial space which is used as a *service course* – the space for mechanics to store and work on bikes.

The decision to combine all the investment and energy in one place demonstrates how serious USA Cycling are about taking their best young riders to Europe and giving them a chance to make the most of their talents. Being close to Maastricht, Brussels and Antwerp, Sittard is a convenient location for travel connections and for the thriving Dutch and Belgian road racing and cyclocross scenes. The landscape is good for training too, for the road riders the Limburg hills around Valkenburg are within easy reach, and for the cyclocross team there are the sandy forests of Brabant.

The objective of each cross camp is to give the group of riders an intensive blast of being a full-time cross racer. The set-up is professional, with coaches, mechanics and *soigneurs*. The riders train together, eat together, attend nightly team meetings, and race frequently. Although they may do the occasional lower-ranked race for training, the races are predominantly World Cups and Superprestige. The group hail from all over the country, though many already know each other from Geoff Proctor's summer camp in Montana, and from the race circuit. For the period of the camp they have no commitments other than racing their bikes. No parents are allowed because the intention is to create as professional an environment as possible.

For Geoff Proctor, head coach, the current development cross camps are not something new, but an evolution of the work he has been doing for many years. In 2003 he founded EuroCrossCamp, a remarkable initiative that, while endorsed by USA Cycling, was independent of them. The idea was the same – take the best American youngsters and give them a chance to develop in Europe, with the guidance and protection of a trusted team. During its eleven years, EuroCrossCamp hosted many riders who went on to have successful professional careers. Being independent, however, meant that it had to fund itself, and because Proctor wanted to keep the fees as modest as possible, the operation was run on a very modest budget. As EuroCrossCamp grew in both reputation and expertise, it was only a matter of time before it was absorbed more formally into the USA Cycling structure. In 2014 Proctor was appointed head coach of the junior and Under-23 cyclocross teams, and the camp made the move from Izegem to Sittard. As well as validating a decade's worth of work, the move gave Proctor some practical benefits too: in the slightly antiquated house at Izegem, by the time all the riders had had a post-ride shower, there was never any hot water left for Proctor.

Like many native New Englanders, Alpine ski racing was Proctor's first love. He rode a bike for training, but it was only when he relocated to Portugal to teach English that he discovered cyclocross. Watching a big old black and white television in his apartment one Sunday afternoon in late January he found himself watching a strange sport where the competitors seemed to mainly carry their bikes through a muddy field. He was witnessing the 1986 World Championships from Lembeek, Belgium, a notoriously muddy edition, and he was intrigued. Back in America, he moved to Montana to go to college, and there began learning about cyclocross. He raced at elite level from the late 1980s and into the nineties, spending two years in Switzerland and representing USA at the World Championships three times. As he matured and learned more about the nuances of performance and preparation, he began to coach children, something that fitted neatly with his day job as an English teacher.

Juggling school and racing is a recurring theme for those taking part in Development Cross Camp. Proctor still combines his cyclocross coaching with teaching high school English back in Montana, and most of the racers are high school or college students, a situation that creates a strange yet not unhealthy tension. To maximise their cyclocross potential, Proctor needs his riders for long intensive blocks, meaning more time out of school. One of the junior team, Spencer Petrov, calculated that he'd missed 40 days of school in one academic year. A talented rider like Petrov, or his peer Gage Hecht, has a real shot at turning professional, so it could be worth sacrificing education for cyclocross. But what if the dream of turning professional turns sour? Having a robust education is always prudent, and few parents of American riders want to throw their kids into the deep end of European racing without some kind of back-up plan. Proctor has to tread the fine line of promoting his sport and protecting his time with the team, while also respecting their parents and the education system he passionately advocates.

This is not a problem Proctor's European counterparts have to trouble themselves with. In 2011 Proctor spent some time with Sven Nys, talking about how Belgian teams, such as Nys's Landbouwkrediet, prepare their Under-23 riders. As well as the obvious geographical benefit of having everyone live, race and train within a hundred square miles or so, the Landbouwkrediet coaches knew that their young riders were entirely focused on their cycling careers. Out of eight riders, none were in college. All were full-time racers.

For Americans to travel to Europe, integrate themselves into the landscape and the racing culture, and take on these dedicated European riders is tough. Cycling, like art, requires hard work and commitment.

Gage Hecht, a resident of Parker, Colorado, is stretching himself even further by maintaining a parallel career ambition to cycling, that of training to become an airline flight officer. This requires studying for a degree in Aviation at the Metropolitan State University in Denver, and putting in twenty hours a month in the air. If you're ever in downtown Denver take a look up, and if you see a small Piper Warrior II trainer plane, chances are there's a multiple national cycling champion at the controls. Reassuringly, to qualify as an airline pilot, trainees must demonstrate a minimum of 1500 hours flying time, and though Gage tries to put in solid blocks of time in the air when he's not racing, he's still a long way off this target. It probably doesn't help that he races both in the summer and the winter. In between time spent at his desk, and time in the air, Gage also somehow manages to find time on his bike.

The travel associated with representing his country on the bike is perhaps the most challenging aspect of this demanding life Gage has chosen. Some of his teachers are less flexible than others, so he's often found crouching over a laptop on a plane, or in a Dutch coffee shop, frantically trying to write a paper for school. To say that Gage is driven would be an understatement but I can't help wondering whether he's biting off more than he can chew. Or, to put it another way, should he focus on cycling exclusively for a few years, see how he develops and then make some choices?

Of course, I know very little of this young man's life, so I keep my musings to myself. He seems to be successful in everything he turns his attention to, and is a calm, polite and friendly person to boot. Perhaps he's just one of those people who overachieve in everything they do, and are so nice you can't even dislike them for it. I feel exhausted just thinking about it.

With almost three decades of experience in cyclocross, there's not much Proctor doesn't know about the sport. He's a consummate organiser and motivator, and he loves coaching (a role which sometimes gets pushed to the rear due to the sheer amount of legwork involved in running a team), but because he's also a well-read and reflective man, Proctor thinks deeply about the sport, and about its connections to literature.

Writing on the EuroCrossCamp online journal a few years ago Proctor quoted the poet Beth Ann Fennelly, who wrote of 'narrowing the aperture' to focus on nothing other than the poem in hand. Proctor shrewdly draws the analogy between a poem and a cyclocross race. Each is the 'One Big Thing' that, when properly focused on, becomes the very essence of living in the moment. Yes, we could argue that a poem has a lasting value while a cyclocross race is banal and temporal, but that doesn't matter. What matters is that the poet or cyclist finds the means to give the task their undivided attention. One of the key objectives of the cross camp has been to give riders like Gage, who lead busy, varied lives, the opportunity to achieve this focus.

Proctor writes, 'A big part of this Camp is learning how to narrow the aperture. While all the riders lead busy, productive lives with school, work, functions and fun, life during the Camp affords the opportunity to focus 100 per cent on the "One Big Thing". Not to say homework, a trip to the sandwich shop or other diversions aren't part of the equation. But, learning how to race your bike fast is certainly at the forefront . . . Not everyone is cut out for this life. For Americans especially, there are a million-and-one worthy things to pursue. But I do think it's an important rite: to experience – even just for a little while, no matter the medium or one's age or stage in life – the purity of pursuing One Big Thing with all of one's worth.'

Of course, pursuing the One Big Thing with total focus for three weeks or even for three months is very different from committing to it permanently. Talented young riders always have options, and the collective view of the American elite cyclocross community is that for a young rider to throw everything into European cyclocross is a very risky move. The scene is small, often defensive, and one season beset by injury or illness could spell the end of a career. As they progress into the Under-23 category, elite American riders may start to specialise in one discipline, but that is also the time when many will go to university. Combining studies with racing is possible, but not if you're living in Belgium and riding for a big cyclocross team.

All of which prompts the question – will we ever see an American win the men's elite World Championship?

9

Into the Dunes

Koksijde is a Belgian seaside town on the North Sea coast, not far from the French border. Like any seaside town out of season, there is a feeling of bleakness, melancholy. There's a theme park called Plopsaland, its gates closed. The sea is grey and choppy. The cafés around the main square are all shuttered. I'm here, in late November, for the third round of the World Cup. It's a dark, cold morning and inland, to the east, sits a bank of charcoal clouds. The forecast is for rain and wind. As he drives us into the town centre, Balint Hamvas is very cheerful. 'This is real cyclocross weather,' he says. 'It's nice to have sunny days, but this is better for the photos. OK, I'm just going to stop at this supermarket then we'll head over to the press centre.'

'Meat paste?'

'Oh yes,' he grins.

On our previous trip to Belgium he'd taken a fairly lengthy detour to find a supermarket, and while I inspected the selection of kids' sweets (for myself), Balint headed straight for the meat fridges. His prize: a suspiciously bright pink paste, made from all the bits of animals you don't want to know about. 'Yes, it's authentic,' I'd said at the time, 'but also revolting.'

In the supermarket he buys two tubs of the stuff. Meat paste and rain; it's going to be a good day.

From the television coverage, with its focus on the lengthy sand-dune sections, you'd be forgiven for thinking that the Koksijde course is close to the beach (indeed there is a cyclocross at Irvine in Scotland which is right on the beach, and is referred to by locals as Joksijde). The course in Koksijde is based around a military airbase a kilometre inland. Whereas the course at Asper-Gavere, another military base, is compact and easy to visualise, at Koksijde there is a weirdly disjointed feeling. It's not just the anomaly of high sand dunes in an otherwise pan-flat landscape, it's also the discovery that the race loops through a holiday village with chalets, an outdoor swimming pool and a children's playground. The barriers run so close to some of the chalets that spectators have to squeeze through one at a time to get past. Beyond the holiday village is the airfield, complete with a recently refurbished aircraft hangar. The finishing straight, VIP tent and all the usual paraphernalia of a major race are set up on a section of the runway.

Using our privileged status as press, we drive into the airbase. It's a week since the horrific terrorist attacks in Paris, in which 130 people died, and Belgium is in a security lockdown. The bombers, including one who survived and escaped, have been traced to the Molenbeek suburb of Brussels. Shops, schools, public transport have all been closed since the attacks, and the public advised not to congregate for fear of further attacks. As Balint and I drive into the Koksijde airbase there are tanks sitting on the boulevards of Belgium's capital. After the initial shock turned to fear and anger, the story of the attacks became intertwined with a ferocious public debate about refugees from the Middle East. The attackers were all EU citizens, but some had travelled to Syria to fight for ISIS then returned to Europe among the flow of migrants from the region. The rhetoric of sport has often been about transcending boundaries, of nations competing peacefully, of ideology suspended. Admirable, but unrealistic. Ever since the atrocities at the Munich Olympics in 1972 we've known that the very public nature of major sporting events, their capacity for visual terror, can make them attractive targets. The Paris attackers tried to get into the Stade de France but were turned away by security guards, and blew themselves up outside the stadium, taking only one innocent life in the process. A bike race is much harder to police than a football match, yet after a midweek meeting with the police, the organisers decided to go ahead with the event. Something of the Blitz spirit prevailing perhaps, or more likely commercial pressures brought to bear. The impossibility of ever fully securing a bike race was brought into focus a couple of days before the race when the media learned that some of the barracks adjacent to the press room, inside the security cordon, were being used to house Syrian refugees. The mayor of Koksijde promised to lock them in for the duration of the event. He probably meant well, but it was a shocking and badly thought through thing to say.

Also well meaning but not particularly helpful was the American embassy in Brussels, which advised its athletes not to participate in any events until further notice. Fortunately USA Cycling decided to ignore them and brought its sizeable team over from Sittard. The media tried to build a story about the team's anxieties but, sensibly, most of the riders restricted their quotes to cycling-related matters. There may have been some worried moms back home, but it was important that the Americans compete, and do so visibly.

Katie Compton, with her team set-up being outside the USA Cycling structure, was able to make her own decision, and did so with characteristic pragmatism. When asked whether it was true the US Embassy was going to stop its citizens racing, Katie's husband replied, 'Haven't heard anything about that. Katie is racing.' Those last three words, simple and emphatic, speak volumes about Katie's approach.

After leaving Balint in the press room to fiddle with his massive lenses, I set out across the sand dune to see Gage Hecht ride in the juniors' race. At ten o'clock in the morning the course is quiet but the beer vans are serving their first customers, and at the stall where you can buy a yellow poncho emblazoned with either SVEN or WOUT, the staff are piling their product high.

Having won the juniors' race here last year, and finished fourth in the Junior World Championship the following February, Gage is a big favourite. As the race starts, I head over to the first sandy section. Only when you see the sand, how deep it is, do you realise the artistry and power of anyone who can ride through it on a bicycle. The lead riders come flying out of the woods, through the pit area and into the sand. It's important when riding the Koksijde sand to carry as much speed as possible into the sections, follow the firmest line and keep pedalling. Above all, keep pedalling. Hesitation is fatal. As soon as a rider loses momentum he or she comes to a grinding halt and is forced to dismount.

Two Dutch riders in blazing orange skinsuits lead, Gage is in third. But he picks the wrong line and his front wheel digs deep into the sand. If the course had been dry he might have pushed through this mishap, but with the sand soaked by a week of rain showers he hasn't got a chance. His bike flips forward, and although he avoids crashing, it's a less than graceful way to dismount. I hear him grunt in frustration, wrench his bike off the ground and pound away on foot. Riders directly behind him have to stop and do the same thing. Those able to pick a clear line shoot past. In a moment Gage has lost half a dozen places, and this is going to be the story of his day.

This is the first time I've seen Gage compete, and it's easy to see why he's won so many races back home. He's a powerhouse of a rider, tall, with a broad chest and strong shoulders – a stature reminiscent of a Miguel Indurain. On his titanium Moots bike, in the stars and stripes, he stands out from the Belgian and Dutch riders around him, who generally seem to be small and very skinny. But today Gage's strength isn't translating into a high placing. Despite pushing himself to the limit he slips further back into the field, eventually finishing 21st. Afterwards, the disappointment is written across his face. He doesn't, however, look for excuses. In cyclocross everything within the rules is considered part of the race – crashes, punctures, mechanicals. Which means that any rider learning his craft, as Gage is, has to accept such mishaps as occupational hazards rather than excuses. Even beyond the rules, there is the unwritten code of not looking for excuses; if someone elbows you in the ribs or flicks you into a ditch, you don't tell the media, and certainly not a commissaire.

'I didn't give the course the respect it deserves,' he tells me, somewhat cryptically. Is he admitting to a degree of overconfidence? If so, and if he was expecting to blast his way to a high finish with relative ease, his race must have come as quite a shock.

After the juniors' race, the crowd begins to grow. But it's a trickle rather than a flood. The combination of bad weather and the terror alert seems to be keeping people away. The average West Flandrian cyclocross fan doesn't share the spirit of the organisers: why make the effort when both elite races are televised live? By early afternoon there are an estimated eight thousand fans at the circuit, and except for the critical sand-dune section it's easy to get to the barriers beside the course. Hard, then, to imagine being here among 61,000 fans, the estimated crowd at the World Championships held here in 2012. The winner of the elite race that day was Niels Albert, one of the few riders able to consistently compete with Sven Nys. Albert's career was cut short when he was diagnosed with a heart condition, and though he professes to being content in his new career in team management, Albert cuts a rather disconsolate figure as he stands in the pits watching his charges come and go. Also notable from that World Championships are the names of the junior champion and runner-up: Mathieu van der Poel and Wout van Aert.

But we have to go further back to understand why this race is so revered as a cyclocross Classic. After Eric de Vlaeminck left the sport and took to driving a dump-truck around Eeklo, Belgian cyclocross suffered a crisis of confidence. In the late seventies, success at the World Championships switched to Switzerland, the new dominant force in the sport. Between 1976 and 1979 Albert Zweifel won four World titles, and on each occasion one of his countrymen took silver. Roland Liboton, a charismatic young man from Leuven, restored some of Belgium's self-confidence with his four titles won between 1980 and 1984. Liboton appealed to the mythology of a Flandrian working lad done well, which is why the fans loved him for turning up to races in a Porsche, with a glamorous girlfriend dressed in a fur coat. If he won a big race Liboton would privately hire a nightclub just for him and his friends, and party all night. His behaviour was more befitting a footballer, but the Belgian fans loved him for it.

On his own, Liboton couldn't prevent the Swiss scene becoming still more prestigious and economically successful. During the late eighties and early nineties, Swiss and Dutch riders did better than the Belgians at the World Championships. Between 1990 and 1993 there was no Belgian on the podium in the professional men's race at the World Championships (at that time the event was split into professional and amateur races). Unthinkable. Eric de Vlaeminck was the national team manager and he was under pressure. In 1994 Koksijde hosted the World Championships and the pressure on the Belgian squad intensified. Here was a World Championships in deepest Flanders, the public expected medals. At that time the only events in the World Championships were juniors' and elite men. No one had thought of having an Under-23 category, and as for women, well, they didn't ride cyclocross, did they? Incredibly the first women's World Championship race was in 2000. In the world of cyclocross, gender equality has a very short history.

De Vlaeminck's wunderkind in the junior category was a teenager called Sven Nys. De Vlaeminck saw in Nys the champion he was to eventually become, and the respect was mutual – Nys followed the old master's instructions religiously. During his career De Vlaeminck was the best bike handler on the circuit – acrobatic, technically brilliant. One urban myth has it that De Vlaeminck could ride along a train rail for several kilometres without falling off. And as a coach he passed on his secrets to Nys. In one training session De Vlaeminck would tell his juniors to ride down steep muddy slopes with their hands in the air. Only Nys, and his coach, could do it without crashing. De Vlaeminck could teach Nys technical tricks, but the psychology of victory was altogether more complex. At Koksijde, in the race destined to be his first rainbow jersey, Nys faltered. He could only finish fourth, overcome by the magnitude of the moment. The Belgians did take a bronze medal, with Ben Berden, but for De Vlaeminck this was barely a consolation prize. In tears, he got up on stage and apologised to the crowd.

A few hours later, inside the last two laps of the elite men's race, 40,000 spectators were going berserk. The young Dutch rider Richard Groenendaal had led for much of the race, but Paul Herygers was chasing him down. Herygers, at 31, was having the best season of his cyclocross career, having already won the inaugural World Cup and the Superprestige at Gieten. A former postman, brickmaker and farmer, Herygers was the most photogenic and charismatic of the Belgian team. He always dressed well, rode an unusual black bike with four-spoke wheels, and was good for a post-race quote. Could he become World champion?

When he caught Groenendaal, Herygers rode alongside and slapped the Dutchman on the back. And with this audacious stunt the gold medal was effectively his. Groenendaal led Herygers around another lap but was powerless when the Belgian attacked on a steep climb. That slap on the back was condescending, dramatic. If Herygers had been able to make himself heard above the din, he might have said, 'I'll take over now, son.' The slap was the same thing. It spoke of such supreme confidence that the whole nation, Flanders anyway, found they had a new hero. A showman, Herygers celebrated all the way down the finishing straight, at first pointing to his exposed hairy chest, then zipping up his skinsuit, hopping on and off his bike, punching the air in a variety of interesting ways, clapping his hands and blowing kisses to the crowd. All while Groenendaal pursued him, in vain, to the line. In Paul Herygers the public found a classic Flemish hero – like Roland Liboton he was another working-class lad made good. In an age of live television coverage and talk shows, Herygers was good value. With a new and popular Flemish World champion appearing on television every Sunday afternoon, local sponsors began to see the commercial potential in the sport.

As Herygers pulled on his rainbow jersey Eric de Vlaeminck stood beside the podium, crying again, this time tears of joy. Herygers never repeated his Worlds win, but he didn't need to – his place in Belgian lore was assured. Three years later in Munich, in the newly created Under-23 category, Sven Nys was crowned World champion and the Flemish public had a new idol.

At Koksijde today, though I barely know him, I'd turned up hoping to see Gage win, so as I leave the finishing area and go off in search of the team vehicles, I feel a little disappointed. It's a dose of reality, of course. No matter how much natural talent a young rider has, he cannot simply swoop in and claim the honours. Courses like Koksijde have a thousand obstacles that can impede your progress – one has to respect that, and the opposition.

Usually at cyclocross events the spectators' tickets are collected by stewards standing at a gap in the fencing. Today there is a covered bag check manned by the police, and a queue is starting to form on the other side. Two policemen, wrapped up as if for a day out in the Arctic, motion spectators forward, check their bags, rolled-up flags and inflatable animals. Perhaps not thrilled at being pulled out of bed to work outside on a Sunday morning, they perform their duty silently and with stony faces. The incoming spectators are good-natured about having to queue, and occasionally break into song. The mechanics, brandishing identification wristbands issued by the organisers, are able to march through a fast-track lane.

Beyond the gate is a single narrow lane stretching to the horizon. On one side is a ditch, ploughed fields and some piles of beets. On the other side a continuous line of cars, campervans and trucks, loaded with kit, nervous riders and busy helpers. The parking tsars have again managed the hierarchy: the big Belgian teams are positioned close to the course; anyone who doesn't speak Dutch is further away. As the junior men are rolling back, muddy-faced and voluble, comparing notes on the race just done, the Under-23 riders are on the rollers, warming up, and the elite women are out on the course doing their reconnaissance laps. At a cyclocross race knowing your timings is important.

Fans stroll along the vehicles, peering into windows, studying bikes and murmuring to each other. Riders weave through the crowd, their soft tubular tyres swishing on the tarmac, brakes honking and grinding. On a day like today, if you're not racing, your focus is on staying dry and warm.

At the British Cycling campervan there are mechanics at work, but no riders around. The door is shut and the windows foggy. Standing on a nearby grass verge, talking on his mobile, is Dan Tulett's father, Allister. Dan is one of Britain's most promising young cyclocross riders. He's also one of Britain's most promising young road and mountain bike riders. Still only 16, so at the younger end of the junior category, Dan is a multiple national champion, and having won the Nieuwelingen (the equivalent of the British Youth category) race at Koppenbergcross last season, he is on the radar of many European team managers. However, today in Koksijde, his race was disappointing.

When he finishes the conversation Allister tells me that he was talking to Dan's coach, giving him a report on Dan's performance. He advises me not to speak to Dan for a while – he's feeling very down. The problem, for Dan and his peers in the British Cycling Mountain Biking Academy, is that winter training for mountain biking involves lots of long steady road rides, three hours or more. This is the foundation on which to build good form for the following summer. But it's incompatible with cyclocross. The European riders that Dan is competing against here in Koksijde are already specialising in cyclocross, and their training is completely geared to the discipline. Long steady rides don't help you win cyclocross races. Training for cyclocross is all about short intense efforts. You should feel like your eyes are popping out, your lungs on the brink of spontaneous combustion, and your legs filled with battery acid. Then you stop, recover, have a drink, and do it all over again.

Dan's first love is mountain biking, and that's where he sees his future, but he also loves cross. Trying to combine the two, even at 16 years of age, isn't easy. When I see him later in the day he is down but philosophical, hoping that if he can change his training he will get the speed to make him more competitive. First, though, he has to persuade his mountain biking coach this is a good idea.

Next door to the British encampment is Katie Compton's van. For such a big star, this parking position seems almost an insult. Katie and Mark laugh it off, but it still hurts that after so many victories at the highest level, and a decade on the circuit, the parking marshals send them up here to park beside juniors. Sexism? Xenophobia? One thing is clear – being an independent American woman is not an easy ride in Belgian cyclocross. I can't help but wonder whether their natural modesty is a disadvantage; would the marshals behave differently if Katie turned up in a brightly coloured campervan emblazoned with sponsors' logos, a cheesy picture of herself and her name in huge letters?

She's standing in the tent attached to the side of the van, giving a debrief to Mark about the course. As Mark files down her chain, Katie tells me she's feeling good, that the course is heavy, which suits her. As befits a rider of her experience, she's relaxed and chatty. We talk about the terror attacks and the security situation. Katie points out that there are shootings in malls and schools practically every day in the States. Being on a military airbase, surrounded by men with guns, seems to reassure her. When she starts to shiver I excuse myself so she can get into the van and get warm.

When I next see her it's on the start line, a few minutes before the race. To keep the legs turning and the body warm, the women roll up and down the start–finish straight, bundled into many layers of thermal clothing. With five minutes to go, the commissaire shepherds them all into their grid positions, and the gradual unpeeling of clothes begins. Were I on the starting line, this is where my ever-so-slightly obsessive punctuality would mean peeling off my leggings, over-shoes and thermal jacket far too early, and starting the race with frostbite. Katie and her peers are far more sensible, keeping their jackets on until one minute to go, then tossing them over the heads of the other riders to a waiting helper.

Here, in this last minute of tense silence, I witness something that seems deeply symbolic of the relationship between American riders and the European races. Towards the back of the grid is the young American rider Ellen Noble. A member of Jeremy Powers's JAM Fund development squad, based in Easthampton, Massachusetts, this is Noble's first trip to Europe, and her first World Cup outside America. Her rise to the top of the domestic scene has been swift, but this is another level altogether, and the most demanding cross course she's ever raced on. She looks very nervous. Catching herself fidgeting she closes her eyes and takes some deep breaths. Next to her on the grid is a Dutch rider. The lanes are marked in white paint, but this rider still puts her bike into Noble's lane, and a tense conversation ensues. Noble politely asks the Dutch rider to move her bike, but is ignored. Exasperated, she looks at me and rolls her eyes. Eventually another rider intervenes and the Dutch girl reluctantly edges just back inside her own lane.

After crossing the finish line the women roll to a halt, have the transponders removed from their bikes and look for those same helpers who took their jackets at the start. The contrast in expressions is remarkable. Some look harrowed by their experience, their faces wracked with pain. Others are elated, alive to these extraordinary sensations. Some of the women stand chatting, apparently not noticing the freezing rain falling upon their shoulders, while others hurriedly grab clothing and scurry away. The rain turns to hail, but Ellen Noble doesn't even care. Her eyes tell the story. 'I'm hooked,' she tells a journalist. 'I love it. I love these technical courses, so much better than back home. I'm gonna move out here.'

Sanne Cant, the Belgian and European champion, and something of sand specialist, wins the race. Cant is only 25, yet already has a string of wins and podiums to her credit, and is ranked number one in the world. As young as she may be, Cant already has many years of racing cross behind her. She is from a cyclocross family, and took part in her first race when she was six years old. Her nickname, which she has only recently come to fully endorse, is 'Lynx'.

Katie finishes third, using her strength on the muddy sections to overtake Pavla Havlíková late in the race. As she crosses the line she punches the air. To finish on the podium after her poor start to the season is a sign that her form is returning. The patience and hard work are paying off. Katie has won in Koksijde four times, but this third-place finish today feels pretty close to a victory.

With the women's race finished, the fans turn their attention to the next big event of the day – lunch. At your first Belgian cyclocross event you will almost certainly make a fool of yourself by offering cash for your choice of calorie-laden sustenance. The correct procedure is to buy food and drink tokens from a bored teenager in a booth. Invariably these booths have a metal-grille window for security, but the back door is wide open to let cigarette smoke out. With tokens in hand, you make your way to the vendor selling what you fancy. There are many vendors, but they all sell the same thing: hotdogs, burgers, sausage patties and chips. The chips are always good: thick-cut, fresh and hot. The critical decision with chips is the sauce. The woman – it's always a woman – serving you will shovel your portion from a huge steel cauldron into a cardboard cone, then ask you which sauce you'd like. In front of you will be an array of industrial-size dispensers. The safest bet is mayonnaise. Thick, creamy, traditional. Tomato sauce is a very brave choice. You've got to be pretty confident to ask for tomato sauce in Belgium, but I have seen it happen. There are also some other, more mysterious sauces; the Dutch labels don't give the non-Dutch-speaker any clues – you'd be taking pot-luck to choose one – and do you really want to take that kind of chance with your chips?

As the rain eases off, I go for chips (with mayonnaise), a hotdog and a black coffee. Refraining from putting cream in the coffee makes me feel like I'm being healthy. Trying to consume this wholesome meal while walking is rather tricky, so I head over to a large digital screen and set up temporary camp on its base. On the other side of the finishing straight, cloistered behind barriers and burly security guards, lunch is being served in the VIP marquee. Among those tucking into the salmon and champagne are businessmen, local dignitaries, celebrities, former riders and anyone else with good connections to the organisers. Tickets aren't cheap, and the VIP tent represents a sizeable revenue stream for the event. Of course I'd rather be out here eating chips in the rain.

The Europop is pumping from every speaker around the course, the crowd are staking out their positions on the barriers, the announcer is beginning to get breathless with excitement. The men's elite race is drawing close. As I wander around, mainly to keep warm, I hear some American voices from a group of men and women walking across the paddock. One of them is wearing a jacket that says *Jingle Cross*, which is the name of a UCI-ranked race in Iowa City in December. Intrigued I say hello and congratulate them on making such a long trip just to see a bike race. 'We're here to check out the organisation,' the man in the promotional jacket tells me. 'We're bidding to get our race to become a World Cup.' Then he says that they've been surprised how quiet the crowd are, they'd expected it to be a lot more raucous. 'In Iowa City our fans are louder,' he says proudly. I shrug and mumble something about the crowd numbers being down because of the terrorist threat and the weather. But I know that's not the real reason; Koksijde with a very small crowd is still bigger than Jingle Cross. The difference in volume is cultural. American fans are engaged with the whole *idea* of racing, of suffering as a noble pursuit, and they're a lot more confident to shout encouragement at complete strangers. Belgian fans have paid to get into Koksijde. They want to be entertained, and when they see something dramatic, or their personal hero, they will cheer. Otherwise they stay silent and concentrate on drinking.

Miraculously the rain stops and the sky clears. There are even hints of pale blue between the clouds. The riders gather on the starting grid, nudge their bikes into position. In front of them is a swarm of photographers, helpers wearing team-issue rucksacks, and UCI commissaires. Standing near the front of the grid, just behind the barrier, I'm within touching distance of Sven Nys. Maintaining the exterior illusion of being a serious and seasoned journalist, inside I'm hugely excited to be this close to the great man at the start of his last race in Koksijde. He has won here six times, is in good form, and he's always done well on courses made tough by a thorough soaking. His presence at any race this season adds an emotional layer to the event, as he is saying goodbye to his fans, and they to him, but he is also saying goodbye to the courses that have been so much a part of his life. Nys's superstardom may have been founded on the cult of his personality, but the fields and ditches and sand dunes of Flanders were the stage upon which his most famous feats were performed. Despite being the very epitome of Belgian cyclocross, there is still something of the outsider about Nys in this, his last season. His kit is all black, with fluorescent green flashes, making him stand out among the mish-mash of primary colours worn by the other riders. His bike too is instantly recognisable, a fluorescent lime-green Trek that seems to float across mud and hardly get dirty. And now, as the other riders fiddle with clothing, chat, compare equipment, take a few last sips of an energy drink, there is a peculiar stillness to Nys. He stands astride his bike, hardly moving, not engaging with anyone else, staring down the finishing straight. As the minutes count down he performs the same functions as everyone else – taking a drink, pulling off his jacket – but does so unthinkingly. They are mere movements. His eyes do not waver from whatever he is seeing in the middle distance. I sense his mind is hovering somewhere above this race, this place. He doesn't need to visualise success, as sports psychologists instruct athletes to do, because success has been his life. It informs everything he does. He doesn't need to visualise the course, because he's raced it a dozen times. He knows every tree root, every drain cover, every little compression. I'll never know what he was thinking in those final moments before the race, but I like to imagine that he was looking down on this world of his, like a god of the fields, absorbing every element, and bidding it a silent farewell.

Green light. The swift clip into pedals and then a full-speed sprint into the first corner. In the first two of seven laps Nys rides a short distance behind the leaders, allowing himself to settle into the race, find his rhythm. The World champion, Mathieu van der Poel, has made a welcome return following knee surgery and in his eagerness to get back to the top he pushes too hard too early. Wout van Aert follows him, then surges into a lone lead when Van der Poel falters on a technical section. The crowd, though happy to see the World champion back in the mix, are even more happy to see Van Aert getting away from his Dutch nemesis. But the cheers for Van Aert are but a whisper compared to the roar when the big screen shows who is closing down on the young pretender. Yes, it's the old king himself. Nys is reeling in Van Aert. By the end of the third lap the two are together: the 39-year-old versus the 21-year-old. Nys's first win at Koksijde was in 1999, when Van Aert was just starting school. For the remainder of the race they ride together, swapping turns to lead, testing each other, trying out different lines through the sand and mud, watching, waiting. Sven in black, Wout in white. Each knows that an error will be ruthlessly capitalised upon. A moment of inattention could be the end of the race. Apart from the respective fan clubs, the crowd are quiet, caught in the same tense game. As the laps tick down the prospect of a sprint finish seems more and more likely.

Many of those watching will remember the controversial sprint finish in 2011 when Nys arrived at the finishing straight with Kevin Pauwels. Like Van Aert today, Pauwels was wearing the white skinsuit of World Cup leader, and like Van Aert, on paper he was the faster sprinter. But as soon as the pair got through the final corner and opened up the sprint, Nys deviated from his line to shut the door on Pauwels. Having to take evasive action to stop himself crashing into the barriers, Pauwels lost all his speed and could only watch as Nys sped away to the line. Pauwels and his team manager Mario de Clercq were so angry they chose to lodge a formal complaint, but the commissaires rejected it. Nys held onto his victory, and the polemics continued through press conferences, interviews and newspaper articles. 'The commissaires have no balls,' claimed De Clercq. 'If you do this in the Tour de France you'd be sent home.' Nys freely admitted to shutting the door on Pauwels but maintained that the sprint was safe, and within the spirit of the sport. At the press conference after the race Pauwels and De Clercq fumed. Nys made jokes.

There will be no sprint today. At least not in the finishing straight. Nys has spent an hour calculating the best place for an attack. The section just before the finishing straight is flat and grassy; in dry conditions it's fast and fairly innocuous. Today, after a week of heavy rain, it's a quagmire. This is where Nys attacks. He goes to the right of the track and gives it everything. Van Aert sticks close to the left-hand side barrier and tries to respond. For a few seconds they race side by side, both pushing deep into their reserves of strength and energy. Mud flies up from their wheels. Their shoulders, biceps, wrists, all wrestle the bikes forward. The announcer shouts as the crowd yell for their favourite.

I'm standing in a meadow on the other side of the course, watching the big screen. On one side of me are the Sven Nys fanclub, on the other side are the Wout van Aert fanclub. Everyone screams, shakes their fists, spills their beer. The noise is incredible. From the head-on camera angle it's impossible to tell who is winning this drag race. We all know that because the finishing straight is short the first rider through the last corner will win the race. Then Van Aert adjusts his line and we can see that Nys has three bike lengths' lead. He hits the tarmac and sprints hard for 50 metres, and Van Aert, exhausted, cannot respond. Nys throws his arms in the air, then after crossing the line he covers his face with his gloves. Even cannibals have emotions. This is the fiftieth World Cup win of his career, and his first since 2012. On a tough day, on a Classic course, he has summoned strength from deep within. It's so emotional for him because it's an endpoint, a climax to a phenomenal career.

With the podium celebrations still going on in the background, I follow the crowd trudging across the sand dunes towards the exit and their parked cars. When we step onto the road there is the customary banging of boots on tarmac to shake off excess mud. Ahead of me some Sven supporters are singing a raucous tune. I'm exhausted, but buzzing. At the gates to the barracks I turn away from the crowd, go past a security check and towards the press room, where in twenty minutes there will be a press conference with Nys, Van Aert and third-placed Van der Poel. For now there will be hot coffee and cheese rolls. As I cross a grassy quadrangle my eyes wander up to the windows of the surrounding buildings. But there are no faces of Syrian refugees pressed to the glass. If they are in there, locked in, they're surely not interested in this strange event happening on their doorstep.

10

The Method of Torture

Gravesend is like Belgium, but without the glamour. Sitting on the north Kent coast, facing into the bleak brown horizon of the Thames Estuary and the North Sea beyond, it's a town that has sprawled out from its now 'historic' port in a series of unlovely concrete housing estates. It has high crime, high unemployment and poor educational results. It's also where my father-in-law has chosen to live.

The perfect place, then, for a cyclocross race. Round ten of the London Cross League is situated at a dedicated cycling centre built as part of the London 2012 Olympics legacy. There's a road circuit, BMX track, skate park and mountain bike trails, all landscaped on a strip of wasteland beside the A2 dual carriageway. Being a modern venue there is a café, changing rooms, bike shop and even a children's playground on-site. Never one to miss an opportunity to indoctrinate my children in the lore of cross, I bring them and my wife along with me.

While it's great for the cycling community to have a dedicated facility, Gravesend Cyclopark's position above the town, and a lack of mature trees means that it's so exposed that even on a pleasant summer's day it can feel like being on top of Ben Nevis.

And today is not a pleasant summer's day. The wind is a harsh north-easterly, and the dark clouds overhead are sprinkling showers which on a calm day would be refreshing, but in this wind are grievously vicious.

Not that any of that puts off a nine-year-old who wants to race his or her bike. In a paddock area in the centre of the full course, the Under-10s are lining up for their race. There are perhaps twenty children, and while there are a few on mountain bikes, wearing clothing from a variety of sports, most are on mini cross bikes, wearing their club colours. There are some decidedly Sven-like stares. The British Cycling commissaire calls them forward onto the start grid. The riders whip off their jackets and pass them to their parents. With everyone lined up the commissaire calls out the race timing, wishes everyone luck and blows a sharp whistle to release the riders. The group sprints away and into the first set of bends.

'Does that look like fun?' my wife asks our daughter Anya.

Anya, screwing her face up against the cold wind, is fairly vehement in her reply. Gamely, my wife turns to a boy in racing kit sitting beside us at the barrier.

'Is it fun?' she asks him.

'Does it look like fun?' he replies.

'Well . . .'

'No it's not,' he cuts in. 'I can assure you. It's torture.'

Twenty minutes later he's lining up in the Under-12s race. The speed and skill of the best riders in this race is breathtaking. A boy from the Barking and Dagenham Wheelers (another unlovely place facing into the Thames Estuary) leads by some margin and is lapping riders with alarming speed. He rides the three off-camber hairpins with a natural flowing style, absolutely in tune with his white Cinelli bike. Trailing the Barking and Dagenham virtuoso is another rider with clear talent, just missing that blend of smoothness and power. Despite his best efforts he is never going to get back on terms. And unlike Wout Van Aert, this kid will probably not be able to take revenge next Sunday, nor any Sunday. He'll probably never beat his arch-rival. At 11 years of age, when you're the best, you're the best.

Watching the two boys brings back memories of my own brief cross career. I was lucky to race alongside a boy called Roger Hammond in the local Oxfordshire and Buckinghamshire races that I dragged my father to. Roger was almost exactly my contemporary – he was born a week before me – and we were the same height and stature. There the similarities ended. A natural on the bike, Roger was blessed with the genes of a professional-to-be, a destiny he fulfilled with a long successful career riding the road, his highest point being a third place in Paris–Roubaix. In every race we rode together I floundered in his wake, watching helplessly as his beautiful silver Alan bike skipped away through the mud. For the spectators it was a pleasure to watch a rider so prodigiously talented as Roger; for me it was – to echo the boy at the barriers – torture. Roger was the rider I wanted to be, and at the time I couldn't figure out what separated us. Now, with the benefit of many years hindsight, I can imagine just how exciting it must have been for those involved in the British cross scene to have seen Roger develop into the rider he became.

British cyclocross has always had an uneasy relationship with its continental counterparts. Geographical proximity hasn't meant integration. The top British riders have frequently competed in Switzerland, Belgium and Holland, but have never quite established themselves in the top tier of the sport. For the British riders the problem is the same as the Americans, but for different reasons. Like the Americans, the British riders haven't gone to live in Europe, immersed themselves in the culture, learned the language, but for the British that's because they are so close anyway, what's the point?

British cyclocross is growing fast, and is following the American model more closely than the Belgian. Every weekend throughout the winter events like this one in Gravesend are attracting huge numbers of participants, particularly in the children's categories. This explosion is part of the legacy of British success at the Olympics and Tour de France, a legacy to be celebrated – especially if it gets more kids on bikes. Yet while British Olympic success may bring more people into cyclocross, because it's not an Olympic discipline (and never likely to be, given the maxim of the Winter Olympics that all its sports must be based on snow and ice) the governing body, British Cycling, is also marginalising cyclocross. The investment in cross, in terms of finance and resource, is considerably lower than in road racing, track and mountain biking. And when a talented rider comes along who enjoys cross, like Dan Tulett, he or she is firmly guided towards mountain biking. So cyclocross may be enjoying a populist boom, but for a British rider to break through at elite level requires not only talent and hard work but a strong independent streak. You have to be willing to travel to mainland Europe regularly, create your own support network, and ingratiate yourself with the local race organisers.

Before cycling became Britain's national sport, before Bradley Wiggins was a household name, even before Chris Boardman and his revolutionary Lotus, Britain's best cross riders ploughed this furrow. In the eighties a trio of riders from the Derbyshire-based Ace Racing Team undertook probably the most concerted onslaught into the continental scene by a British team. Managed by Simon Burney, himself a former professional, and now the UCI's Mountain Bike Co-ordinator, the three riders – Tim Gould, David Baker and Fred Salmon – based themselves in Switzerland and rode there every weekend, only coming back to the UK for National Trophy races. This was a time when Switzerland, not Belgium, was the home of cyclocross. Events there were attended by huge crowds, and the circuit was lucrative for riders who committed to it – a British professional who might only finish in the top twenty could expect to receive around a thousand pounds start money. In part this was because the Swiss authorities and sponsors invested a lot in the sport, but also because of a neat trick the race organisers pulled off. Every rider, in addition to riding for their usual team, would be sponsored or patronised for that specific race by a local business. So while David Baker might be riding throughout the season for Ace Racing Team–Peugeot, for a specific race he would also be sponsored by a local car dealership. The business paid his start money and in return got to put their name alongside his in the programme, and got to shake his hand afterwards in the VIP tent.

Gould, Baker and Salmon were, along with Surrey's Steve Douce and Yorkshire's Chris Young, a generation that dominated the sport in Britain during the eighties. In the British championships Douce won seven times between 1983 and 1993, and he also competed regularly in Switzerland and Belgium. For many years during that time, the BBC's flagship sports programme *Grandstand* showed a re-run of the national championships (it was a good filler when the football had been rained off) and publicity of that sort, even for only one event, was enough to attract sponsors to the sport, so the top British riders could make a decent living without going to ride for a Swiss or Belgian squad. There were even events in Britain which the top Belgian and Swiss riders considered worth travelling across the Channel for. The Halfords International and the Smirnoff Scramble (echoes of the Martini International?) gave the British riders a chance to compare themselves to the elite of the sport on home turf.

Before Douce and his cohorts, the lanky figure of Chris Wreghitt was exciting the British cyclocross community. Wreghitt won the national championships five times in a row, the first of which when he was only 18 years old. He went on to take a history degree at Birmingham University and after graduating moved to Switzerland to ply his trade. He was successful immediately, winning the prestigious Zürich-Waid event, and ironically that spelt the beginning of the end of his cross career, because he was soon lured into a road racing career, eventually signing for the Bianchi team.

Britain's biggest successes in international cyclocross have historically been at junior level. In February 1986 I was 12 years old, and a cyclocross veteran. I had some wins on my *palmarès*, but I was about to take a step up, from the safe environment of the Under-12s to the rather more formidable Under-16s category, which now goes by the title of 'youth' but in those days had the rather cringe-inducing title of 'juveniles'. I was obsessed by all things cycling, and one of the high-points of my week was Thursday morning, when *Cycling Weekly* was published. *Cycling Weekly*, or the *Comic* as it was called by those inside the sport, was essential reading. It was devoted to racing, because back then you either raced or you toured. To the racing community, the latter activity was for eccentric old chaps with mudguards, panniers and soggy bikes. There was, of course, no internet and no social media, so the only way to find out who had won a major race was to wait until Thursday to find the results in *Cycling Weekly*.

Like all responsible boys, I had a paper round. The newsagent, knowing me to be a keen cyclist, had given me the most physically challenging of his routes. No quick jaunt around a flat housing estate for me. My route took me up a long climb into a nice middle-class suburb where everyone read broadsheet newspapers, so the orange plastic bag I had to carry was so heavy that when I set out I could barely lift the strap over my head. Still, it was character-building, probably. Cruelly, an hour after my paper round, I then had to climb the hill again to get to school. By my first lesson I was already exhausted. But on Thursdays I got my reward. I returned my orange bag and the newsagent produced *Cycling Weekly*, which I had on special order. Sometimes I would stand outside, skimming every article and devouring the adverts for replica trade team clothing. Other times I curled my precious cargo up and belted home, to read it as I ate toast and jam before school.

On the first Thursday in February 1986, I was stunned to discover that a British rider had just won the Junior World Cyclocross Championship. Stuart Marshall, from Lincoln, plugged his way through the glutinous mud of Lembeek, Belgium, to take the title by 17 seconds from a Swiss rider, Beat Brechbühl. Marshall was only the tenth British rider to win the rainbow jersey, and the first in cyclocross. His win was founded on his strong running ability – he'd been a schoolboy cross-country running champion. In practice the course had been heavy but rideable, but heavy rain on the eve of race-day turned it into such a quagmire that arguably it contravened the UCI rule which states a race must involve more riding than running. (Lembeek wasn't the most muddy World Championships however, that honour goes to Saccolongo in Italy in 1979. The Italian Vito di Tano was favourite for the amateur race, and preferred a heavy course, so the local fire brigade was pressed into surreptitiously watering the course a few days before the event. It then rained heavily, turning a heavy course into a completely unrideable course. Only the tarmac section could be ridden.)

Marshall didn't mind the Belgian mud. Recovering from a relatively poor start, he picked his way to the front of the race then, with two laps to go, having just carried his bike across a shoe-sucking field, he found he had a gap, and in his own words, 'just kept going'. That final lap was nerve-twisting for the British team manager, George Shaw, and the coach Chris Wreghitt.

But in the pits there was stress on another level altogether. Halfway through the race Marshall had thrown his bike at the mechanics and shouted at them that something was wrong with it. On inspection the British team's head mechanic Sandy Gilchrist found that Marshall's crank was loose. He tightened it, and Marshall took the bike back next time round. But when he came round again the crank had worked itself loose again. Gilchrist realised that the crank was in such a poor condition that the conventional method of tightening wasn't working. With a degree of lateral thinking that astounded his colleagues in the pit, Gilchrist saw a spectator drinking a can of Coke, jumped into the crowd, took the can from them, poured the drink out into the mud and began snipping it into a collar for the crank, to give it something to tighten on to. He was still tightening as Marshall approached the pits on his last lap, alone in the lead but without a gap big enough to give any sense of comfort. Simon Burney, in the pits with Gilchrist, shouted to him that Marshall was approaching. Fifty yards, 40 yards, Gilchrist was still tightening, 30 yards, 20 yards, one last turn of the wrench and the bike was flung onto the course ready for Marshall to collect.

At the finish line there was no big screen to watch his progress and crowd control was much more lackadaisical back then, so the scenes were chaotic. The British team managers and journalists strained to see down the long uphill finishing straight. Marshall appeared at the bottom of the hill, alone and furiously pumping at his pedals, elbows thrust outwards. With barely the strength to raise an arm in victory, he crossed the line, the

Belgian announcer duly calling out in French the words which make every cycling fan's nerves jangle, '*Le nouveau champion du monde cyclocross juniors!*'. Marshall collapsed into the arms of Shaw then draped himself over his handlebars, trying to regain his breath. A few minutes later, cleaned up, fully recovered yet in a state of total shock, he was standing on the top step of the podium.

I read about all of this in Dennis Donovan's evocative race report in *Cycling Weekly*. I devoured the black and white photos of Marshall and others tackling this epic course. And though my own first experience of cyclocross, aged 11 in that farmyard in Oxfordshire had left an indelible mark, it was probably this victory of Marshall's that made me fall in love with the sport. Then, as now, any British success was considered 'against the odds'. The language was of 'raids across the Channel'. We were plucky underdogs, and in this scenario the mud of Flanders, though it was never mentioned, had other connotations.

Stuart Marshall didn't make a successful transition to the senior ranks, and disappeared from the sport soon afterwards. Now, all that remains of his win, other than his rainbow jersey and gold medal, are a few grainy photos and a short video on YouTube. And a famous umbrella. Lembeek was so wet and muddy that it became infamous even among Belgian fans. One fan decided to commemorate the event by painting the name of the venue in large yellow letters on a black umbrella. He or she – the umbrella owner's identity is a mystery – goes to a lot of cross races, because that umbrella can be seen bobbing above the crowd at most Belgian events. I wonder whether it's some kind of communication to the weather gods: 'Bring us rain and turn every weekend into Lembeek,' the vintage umbrella says.

*

Back in Gravesend, behind the two leaders follows a long string of riders, many of whom have parents providing a vigorous in-race technical analysis. 'Change down . . . jump off . . . jump on . . . take the inside line . . .' if the kids resent their parents' pushiness they don't show it; they're too exhausted to shout back anyway. It's easy to scoff at these cyclocross equivalents of soccer dads, but would I be more restrained were either of my children to take up the sport? It seems a problem I'm unlikely to encounter. Anya is watching the race with an expression of curious horror. I can tell what she's thinking – 'There's a warm café nearby with cake and apple juice, why isn't everyone in there?' My two-year-old son is gazing around with a look of detached bemusement, as if to say, 'This is all very silly – where are the swings?'

Still, for the good of the sport, it's encouraging to see so many children racing their bikes. Whether it's peer pressure, parent pressure, or some kind of instinct for what it means to race, most of the riders are pushing themselves deep into the tunnel of pain that experienced cyclists know and love. In no other part of their lives will an 11-year-old push themselves to the boundary of what they're capable of.

The Essex Sven Nys is approaching the bell. Then disaster strikes. He rides into the finishing straight frantically gesturing at his front wheel. Puncture! His dad brings him to a halt, heaves the bike over the barriers and into the crowd and sets about changing the wheel. It's a painfully slow change. Dad struggles with the cantilever brakes, and while the crowd gathers round to watch, his son is jumping up and down in exasperation. The second-placed rider, previously completely out of the running, is fast approaching. I feel for that father – having to do a speedy mechanical to save your son's race in front of a knowing crowd is my idea of hell. He gets the wheel in and flips the bike back onto the course to his waiting son. But the second-placed rider is there now, shooting through the finish line as the commissaire rings the bell: '*Laastse ronde*.' Dad yells encouragement at son. The pair of riders disappear into the bends locked together. The crowd, suddenly animated by this dramatic turn of events, runs over to the back of the course to see who's going to emerge in front.

When they reappear the Barking and Dagenham rider is back in the lead, but his rival, sensing a rare opportunity for a scalp, is fixed on his back wheel. Coming into the off-camber section for the final time there are a number of lapped riders blocking their path. No amount of shouting from the parents will get these lapped riders out of the way, there just isn't room. Now comes a moment of pure cyclocross heaven. Slowed by the lapped riders and facing a stiff climb, the Barking rider has to dismount. He runs well, but somehow his rival manages to stay on his bike and find enough traction and momentum to threaten a pass. Coming around a sharp turn, with the ground now sloping downwards, the Barking rider moves sideways, blocking the pass and securing his position in front. He then leaps back onto his bike and sprints away into the next obstacle, creating enough of a gap to secure victory. His move was subtle, and probably wasn't even done consciously, but a professional would have been proud of it. In cyclocross position is important. This youngster knew that intuitively.

One by one the kids stream across the finish line then collapse in melodramatic, panting heaps at their parents' feet. It's not long before they've jumped up to compare notes with their friends. In last place is a girl who is grinning from ear to ear, despite the fact that she's so exhausted she can hardly keep the bike moving forward. Embarrassed at her position, not wanting to ride past the crowd of parents at the finish, she attempts to leave the course at the final bend. We wave her on, telling her she's got to cross the line to finish, but she's already off her bike. So the commissaire holding the chequered flag makes a lightning decision. Flag in hand, he runs down the finishing straight and waves it over the girl's head. Who says finishing lines have to be in a fixed position anyway?

Much to Anya's relief, we make our way up to the café in search of hot drinks. In the entrance foyer I bump into Jim, a friend and sometime cycling companion. Jim is a relatively recent convert to serious cycling, and has thrown himself into it with the same passion that he shows for music, coffee and a host of other interests. We know each other not through cycling but through playgroups – he has three young daughters. Having vaguely heard of this strange beast called cyclocross, Jim checked it out on the internet, found this race meeting, and entered. And here he is. I'm rather jealous of people who have that ability to do stuff without the months of careful planning and analysis that I would have to go through to get to the same endpoint.

Today, though, Jim seems pretty stressed. Having run in from the car park with bike and backpack, he has entered into a protracted negotiation with the parking machine. His race starts in half an hour.

'We're late for bloody everything,' he mutters.

'Your first cross race?' I say. 'How are you feeling?'

'Tired. The kids had me up in the night.'

To show my deep understanding of the sport, I pinch his tyres and tell him they're too hard for the conditions. He does not look impressed.

While Jim heads out for a warm-up, I button up my coat and walk up to the highest point of the course. The organisers have made good use of the limited space and natural topography by looping the course intricately up and down and around and around. Even from here it's impossible to follow. Some sections are just baffling cacophonies of fluttering plastic tape. Like the huge grassy spiral at the top of the course, which riders enter into, go round and round, then emerge apparently where they came in. It seems to defy the laws of physics and common sense. It's a curious task, creating a cyclocross course. Part jigsaw puzzle, part theatre set design, part sadism. The principal objective is to create a course which enables good racing, but beyond that there are many nuances. The UCI, naturally, are more interested in rules. Their rulebook runs to dozens of pages, and one could forgive the average course designer for losing the will to live when faced with so many constraints. But true creativity lies in working within constraints. Our architects know that the course must form a closed circuit of a minimum length of 2.5 kilometres and maximum 3.5 kilometres, of which at least 90 per cent shall be rideable. They know that rule 5.1.018 states the course must be at least 3 metres wide throughout and clearly marked and protected on both sides. Such things go without saying. And once the location of the start–finish straight and the pits – which have to be halfway round the lap – have been determined, then the real fun can begin.

I wonder whether course designers go about their lives always with one eye out for a possible course locations, or even just a feature. Do they take their children or grandchildren to the park and mentally stake out a series of loops across the grass, while their children play on the slide? Through the eyes of a course designer a quiet wooded slope becomes a technical descent, a grassy knoll becomes a run-up, and a beach becomes a November battleground.

As the wind whips some fresh rain across my face, the seniors line up on the road circuit for their start. There are separate prizes for women, veteran men and veteran women, but all ride together. It's a sizeable field, perhaps fifty riders. I move down to the road and stand a hundred yards away from the riders, to see the opening sprint. Beside me are Jim's wife and three girls. At the front of the grid are some slender, skinsuit-clad, stony-faced dudes. They've done their reconnaissance laps, warmed up on rollers, downed some energy drink and thrown their jackets to their mothers. They know the drill. Several rows further back is Jim, the cross virgin on a borrowed bike, wearing a plain long-sleeve jersey and with absolutely no idea what he's about to encounter. The commissaire gives the riders their instructions and steps off the road, his whistle already between his lips. I try to remember whether I told Jim that in cross the sprint is at the start, that positioning is crucial.

The whistle blows. The skinsuit dudes charge up the hill and past us with grunts and swishes, the rest of the field comes charging after them, and at the back, smiling and waving to his delighted children, comes Jim. The smile doesn't last long.

He might not be carrying his bike or remounting in the right way, but Jim has got his race face spot on. Riding cross requires concentration, because the moment you get distracted is the moment your wheels slide out from under you. Still, by lap two he has the time and energy to ask me, 'When will it be over?'

On another section of the course there is a steep, gravel descent with a sharp left turn at the bottom. Standing at the bottom, I watch the riders slide, wrench and teeter around the bend. They might have been smiling and exchanging jokes with spectators a few seconds ago on the climb, but now their eyes are totally focused on making this turn. Jim comes rattling down the gravel path at the speed of a man who has forgotten how painful crashing is. He's in the zone. He's on his A-game, and all the other sporting clichés. Arms bent, back wheel skipping cheerfully, his fingers clutching the brakes. It seems highly doubtful that he will make it round the turn. But I've underestimated his skill, or his luck. He makes it, drawing a gasp from the spectator standing next to me. And as he passes I glimpse a change in Jim's expression. It's only tiny, he's still focused on the bike and the path and the race, but it's definitely there – a half-smile not intended for anyone else. It's an instinctive expression of joy. 'I made it,' his face reads.

That fleeting moment was redolent of another rider's expression I detected recently as I watched the Superprestige at Asper-Gavere. Experienced elite Dutchwoman Sanne van Paassen, possessor of one of the broadest smiles in the sport, was on the front row of the grid, but a bumpy gear change during the initial sprint from the line pushed her back down to twelfth by the first bend. By the top of the long muddy slog-climb at the start of the circuit, Van Paassen had ridden into ninth place and was a few seconds behind a group of six. Then came the descent. Whenever cross organisers install inflatable crash barriers, you know there's a tricky descent. Halfway down Nikki Harris lost control of her bike, two other riders couldn't help but crash into her, the three of them almost blocking the course with bikes and bodies. Two more riders had to slam their brakes on and put a foot down to avoid falling, but because Van Paassen had been sitting a little way behind this bunch, she was able to adjust her line and pick a way through the mayhem, passing five out of the six riders ahead of her and hardly losing any speed as she did so. Van Paassen was then able to carry her speed into the steep climb that followed the descent, and ride up it, whereas most other riders were forced to run. As she crested that climb you could see an expression of exhilaration on her face. For professionals and cross virgins alike, clearing an obstacle is a delight in itself. The fiercest competitor in a cross race, the one everyone wants to beat, is the course.

In the café after the race, Jim enjoys a well-earned slice of cake. Red-faced and ravenous, he shares stories with fellow competitors. One comes over to apologise for nearly knocking him off.

'After thirty-five years I never thought I'd have so much fun riding berms,' Jim says. 'Oh, man, that was so hard. And so much fun.'

Cake eaten, tea drunk, he starts packing up his bag and ushering his children towards the exit. It's a Saturday lunchtime, there's a three-year-old's birthday party to get to.

*

After her third place in Koksijde, Katie Compton flies home to spend Thanksgiving in Colorado Springs. She and Mark spend the day with friends, eating maple syrup and bourbon pecan pie and drinking good wines, but the following day it's back to training.

A few miles west of where she lives, Pikes Peak dominates the landscape, its snow-covered summit sits at 14,115 feet, making it one of the highest in the Rocky Mountains. There's a road to the top, 19 miles of switchbacks and incredible views that you really shouldn't be looking at if you're driving, and every year racing drivers come here to compete in the annual Pikes Peak International Hill Climb. There are also bike races and organised rides to the summit, and anyone new to the area will soon discover the lung-busting effect of riding uphill at altitude – oxygen pressure here is 60 per cent of what it is at sea level.

During the cyclocross season, when Katie comes here, she brings nothing more than a pair of running shoes. She heads for the Manitou Springs Incline, known locally simply as 'the Incline'. A hiking trail that starts in the town of Manitou Springs and heads straight up one of the foothills of Pikes Peak, the Incline has gained notoriety as the ultimate cardio workout challenge. Built upon the sleepers of a funicular railway that got swept away by a rockslide, the trail climbs for just under a mile, gaining over two thousand feet. That's steep. Very steep. The slope is relentless, a never-ending stack of timbers for the hiker to clamber up. A fit person can climb it in an hour or so. Katie runs up it, in under half an hour.

Like many other athletes based in Colorado Springs (the US Olympic training centre as well as army and air force bases in the town ensures that there are always many similarly masochistic athletic types around), Katie loves the idea of the Incline, and she loves the pain it causes her. There's something pure about running up a one-mile staircase that climbs a mountain. Plus, stair-running is a brilliant workout for cyclists because it's so hard on the quads.

At the top of the Incline Katie turns onto a hiking path called Barr Trail and descends the hill she has just climbed. If she'd turned the other way, the trail would take her all the way up to the summit of Pikes Peak, but cyclocross racers do not use 14-mile hiking trails to get race-fit. By the bottom of the hill, she will have recovered from her effort, and will turn to face the Incline once again.

When I was racing, my training mainly consisted of taking my bike out into the woods near my house and riding deep into the muddy trails until exhausted. There was no science, no plan, no structure. Now all elite cyclists train according to the data. Everything is measured, everything is done for a specific reason. Cyclocross, however, does retain a more intuitive mindset, partly because of the nature of the discipline. Without technique, mind-blowingly good physiology is useless. So riders have to practise their skills, and that means heading out into the woods.

Everyone has their own local training routes. For Dan Tulett it is the sinuous paths that climb the North Downs, the line of hills behind his house in Kent. For Katie in Colorado it's the mountain bike trails of Oil Well Flats and Pueblo Reservoir, and in Belgium the flowing single track of the Kalmthoutse Heide forest. Most riders train alone or in small groups, but there are larger group training sessions. The most famous takes place every Wednesday afternoon at 't Zand, near the Dutch village of Alphen-Chaam, just across the border from Belgium. Go to 't Zand on a summer weekend and you'll find a sandy car park in the middle of a forest, filled with cars and families carrying picnics, towels and windbreaks, for here in the middle of a forest is an expansive, welcoming beach. During the autumn and winter the forest is much quieter. There are dog-walkers and joggers, and every Wednesday the elite riders of Dutch cyclocross come here to train. The car park is full of mechanics, riders and parents unloading bikes and wheels. It's a chance to compare your form with your peers', and group sessions make you focus, work hard. The coach leading the session will put the riders through a variety of drills, each aiming to develop specific skills or types of fitness. The forest has a mixture of terrain, so the training circuits can be modified to replicate whatever terrain the riders will face the following weekend.

While group sessions are useful, particularly for riders prone to losing focus, most elite riders train alone or in small groups. Sven Nys was famous for his dedication to training and recovery. During the summer Nys averaged thirty hours per week on the bike, building up endurance with long rides in Belgium or Majorca, with road or mountain bike races thrown in for their higher intensity. Then, once the cyclocross season started, his training changed. The overall volume decreased but the intensity increased. Intervals, sprints, hill sprints and running all played a part. And, of course, racing – the best training of all. Jeremy Powers, who used to be a professional road racer, had to undertake a carefully planned training programme to change his body to suit cyclocross. He likened it to training to become the ultimate fighter. Cross requires strength and agility throughout the upper body as well as the legs.

The professionals will tailor their training to specific target races. Lars van der Haar, for example, is training specifically for the World Championships in Zolder by doing short uphill bursts to increase his power. He believes this is where the race will be won. Training and racing aren't always in full alignment. Van der Haar has planned to have a particularly hard period of training in early November that will negatively affect his form at the time but bear fruit in January, when it's important.

Over the last decade professional road racing has become a slave to analysis. Every training ride is planned in terms of power and heart-rate levels. After training the riders download their data, and their coaches peer into spreadsheets. Selection for major races is based as much on data as on results. It's fascinating, if you're into that sort of thing, but it doesn't seem to have a great deal to do with sport. In cyclocross the numbers are still important, and professional cross riders also have coaches who stare into spreadsheets (often in the middle of a forest). But in cyclocross the difference is that technique plays a critical role, and every rider must continue to refine their technique. Riding through deep mud, using your bodyweight to rock the bike over obstacles, smooth dismounts and remounts, cornering on soft tyres, even changing bikes in the pits – there are dozens of moments when a cyclocross race can go disastrously wrong if your technique isn't good enough. Fortunately this gives cyclocross riders of every level an excuse to go out and blast their bikes around a forest, bunny-hopping logs, plunging down steep cliffs and splashing through muddy puddles.

The joy of riding a cyclocross bike lies in the necessity of combining pure fitness with the challenge of clearing obstacles. On a good day, the endorphins will be flowing through your body, and your wheels will be flowing through the mud. On a bad day, your lungs will feel as if they're going to pop, and everywhere you point your front wheel it gets stuck.

11

Live Transmission

Leaving my children on this Saturday is particularly hard. In the morning it's my daughter's school's Christmas fair – an intense and exhausting affair involving lucky dip, tombola, raffles and a high-stakes visit to Santa's grotto. Hard work, but on those moments when I lift myself out of the chaos, there's a poignancy that is heart-breaking. These are the moments that a parent wants to freeze, to always remember: the choir piping out 'Away in a Manger' – impossibly cute – and the banter between my daughter and the local out-of-work actor who's been drafted in to play Santa. Afterwards we head off to a local Christmas street fair, with stalls for local shops, mulled wine and mince pies and hotdogs. I'm reminded of the northern European tradition for Christmas fairs: part commercial, part social, only a very small part religious. In a couple of hours I'll be heading into London to get the Eurostar to Brussels. But first there's the Christmas tree to put up.

We get in out of the cold, make tea, and I venture into the loft to get the fake Christmas tree and the accompanying box of decorations. Opening this box of delights and cooing over its kitsch contents is becoming something of a family tradition. *E.T.* is on television as the children hang baubles and switch the fairy lights on and off, on and off, on and off in migraine-inducing fashion. Small children love to decorate a Christmas tree, but their height means that you end up with a band of intense baubling around the bottom of the tree and nothing above. As darkness falls I say my goodbyes and head for the train station.

Living in a city as large as London it's all too easy to let the seasons slip by. Life is so fast, and so sheltered from the raw elements, that you can arrive at midwinter without really noticing autumn. As I navigate central London I see signs of Christmas in shop windows, on advertising billboards. I move between trains, bundled into a big coat, earphones plugged in, reading my book. The weather barely registers on my mind.

Perhaps that's why we love cyclocross so much. It's a very visible and very visceral battle against the elements. Cyclocross fans and riders get unnaturally excited about mud, snow, rain and wind. It is, after all, a winter sport, and like all winter sports it's a test of courage, facing into the destructive power of nature. For a racer to float across the stickiest mud, plastered in wet snowflakes, wearing only a skinsuit and sunglasses, is a nose thumbed in the face of winter. We fans, wrapped in layers of fleece and Gore-Tex, and warming our mitts on cups of coffee or mulled wine, applaud our mad heroes. Winter might not feel real to us but it certainly does to them, and we'd rather suffer it vicariously.

Druivencross is a Classic race, the epitome of Flandrian cyclocross. Its status is built on its longevity – the race has run continuously since 1960 – and on the quality of its previous winners. Flandrian legend Roland Liboton has fifteen wins here (his tally helped by it being run more than once in some seasons), Sven Nys has six wins and Erik de Vlaeminck has nine. In the women's race, which has only run since 2000, Katie Compton has won three times. The race's nickname is 'the mother of all crosses'.

But its Classic status is also related to its setting. Overijse, an affluent village to the south-east of Brussels, is one of the more picturesque stops on the cyclocross merry go-round. There are a couple of large duck ponds, ancient red-brick barns, cobbled streets, and a steep wooded hillside. Brussels, and London, seem a long way away. Nestled among the Flemish quaintness are some modern municipal buildings – a swimming centre in the shape of a glass cube thrown into the ground at an odd angle, and a crescent-shaped cultural centre. Somehow the Belgians seem to get away with mixing modern architecture and old, or perhaps I'm just predisposed to approve because this is the venue for a great bike race.

The course, which hasn't varied much for over fifty years, sends the riders out of the village streets and up a steep grass slope onto open farmland, then runs past the local football ground and into a long intricate series of woodland loops, before plunging back down into the village. It's actually a lot more complicated than that but to describe it accurately is like trying to give someone directions through a maze. It's a hard course because it climbs the hillside three times each lap, and the woodland paths are fast but often slick. It demands supreme fitness and powers of recovery, alongside technical ability. To win here, as in Koppenberg, is a significant addition to one's *palmarès*.

I'm here to spend the day with the Telenet–Fidea team. When I arrive at ten o'clock in the morning, there are only three campers and a couple of team cars. The head coach, Kris Wouters, is busy helping a junior rider get ready for his race. A fit-looking forty-something, trim in a tasteful grey Castelli down jacket, black beanie and black mechanic's trousers, Kris is coach to all twenty-three riders in the squad. After he sends the rider on his way towards the start line, I suggest that twenty-three riders is rather a lot to coach.

'It's too much. It's OK during the week, but on race days it's too much, so I have some help. Particularly for the juniors because they can't park here so we have to do a lot of running around to get to them.'

Ah, parking. I've been in Overijse twenty minutes and already the subject of parking has come up. Telenet–Fidea, with their phalanx of yellow and blue campers, have been allocated a prime spot – a long stretch of car park alongside a small lake. It seems pretty good to me but Kris isn't happy. The first three campers arrived before he did, and took the insane decision to park lengthways.

'Look, if they'd parked across we'd get more campers in. The organisers never give us enough room. They say, "OK, you can have this 120-metre stretch," and that sounds OK, but then if you measure the campers it's not going to work. But they don't want to listen.'

Assistant manager, Karen Ramakers, tells me that for the team, parking is important because it enables them to make a big visual impact for the fans. That's good for the sponsors, so it's good for the team. And there are practical benefits. The mechanics want to be close to each other, and to the course, to avoid any unnecessary travelling loaded up with bikes and wheels.

For the next hour I loiter, somewhat self-consciously, as more campervans arrive. The routine is always the same, wherever you're racing. Once you've got through the parking stewards, gatekeepers to the world of cyclocross stardom, there is a careful reversing manoeuvre, then the setting-up begins. Roll out the canopy, unpack the storage compartments, begin assembling bikes. The riders stay inside, in the warm, with the television on, while outside their mechanics get to work.

About three hours before their race, the riders will go and sign on, collect their numbers, stop to chat to friends and acquaintances, members of the press. Then they disappear back into the camper. A little later they ask their mechanic for a functioning bike, perhaps have a brief debate about tyre pressure, and head off for a course inspection.

Meanwhile, at the campers, the crowd is slowly growing. Fans stroll along the line, staying respectfully behind the barriers, looking for their heroes, or at least their heroes' bikes. There are more team helpers too. Predominantly these are parents or other relatives of the riders. All are voluntary.

Nikki Harris's helper, a friendly woman in her fifties, bundled into a team fleece, tells me that during the week she works for the Belgian government in their housing procurement department. At weekends she works for the team, travelling to races and looking after Nikki. When I ask her what this entails she shrugs and says simply, 'Everything.' As far as I can tell this means preparing food and drinks, carrying clothing, and after the race pouring everyone a glass of apple schnapps.

In short, these unpaid helpers, who generally seem to be women in their fifties, do anything required to make their rider's life easier before and after the race. The distribution of items of clothing is more important than it might sound; riders want to retain the body temperature achieved during warm-up for as long as possible. Only with three minutes to go do the riders start to disrobe. By this time the television cameramen are standing in front of them, a gaggle of commissaires and official-looking types, and the team helpers. This is their time. For this handful of minutes they are part of the race. Often you will see a subtle smile on their faces as they wait for their rider to unzip their jacket, roll it into a ball and lob it over the other riders to their helper. There's a strong maternal feeling to this moment. Indeed, for many riders it is their mother who they're throwing their jacket to, and it's a moment they've been repeating since the beloved was a child riding local races.

Nikki's mechanic is working on one of her bikes outside the camper. He is amenable, but taciturn. 'Nikki is the boss. Whatever she wants, I do,' he says before knocking the hell out of a bottom bracket.

'Who decides her tyre pressure?' I ask.

'She does,' he says with a frown. Stupid question. Then with an eyebrow raised he adds, 'But it can change very late before a race.'

As the women's race starts I talk to Karen Ramakers about the team. Like most Belgian cyclocross teams the title sponsor operates only in Flanders (Telenet is a broadband company) so its interest is in securing television and media coverage in Flanders. Cyclocross is an attractive proposition because it has extensive television coverage at weekends, and it can connect the brand to a broad base of the population.

The team comprises the twenty-three riders and thirty sponsors. Telenet–Fidea is unique in that it has riders in all categories – juniors, Under-23s and elite men and women. Only the professionals get a salary, but all riders get a bonus for a good result. The managers and coaches are on a full-time salary but everyone else is a volunteer. Karen's job is logistics, in its broadest sense. This means agreeing contracts with sponsors, contracts with riders, travel arrangements, buying campervans, buying snow tyres for campers . . . she rolls her eyes as if to say, 'The list is endless.' Her background is in tennis and basketball but she saw *Wellens en Wee*, a reality TV show featuring Bart Wellens and his family, fell in love with cross, saw the job and applied.

Because cyclocross is an individual sport rather than a team sport – unlike road racing – even the biggest teams like Telenet are little more than confederations of the smaller groups that collect around each rider. Each rider has his or her own mechanic and helper. At the camper of Eli Iserbyt I speak to a man in team overalls, cleaning Iserbyt's bike after his course inspection.

'I'm not paid! I'm his uncle,' he moans, but he clearly loves it.

Next door, two mothers in their fifties are comparing notes. Their sons used to be in the same cycling club, but now ride for different teams and live a long way apart. One says, 'We work Monday to Friday then we work at weekends for our children. It's hard. Early starts. We eat here as a family before driving home. Sometimes we sleep in the camper.'

There is a great deal of hanging around the campers. They function as transport, storage, refuge. All are very organised, with bikes, spare wheels, kit and food all neatly stored away. The financial arrangements relating to the campers vary. The team owns some, mainly those of the top riders, or at least the riders with good agents. Other riders own their own. Others still have leased their camper for a season. Whoever owns the vehicle, the team always pays to have them 'wrapped' in the team colours – no small expense, since wrapping a camper costs around 5000 Euros. As Kris talks me through the process for wrapping a camper, I don't quite have the nerve to ask who on earth thought it a good idea to have huge, cheesy pictures of the riders on the sides.

Every camper has a different vibe. Karen walks along the line with me and gestures to Tom Meeussen's. 'A real man-cave,' she says, with a wry smile. In contrast the Dutch rider Corné van Kessel has one of the most clean and organised campers. His girlfriend Nicky comes to every race, makes food and drinks for everyone, looks after his clothing and generally keeps him in check. As she opens the door for me, she looks anxious. I try to reassure her that I'm not going to judge her on the cleanliness of her camper, but something seems to get lost in translation. Inside it is, of course, immaculate. There is a television, a small kitchen area, soft seating and a bed. Other than a bag full of kit there is nothing to denote that this is a professional bike rider's home for the day. Nothing on the inside at least – on the outside the camper is wrapped in Telenet–Fidea's blue and yellow livery, with lists of sponsors' logos and the obligatory cheesy rider shot. I wonder whether there's a photographer who specialises in taking pictures of Flemish cyclocross riders to be used on the side of campervans. Now there's a niche occupation.

As Nicky and I talk, standing under the pull-out canopy over the door, Corné rides up and hands his bike to his mechanic. Like most professional bike riders he has a grace and fluidity in his movements, even just riding through the car park. To me he gives a little nod, acknowledging the media pass that hangs around my neck on a lanyard. To Nicky, his girlfriend of five years, he says something in Dutch then disappears into the camper. Whatever he said, it made her smile. She tells me that he is generally a quiet person, but determined. They met through cycling, her family have always been involved in the local racing scene in North Brabant, where they are both from. Nicky has a hairdressing business, but Corné's riding comes first, so she often has to shut on a Saturday if they are travelling to a race.

That blend of quietness, humility and steely determination is becoming something of a theme. It is integral to the Dutch and Flemish perception of a great bike rider, but it also seems to sit uneasily alongside the demands of modern sport. When athletes are brands they must have a presence, a personality, a story. Results on their own do not bring fans, sponsorship money, start money. Sven Nys understood this, Bart Wellens understood this. When you are at the top of the sport in Belgium you'll be invited onto television chat shows. Journalists will ask you for opinion on matters completely unrelated to cyclocross – the Tour de France, Belgian politics, the Middle East.

In October 2010 *The Last Show*, the Belgian equivalent of *Letterman*, if you can imagine such a thing, did a cyclocross special. They had four stars of the sport in the studio, and challenged them on their knowledge of Belgian mud. Three unlabelled pots of mud – three guesses which famous course they came from. In a studio bedecked with bikes, and in front of a live audience, Sven Nys, Niels Albert, Bart Wellens and the flamboyant Czech star Zdeněk Štybar sat on the sofa and chatted amiably to the host. They only needed a quick sniff to guess the mud correctly.

If you want to be a Belgian cyclocross superstar you need to be as comfortable appearing on television as you are getting plastered in mud. For as well as the live coverage of racing, there will be post-race interviews, chat shows, news reports and invitations to reality television programmes. Indeed, Wellens, a craggy-faced veteran of the sport whose career has included World Championship victories, the World Cup, Superprestige and Belgian national titles, had his reality television show, *Wellens en Wee* on Flemish channel VT4. The show followed Wellens and his family and teammates through the weekly routine of training, racing and facing the media. Something like *The Osbournes*, but focusing on Flemish cyclocross.

Developing your personality for the television audience doesn't necessarily mean becoming brasher, louder. At the end of every season the television channel Sporza creates a 'humorous' sketch show to celebrate the stars of the sport, and to show the viewing public their human side. In February 2015 the concept was that of a rap battle. Kevin Pauwels's contribution was a video of him cruising around an Antwerp suburb in a vintage American car, wearing a baseball cap, shearling coat and sunglasses, rapping about how success brings money and women. It was a vision both hilarious (it looked to have been filmed on a typically grey and cold day, and the girls in the video were rather pasty and unconvincing) and disturbing. How did Pauwels, the quiet man of cyclocross, who clearly hates doing interviews and press conferences, end up pretending to an American gangster rapper? How much pressure was there from the television company, his agent, his sponsors? 'People think you're quiet, aloof,' I can imagine them saying to him. 'Show them your funny side. Show them the Kevin *we* know.'

Television coverage has transformed cyclocross. If you're looking for one reason why the sport has become so popular and professional in Belgium, it's television. Sporza's live coverage of races on a Sunday afternoon now resembles what I remember the FA Cup final coverage being like on the BBC. There is build-up, expert pundits, interviews with key riders before the race, sometimes a clip of races from yesteryear. Then the men's and women's races live, all the podium celebrations and further interviews and analysis. Perfect viewing for a lazy Sunday afternoon. Viewer figures are phenomenal: Sporza consistently attracts over 600,000 viewers for World Cup and Superprestige events. A World Championship, particularly if it's being staged in Belgium, could attract over 1.25 million viewers. That's in a country whose total population is 11.2 million. Naturally, with such reach into the households of Flanders, sponsors are keen to be involved in the sport, money comes in, and the virtuous circle begins.

Yet this comprehensive approach to televising cyclocross is relatively young. For decades, from the sixties through to the nineties, only a handful of races were shown on Belgian television. These were the classics – Asper-Gavere, Overijse, the national championships and the World Championships. Paul Herygers' 1994 win at Koksijde may have captured the imagination of the Belgian public, but without consistent television exposure for racing, all his chat-show appearances alone weren't going to bring in serious investment.

The sea change came in 1997, in the rather unlikely setting of Munich. The World Championships were staged there on a bright but cold day in early February. The course, based in the impressive Olympic stadium, was packed hard and treacherously icy. Sporza, the sports arm of the Belgian public broadcaster, had just lost live football rights to a new commercial station. This loss meant that it needed something new to compensate, and also that it had surplus budget. Throughout the nineties professional cyclocross had been a battle between the Swiss and the Dutch, with Belgian riders having limited success outside of their own country. As most Swiss races were not televised, for a Belgian station to show them would have meant transporting a huge load of kit and people over to Switzerland – all to watch Belgian riders being beaten; hardly an attractive proposition. But someone at Sporza knew cross well enough to know change was coming. Two charismatic and talented riders, Sven Nys and Bart Wellens, were about to burst onto the world's stage. A live feed from Germany was secured, and on that Saturday afternoon Belgium watched with joy as Sven and Bart dropped the rest of the field. Coming into the last lap the pair were inseparable. They cleared the log staircase and the slippery off-camber descents, they went through the pits, together they approached the stadium. Their final obstacle before the finish on the athletics track was two 40-centimetre planks of wood. They arrived side by side. Wellens jumped off, as they had both been doing all race, but Sven did not. He bunny-hopped the planks, got a small gap, and that was enough. He took his first rainbow jersey and Belgium had a new hero. Even better, Belgium had a new duel to watch – Sven versus Bart.

The following season the number of live televised races rose from four to twenty-four. A commercial station snapped up rights to the Belgian championships and the Superprestige, so Sporza responded by buying rights to the World Cup and Gazet van Antwerpen Trofee. It was a clear-cut business decision. Wintry Sunday afternoons had nothing important in the schedules, road cycling already pulled in strong audience figures, and filming a cyclocross race is relatively straightforward. It requires a legion of static cameras and some outside broadcast trucks, but you don't have to get any aircraft off the ground, which is where things start to get expensive. Live televised cross was an immediate success and the figures grew when Nys and Wellens turned professional.

It's easy, and romantic, to attach the growth of the sport to Sven Nys. With one bunny-hop, he single-handedly created a twenty-year boom. To some degree that is true. Nys has such celebrity status in Belgium, and has been so prominent and successful in the sport, that during his valedictory season there were rumblings about declining television figures after his retirement. His coming of age in Munich marked the start of a new generation of riders, one in which Flandrians would be leading not chasing. What triggered success was the timing of that moment. Ultimately we have the Royal Belgian Football Association to thank for the growth in cyclocross: their decision to sell the rights to their games to commercial broadcasters created the space for the public broadcasters to dive into.

In professional sport more television coverage means more exposure for sponsors, which means bigger budgets, and more sponsors becoming involved. Cyclocross in Flanders is phenomenally successful but none of the key components have an interest in expanding that success beyond Flanders. Flemish television broadcasters have no mandate to sell their coverage abroad. Flemish sponsors are understandably focused on their market alone. Telenet sell broadband services to Flemish communities, what interest do they have in developing awareness of their brand in America, or even in Britain? Flemish fans want to see Flemish riders win. It's a closed system, and while it is operating successfully, Flemish cyclocross will continue to be the international figurehead of cyclocross. But the outlook in Flanders is short-sighted, parochial, even protectionist. What if Flandrian riders fade from the top level of the sport? Or some kind of scandal rocks the sport, denting its appeal to everyday fans at home? The cyclocross enthusiast will always love the sport, but not everyone will be so faithful. If the cycle of prosperity turns vicious, will the sport be in trouble?

*

As I wander down the line of campervans, meeting some more of the helpers and mechanics, I'm starting to tune into the atmosphere. The riders, understandably, are in their own little emotional bubbles, some more tense than others depending on what's going on with their recent form and results. Ellen van Looy, the experienced Belgian rider on Telenet, has had a good run of results recently and is relaxed, chatty. Her husband, who helps out as part of the pit crew, tells me she's scaled back the hours she does as a carer for disabled adults, giving her more time for training and recovery, and she's reaping the dividends with a string of top-five results. Nikki Harris, by contrast, seems stressed. Her season so far has been disappointing and frustrating. Her career is on an upward trajectory, but she still hasn't broken through to the very top strata of the sport, where victories are a regular occurrence. This season she's still looking for her first win, and you sense that until that comes she won't be able to relax.

The team helpers and mechanics don't have such emotional flux. They are professional and serious about their job, but genial and relaxed. They are, of course, older, and that maturity shows. There's a sense of routine, another day at the office. Whatever happens today, they've seen it all before. It's what young riders need – the steadying hand, the quiet word in the ear that instils confidence.

At the press room, situated in a meeting room on the ground floor of a municipal arts centre, I bump into Renaat Schotte, Sporza's roving reporter. Renaat has been a broadcast journalist covering cycling for Flemish television since 1998, and with his famous green microphone he is a fixture on the scene. Before and after races he buzzes around the riders, cameraman in tow, getting the inside line on how they're feeling, how the track is riding. The riders know and respect him, partly because of his integrity and knowledge on a personal level, and partly because Sporza is an important television channel for cyclocross. That green microphone is not one to be pushed away.

In a corridor outside the press room, decorated with framed photographs of tractor racing (in which the weather looks warm and sunny – Belgian tractor racing must be a summer sport, presumably because the tractors are busy in the autumn, or all the fans are at cyclocross races), we talk about the history of Druivencross, its heroes and its place on the calendar. The race is unusual in its independence. All other great races have been subsumed into one of the season-long competitions, which provides valuable funding, structure and resources – but Druivencross has remained fiercely independent, and there are concerns that its future is in doubt. The president of the organising committee, Willy Van Roy, is a charismatic and often challenging figure. Tall, with a ruddy complexion and a bushy moustache, Van Roy has an impressive collection of hats. This year he has had to adapt the course to avoid a field near the top of the hill because of a contractual dispute with the landowner. But the feud the newspapers want to report is with Sven Nys. In 2014, Sven started the race here but dropped out before halfway, suffering from a mysterious lack of form. The organisers took the decision to only pay Sven a third of his start money. The mistake they made was not to tell Sven or his agent. When Sven found out he was furious, calling the action – and the lack of communication – disrespectful. He vowed to never again ride in Overijse, and reportedly said that even if they offered him 30,000 Euros he wouldn't ride. Despite this being his last season in the sport, and living not far from Overijse, Sven made his decision and stuck with it. The fans might want to see him ride the mother of all crosses for one last time, but in professional cyclocross there is no room for sentiment.

With the absence of Nys, and Wout van Aert, who has opted to head to Spain for some sunny training, the men's field has an incomplete feeling. Still, that in itself can't explain the modest size of the crowd. There are probably fewer than eight thousand people here. For a Classic like Druivencross, this is damaging both for its reputation and its profitability. After the similarly small crowd that came to Koksijde, it makes me wonder if there is a deeper dynamic at play? Are people staying at home to watch on television, or choosing to spend their money going to other sports? Is the community spirit on which Belgian cyclocross is founded dissipating?

A day at a cyclocross race goes so fast. Before you know it it's time for lunch. Renaat, Balint and I head out of the press room and go to the town square, where the food vendors are also counting the cost of the small crowd. No queues for chips at this time of day is unheard of, and I stick with the safe option of mayonnaise. Perhaps by the end of the season I'll venture into the realms of the other mysterious sauces. Renaat, I notice, goes for something pink. Surely it's not Thousand Island dressing?

The women's race is a tussle between Jolien Verschueren and Helen Wyman, with the Belgian coming out on top. Chasing this leading duo are Sanne Cant and Nikki Harris. Cant, the Belgian champion, has been the dominant force in Belgian races this season, but doesn't look happy today. It's not for lack of encouragement; the locals are vociferous when her black, red and yellow jersey comes into sight. On the last lap, on an awkward dismount, she bangs her handlebars into her ribs and, winded, slows visibly. Harris takes advantage to jump up into third – remember all's fair in love and cyclocross. At the finish Cant comes to a halt beside a mesh fence and doubles over her bike, clutching at her bruised ribs, her face stricken with pain. Renaat sees a story and talks to her gently, asking her what happened and how she feels. Cant, to her credit, responds. Even when injured, the riders respect the green microphone.

Earlier in the day, Balint introduced me to a man called Julian who produces videos of races for a Belgian website. Julian is one of those men who knows everyone in the sport, and as we stood chatting near the podium, Sanne Cant eased through the crowd astride her white Stevens bike. Julian said something to her in Dutch, she smiled and gave a reply which made him laugh. A little further on she stopped to talk to someone, and was animated, relaxed and cheerful. Her smile when someone cracked a joke was bright and wide. A remarkable contrast to the Sanne Cant portrayed in much of the cycling media. With the sexism so characteristic of cycling media, Cant has been criticised for not smiling as she crosses the finish line with her hands in the air, for looking sullen and moody on the podium when a race hasn't gone her way, and for generally being a bit miserable. Yet seeing her here, among friends and family, before a race, I realised just how misleading television and social media reporting of a sporting event can be. If Cant doesn't smile when she wins a race it's not because she's got a miserable nature, it's because she's pumped full of adrenaline, because she's still focused on the job, because the emotions of victory are more complicated than pure joy. She's an enigmatic, intriguing rider, and does anyone really have the right to criticise her emotional response to racing? Needless to say a male rider wouldn't be criticised for not smiling as they won a race.

I asked Julian whether it was possible for Sanne to maintain her incredible form throughout the season. He shrugged and told me her whole season is based around the Belgian championships in early January and the World Championships in late January. She is sticking to a training regime that will bring her to the form of her life, as the commentators say, by the end of January. If that means a dip in her racing results during December because she's over-training, she's OK with that. A few hours later, as she struggles to hold Helen Wyman's wheel, that seems to be playing out.

For Nikki Harris, third place is a good result. You might think that her rightful position was fourth, on account of Sanne's incident, but Harris would no doubt argue that the injury was self-inflicted and the result of a moment's lapse in concentration. In her typically sardonic way, Harris says to the team helpers standing around drinking apple schnapps, 'That was a bit better, eh?' then clatters her bike against the side of the camper and climbs in to get changed.

At the start of the men's elite race, there is a minute's silence to mark the passing of Eric de Vlaeminck, who died a few days earlier after a long battle with Alzheimer's.

After the men's Druivencross I head back to the Telenet campervans, have another shot of apple schnapps with some of the helpers. Corné van Kessel, having finished eighth, comes rolling back and disappears into the camper to get changed. An anti-doping official with a clipboard follows him to the camper but hesitates and doesn't insist on going inside. He hovers at the camper door for a few minutes, apparently unsure of himself, before Corné reappears, wearing warm casual clothing and holding a flask of recovery drink. Corné gives Nicky a kiss and walks off with the steward.

Earlier in the day Nicky told me that it's often some time before Corné has cooled off after a race, and is ready to talk to her. His emotions run hot and the first person he needs is his coach, not his girlfriend. She understands that, and she knows that when he's ready he'll talk to her. I wonder whether this kiss is his way of starting that conversation. While he is off at the routine anti-doping control, Nicky pulls open a compartment in the campervan and gets out a bowl of chocolate Christmas figures, which she hands out to all the team helpers. She doesn't offer me one, and though I'm not offended (after all, I'm not part of the team) this minor occurrence reminds me that I am still very much on the outside of this sport. I don't speak Dutch, I don't live in Flanders, I don't understand the subtleties.

I leave the Telenet camp and head back to the podium, where I encounter something that I neither understand nor condone. Up on the stage, in front of a row of bemused photographers and a sizeable crowd waiting to see the World champion Mathieu van der Poel, is Father Christmas himself. Saint Niklaas, as he is known here, is resplendent in red and gold robes, a suitably impressive white beard and a red hat reminiscent of a bishop.

Perched on his knee is a blonde podium girl in a short skirt and high heels. Standing beside him and holding his gold staff, is a woman dressed up as a kind of page boy, in black breeches and a red and black jacket with a lacy collar. Her face is blacked-up, in the manner of the Black and White Minstrels, stars of the eponymous television show that was deemed racist even in the 1970s. I look around at the faces of the crowd. Some are laughing, some frowning, some seem completely indifferent to this monstrous sight. That the organisers should even think to include such an offensive little charade in their event is shocking. As Balint and I drive back to Brussels I feel more than ever like an outsider. This world that I've entered is small, powerful, a little odd and more than a little unnerving.

12

Storming the Citadel

Going to a cyclocross race can be a very dark and lonely experience, particularly when you have to leave your warm hotel room before dawn and walk up to the Citadel of Namur.

Deep in the Belgian Ardennes, Namur is the political centre of Wallonia and one of the few cities in the region to give an impression of affluence. The city stands at the meeting of two rivers, the Meuse and the Sambre, and has a bustling centre full of boutiques, independent bookshops, cafés and restaurants. On this last weekend before Christmas there's a market, an ice-skating rink, and many stalls selling Liège waffles. All shut at this hour, of course, as I trudge through the sleeping streets towards the river. Underneath glittering street decorations, past street cleaners atop lumbering machines, I take the Rue du Pont over the Sambre. The Citadel of Namur looms in front of me, impenetrable and forbidding, for all its artful spotlights. I suppose 'forbidding' works for a castle. Dating back to AD 937, the citadel has seen several facelifts over the centuries, but the current layout – protected as a heritage site – was constructed between 1631 and 1675. Given the history of Belgium, there's some irony in the fact that during this period the city was under Dutch control. Now its extensive fortifications, buildings, tunnels and ramparts are a major tourist attraction. And every year on the Sunday before Christmas it's the venue for a cyclocross Classic.

Rather than follow the circuitous route designated for competitors' vehicles, I take a smaller, closed road and begin climbing the hill. The road bends up the hill in a series of S-bends, steadily gaining height. The forest on either side is dark and silent. There is no sign of a bike race. No traffic either. I begin to doubt if I'm in the right place.

In the two weeks since I went to Overijse for Druivencross there have been races at Mol and Spa-Francorchamps – the latter was particularly notable for its heavy mud conditions and horribly steep run-ups and descents. Helen Wyman and Nikki Harris, both lovers of a heavy course with lots of running, battled out the win, with Wyman overhauling Harris on the last lap. Both women went very deep as they sprinted up to the finish line on the tarmac of the motor-racing circuit. The race at Spa is relatively new to the calendar, and with Spa being situated in Wallonia, for the Superprestige series it's practically an international race. It's admirable that the organisers, Golazo, are trying to broaden their series from the very localised success of Flanders. Erwin Vervecken, former World champion and now race organiser for Golazo, tells me that the business model for races in Wallonia is more marginal because the income from ticket sales and VIPs is lower than in Flanders. Even though Spa is no further from Brussels than Koksijde is, there is a perception among Flandrian fans that Spa is somehow further away.

There were more disturbing people on the podium at Spa: two people (impossible to tell whether they were men or women) dressed in white robes with Ku Klux Klan pointed hats, wearing masks with red O-shaped mouths and huge red, erect noses. Harris and Wyman looked genuinely terrified of these creatures, while Sanne van Paassen cheerfully went about getting some selfies with them. It transpired that they were supposed to be *macrales*, witches from local folklore, and while I love a bit of weird folklore, witches are not generally known to enhance the reputation of major sporting events. You could just imagine the meeting of the local organising committee – a group of middle-aged white men sat in a smoke-filled room – where someone suggested, 'Why don't we dress someone up in a Ku Klux Klan kind of robe and give them a spooky mask with a disturbingly phallic red nose? We could put them on the podium with the women. How hilarious!'

In America too, races have strange mascots. At the Jingle Cross in Iowa City riders are (jokingly) terrorised by the Grinch, the Christmas-hating character from the Dr Seuss books. The Grinch leaps and gurns as the riders fight out what is becoming one of the major events on the American calendar. Anyone arriving in Iowa expecting a flat course across the Midwest prairie will be shocked to find a very nasty hill named 'Mount Krumpit' by the organisers in honour of the miserable green creature who lives there. Combined with the usually sub-zero temperature and a stiff wind, the Jingle Cross is festive in a brutal way. This season it took place on the same weekend as Overijse, and the men's race was one of many close tussles between Jeremy Powers and Stephen Hyde. Powers came out on top, but soon both will face the much tougher competition at Namur.

The Grinch and phallic witches aside, since Overijse I've been preoccupied with another dark subject. The sight of the Vlaamse anti-doping officials at that race reminded me that cyclocross does not exist in a cosy, muddy little bubble all on its own. Cyclocross is part of the wider world of cycling, and as such it has to face the same difficult questions that have troubled other parts of the sport – principally road racing.

Is there doping in cyclocross? Well, yes and no. There have been several well-known cases in the last thirty years or so. Mario de Clercq, now the manager of Kevin Pauwels's Sunweb team, was banned from the sport for four years after his involvement in the so-called Landuyt affair, in which several Belgian professionals, including Johan Museeuw, were proven to be involved with the trafficking and consumption of human growth hormones and Aranesp, a derivative of EPO. The substances came from José Landuyt, a veterinarian from a village near Izegem. De Clercq's ban started in 2005 – but he'd retired in 2004, so there was no negative impact on his racing career. A three-time World champion, De Clercq is an influential person in the sport today, and an uncompromising team manager. Investigators from the Belgian police searched De Clercq's house in September 2003 and, alongside some vials of a banned substance, they seized his training diaries from the previous two years. The diaries contained details of his training schedules, results and haematocrit levels connected to taking unspecified products. When questioned, De Clercq claimed to be researching a novel. The training diary entries were all fictitious, he said.

There are other, more recent, cases but they are sporadic compared to the water-torture drip-drip of doping cases we have lived through in road cycling. De Clercq raced with big road teams and was therefore exposed to the endemic drug culture in professional road racing. There is an argument, put forward by Sven Nys among others, that in cyclocross the brevity of the racing together with the importance of good technique means that drugs are less helpful than in a five-hour road race through the Alps.

Here we come back to the gulf in performance between the top Belgian riders and the top American riders. Is it because the Belgians are so much more tuned into the conditions in which they race? Is it because the Belgians are more professional, more rigorous in their training, more demanding of their support networks? If you believe so, then you have your explanation for why American elite men struggle to make it into the top ten of a World Cup.

But it's difficult not to be cynical. I've been watching cycle racing for over thirty years, and over that time I've seen the majority of my heroes unmasked as cheats. I love cycling and I want to believe in it. I do believe in cyclocross, and I do believe that the best Belgian and Dutch men are better than the British, American and Australian men because they have created a perfect environment for their own success. There are no compromises. Everything in their lives is geared towards one thing – winning cross races. Sven Nys, in particular, is known as utterly ruthless in his pursuit of every detail that will together give him the edge. Long before Sir Dave Brailsford was extolling marginal gains, Sven Nys was demonstrating it every weekend in the cow pastures of Flanders. Nys has a son, Thibaut, and a common sight in years past has been Thibaut pre-riding the course with his father, then later doing laps of an improvised course on a rough patch of ground near the car park. By the time Thibaut makes his Superprestige debut, which he's sure to do eventually, he will know the cyclocross courses of his homeland better than any American or Brit, however long in the tooth they are.

So for now, I believe. But I try to be objective, not a fantasist. The same conditions that make it possible for Belgian riders to thrive also make it possible for doping to thrive. The community is small and tight-knit. There is a great deal of money circulating. Riders are supported by family and close friends, meaning loyalty is never questioned. It's in no one's interests for a doping scandal to engulf the sport. Well, apart from any clean riders excluded from results that were rightfully theirs. I want to keep my faith in the innocence of cyclocross, but I won't be shocked if proven wrong.

The forest slopes away. I'm coming to the top of the hill, or so my aching calves tell me. I pass a small church, whose door is being unlocked by a gentleman in an overcoat. Sunday morning rituals. Across the road is a row of cars, the official parking area for UCI officials. The way the parking maps out is becoming as intriguing to me as the races themselves. At Namur there is a broad esplanade area given over to the big Belgian teams, plus the French team, and everyone else has to park on a series of roads running away from this central space. The American team has found its own little niche on a patch of gravel in front of someone's house. Their truck is already here, along with two campervans, two team cars, and a minibus full of sleepy juniors.

'How's the jet lag?' I ask Gage Hecht.

'Not too bad,' he smiles, as he pulls on his shoes and a warm jacket. 'It's usually worse going the other way.' Behind him Spencer and the other lads are getting ready too. It's eight o'clock and as the sun comes up they're about to head out onto the course for a recon.

The pre-race rituals are the same for everyone, junior to pro. The team pull on gloves, fasten helmets and retrieve their bikes from the mechanics. Looking on, Geoff Proctor tells me the atmosphere in the house is good, the team had a positive meeting last night. I suspect that in a house full of teenage athletes, a long way from home, there are plenty of tensions that Geoff is far too professional to tell me about. His focus is on ensuring the riders are following his schedule, and have everything they need. 'Guys, it's 8.15, you've got forty-five minutes until you want to be getting on the rollers,' he calls out.

During their course reconnaissance the team try out different lines, test their bikes, try to gauge how their legs are feeling. Geoff stations himself in the pits with a pump and a pressure gauge and helps them adjust their tyres to the conditions. Afterwards they wash their own bikes and roll back to the trucks. Now the nerves are visible. The riders are quiet, busy, purposeful. There is a great deal of fiddling with bits of kit, and the only words they exchange are with Geoff or the team helpers. Geoff buzzes about as the team get on the rollers for their warm-up. He has a quiet word with each of the riders. The rollers' high-pitched whine attracts the interest of the first fans walking up from the parking areas. They watch from a respectful distance.

Towels draped over handlebars, a bottle of energy drink balanced on the front wheel, headphones giving seclusion, five sets of legs begin to spin. It's quite a hypnotic sight. As I stand watching, I chat to one of the mechanics, a Belgian who has helped the US team for over ten years. He owns a bike shop near Izegem, close to where the US team had their original house. There is no financial reward for his help, he simply enjoys it. He tells me how he has got to know all the top American riders of the last ten years and that he likes American riders because they are more respectful. The Belgians all think they are Tom Boonen, even the children.

I ask him what he thinks of Gage's titanium Moots bike, expecting him to dismiss it as an American oddity. But he likes it. 'It's heavy,' he says, with a shrug. 'But it's strong. Gage breaks bikes too easy.'

Part of the learning curve for the younger riders on the team is about hierarchy. European racing, in general, operates with a strong sense of the hierarchical, and often this relates to respect for your elders. Cyclocross is no different, but the juniors have to learn that just because they are the youngest people around they are not at the bottom of the pyramid. They are, in fact, in the middle, beneath the sponsor and the team director but above the *soigneurs* and mechanics. It doesn't matter if the *soigneur* used to rub Erik de Vlaeminck's legs, or is a close friend of Eddy Merckx – if the rider wants something done in a certain way, within reason he should ask for it. The riders have to learn to be assertive yet polite and diplomatic. If they want to swap wheels at the last minute before a race, that's their call and a good mechanic will do as they ask.

Twenty minutes before the start, Geoff and the mechanics head off to the pits carrying bikes and wheels, the team helpers pick up rucksacks and head off to the start, and finally the team wheels away through the parked cars.

Gage gets a good start, but it's Spencer Petrov who is closest to the front as the race slams into the steep hill just off the starting funnel. At this hour the crowd is scant, the announcer doesn't seem very interested in the race, and there's no interminable Europop blasting out of the speakers, so it's possible to actually hear the sounds of the race: tubulars slithering through the mud, brakes honking, heavy breathing and cursing in many different languages.

Belgium's Jappe Jaspers takes the win from the Netherland's Jens Dekker. Petrov is a strong fourth, and Hecht sixth. They may not be on the podium on this occasion, but they are serious competitors at this highest level of the sport.

After the race, red-cheeked and speckled with Wallonia mud, the boys are exuberant and chatty. The tension has been released, and the adrenaline is still flowing: 'I was just on the wheel of this French guy and he got a gap and I couldn't close it'; 'That was so tough, so much running'; 'Some Dutch kid dropped his chain and then I had to stop between him and a wall'; 'My ears are still ringing, from the pressure in my head of riding . . .'

Half an hour later Gage emerges from the minibus in civilian clothes. He looks completely different without his stars and stripes skinsuit. Jeans and trainers, a hoody – he is the archetypal

American college kid. And he seems somehow less confident. Or perhaps more aimless. This part of the day has no schedule, no objective. There is nothing to do but hang around and privately play back the race, digest the mistakes and the successes.

We talk about his possible career path. Turning professional is the goal, but he's not yet worrying about the specifics of when, or for which team. He'll continue studying, but if a chance comes up to ride full time in Europe he may choose to pause his studies, to see if a career as a cyclist is viable. When I ask him which is his favourite discipline – road or cross – he doesn't give me a straight answer, which is fair enough because the two are very different, and yet also complement each other. At 17 you can ride both, and expect success at similar levels, but two years later and you have to begin to make a choice. Jaspers and Dekker may have already chosen cross as their specialism because for them the career path is mapped out. They will follow in the wheel-tracks of Mathieu van der Poel and Wout van Aert, and Sven Nys before them. For Gage, choosing cross as his specialism would be a much braver choice. He would have to commit to moving to Europe, to riding for a Belgian team, to learning Dutch. Complete integration into another culture.

We talk too about training, about how Dekker and Jaspers train on this terrain every day, and that gives them an advantage. He tells me that back home in Colorado there's a foot and a half of snow on the ground. To train in such conditions you either have to go out on the road, or get a few riders on a grassy field and pack the snow down by going round and round in circles. Neither are perfect training sessions.

Now that all the elite riders have arrived, and the women are warming up, the crowd is getting thicker too. The American encampment seems to hold quite an allure for a certain type of middle-aged Belgian man. In small groups they wander from vehicle to vehicle, looking for someone they recognise, or something novel – like the Bart Simpson attached to Gage's bike. Some of the fans are collecting rider cards. These are small promotional cards that every rider has, with a colour photo and some sponsor logos. Like Panini football stickers in England, they are collected religiously, usually filed in some kind of photo album.

Now, as the juniors sit on the edge of the minibus, waiting to leave, some fans ask them for their cards. They each have a plastic bag with a stack of cards, and hand them out on request, but seem unsure of the etiquette. One fan asks for three cards and the boys exchange looks as if to say, 'Is that OK?' Then, when the fans are gone, they're back to their relaxed and goofy selves. I think of my own children and whether I'd like them to take up the sport, or any sport, at this level. Irrespective of whether they achieve athletic success, these boys certainly are learning something . . . though I'm not quite sure what that something is.

By the time I find Katie Compton she's almost ready to roll off to the start. She's palpably nervous. With a few adjustments of her helmet strap, and a cursory smile that tells me now is not a good time to talk, she takes a bike from the side of the van and rides off through the car park. Mark and I walk down the hill, he carrying Katie's spare bike and a set of wheels, and we chat amiably about Pixie, their beloved three-legged Rottweiler, American versus British healthcare systems and strict New Zealand headmasters.

The conversation comes round to Katie's health, her form, and how long it might be before she retires. 'We'll keep it going as long as we can,' he says. 'It's still better than doing a proper job – doing this every day is a Saturday.'

At the Telenet–Fidea trucks I see Nikki Harris's helper and wave hello. Nikki herself is just about to ride off to the start, and isn't engaging with anybody. Her result at Spa was both encouraging and frustrating. Much like Katie, her form is coming, but she has yet to convert that into a win. A few days ago Nikki announced that she had signed a contract with a new team, Boels–Dolmans, and would be riding the road alongside World champion Lizzie Armitstead. Her mechanic and helper will be going with her. Their loyalty is to Nikki rather than to Telenet–Fidea.

While the men's elite racing is dominated by Belgium and Holland, the women's side of the sport is much more international. The top ten of the Namur World Cup is composed of two Britons, two Americans, two Belgians, two Dutch, one Italian and one Frenchwoman. Out of the top ten is Sanne Cant, who has been diagnosed with a muscle tear between two of her left ribs, the injury she picked up at Overijse. On a tough course like Namur, with lots of running and long climbs, that kind of injury would be particularly painful. Cant finished in fourteenth, just behind the talented young Dutch rider Thalita de Jong. At only 22, De Jong has had a slow start to the cyclocross season, having taken some time to recover from a successful road campaign over the summer, but will be happy to be just outside the top ten of this race. Her targets for the cross season are after Christmas.

In second place is the French rider, Caroline Mani. Originally from Besançon, Mani now lives and competes in the United States. Over the past few years her performances have been gradually improving, but this is her most successful season to date, and second place at a World Cup in Belgium, against a full field, is a significant result for her. As she crosses the line she punches the air, then her chest. Mani is always expressive; she rides on emotion. There is no coolness to her, no mask. Fans love her because they can see written on her face all the pain she is going through, but at the same time they can see the absolute focus and her love for the sport.

Nikki Harris is happy too, though her expression of it is more in the classic British style. The form has been coming, and today everything went right. After a good start she was on the wheel of Eva Lechner towards the end of the first lap, and was able to accelerate past the Italian on a long, on-the-bike slog of a climb. After that she never looked back – at least, not figuratively – and led the race all the way to the finish.

During the women's race I head off in search of the Kevin Pauwels fanclub, whom I've arranged to meet. They're pretty easy to find, as they all wear blue jackets with the club title and logo emblazoned on the back. Before I began spending a lot of time immersed in the Belgian cyclocross scene, I'd thought that the riders' fanclubs were hardly better than the hooligan firms who attach themselves to English football clubs; that they go to races, get drunk and shout abuse at the fanclubs of other riders. And when Dirk, a man of roughly my age, who works in a factory near Antwerp, reaches inside his jacket and pulls out a bottle of cinnamon schnapps, my preconceptions remain intact. The drink is called Gold Strike because it has tiny flakes of 24-carat gold leaf floating in it. Someone points to the label – 50 per cent proof. Dirk looks at me with a wry smile and steady, hard-to-argue with, eyes. 'I'm going to get you very drunk,' he seems to be saying. This is not the moment to tell him that I'm not really much of a drinker, and that my tipple of choice is generally a cup of tea. 'When in Rome . . .' I say to myself, and accept a shot of the precious liquid. I don't cough, I don't sway and stagger. I've passed the first test.

Dirk is the youngest and, it seems, the most mischievous of the group. They are predominantly middle-aged, friendly and courteous people. Connie is Kevin's auntie. Joos, the secretary of the club, is married to Connie. Dirk's father Danny is there, he works as a docker in Antwerp. The oldest of the group is perhaps in his mid-sixties, and tells me he has recently retired from his toy-shop business. Everyone is from the town of Kalmthout, just north of Antwerp, where Katie Compton stays when she is in Belgium. They've been coming to cross races for sixteen years, they tell me, ever since Kevin was a junior. They come to support Kevin, their friend and, in some cases, relative, and because they enjoy the atmosphere and the racing. On most Sundays throughout the winter they meet at the Café T Centrum in Kalmthout, have a coffee and climb on board the bus which drives them to whichever race they are going to. Rarely is the journey more than a couple of hours.

I ask why cyclocross is so popular here. 'Look,' says Dirk. Still holding the bottle of Gold Strike he takes a worrying lunge towards the barriers and thrusts his hand into the air-space above the track, narrowly missing an American rider grinding her way up the hill. 'Because you can get so close to the action. Every week you can see the same riders, the same rivalries, on a different course with different weather conditions.'

A few minutes later the leaders of the women's race are approaching. I shout for Katie and Nikki. Dirk and the others shout most vociferously for Jolien Verschueren then throw in a shout for Sanne Cant almost as an afterthought. Jolien isn't from their region (she lives in Kortrijk) but like many Belgian cyclocross fans they respond to her, perhaps simply to the idea of her. A nursery school teacher riding cross is an idea that sparks the imagination because it personifies the Belgian approach to cross – the riders are one of us, part of the community, yet they work hard to excel in their chosen discipline. They are local heroes, not celebrities who live in Monaco or Girona.

Returning to the conversation about why cross is so popular, Joos makes the comparison to motocross. This track at Namur, he tells me, was a motocross Classic in the eighties and nineties, before the attention turned to cyclocross. Motocross is an interesting sport to compare to cyclocross. Ostensibly it shares many features, having originated in the early twentieth century from scrambling on motorbikes around the common land heaths of southern Britain, then developing into organised racing. Like cyclocross, motocross has a strong blue-collar base, and in Britain it flourished in the eighties when televised. But the development of motocross was driven by evolving technology. When companies like Husqvarna and Greeves created the first two-stroke-engine bikes, which were much lighter and more agile than the old four-cylinder versions, motocross became much more accessible. Then the Japanese companies like Suzuki started making motocross bikes, and the sport expanded rapidly in America. Without the European cultural constraints that hold cycle sport back (what might be called tradition but can look like an obsession with history that stifles innovation) motocross became hugely popular in America during the seventies and eighties, and several offshoot disciplines like Freestyle and Supercross were established.

Being noisy and polluting, motocross has been pushed to out-of-town locations. The track at Namur, Erwin Vervecken tells me later, was discontinued because of environmental concerns, and when Golazo met with the city council to discuss various sports events they were planning, the idea came up of staging a cyclocross event there. The first edition was held in 2009 and because the location was so stunning, and the course so demanding, the cyclocross world unanimously awarded it the status of Classic. In cyclocross no one feels the need to wait for legends to create themselves. It's a very entrepreneurial sport in that sense.

After the women's race I tell my newfound friends that I'm going to head up to the food concessions and ask if there's anything I can get for anyone. Everyone shakes their head. Joos motions towards his rucksack and tells me they always bring sandwiches, and their own alcohol, because it's much cheaper to do so. Ticket prices have recently risen to 15 Euros, and what with the cost of the bus, which they all share, it can get expensive when you add in chips and a hotdog and a few beers from the concessions

– particularly when you come to races week after week. When I return ten minutes later proudly bearing a cardboard cone of *friets*, a can of Coke tucked in my jacket pocket, the Kevin Pauwels fanclub erupt into collective laughter. It takes me a little while to work out that they're laughing at the big globs of mayonnaise dripping down my hand and onto my wrist. 'You're holding that all wrong,' they call out as I grin sheepishly. 'Change your angle, you're in Flanders now!' (Well, technically I am not, but effectively I am.) Connie and Jenny offer me some napkins to clean myself up. Realising that I am perhaps more drunk than I seem, someone produces a hip-flask filled with cactus genever, the juniper-flavoured national liquor. 'Oh, go on then.' I'm still in Rome, or Flanders, or Wallonia . . .

Over the loudspeakers the announcer is calling out the favourites for the men's race. The usual suspects – Van Aert, Van der Poel, Nys, Van der Haar, Vanthournout, Pauwels. Now that I have some Dutch courage, I bring up a subject about Kevin that fascinates me, but which I suspect may be contentious with his friends and family. I ask if he is autistic, as some media channels have reported.

Joos and Connie, who know him best, are good-natured about the question. He's never been tested, they tell me. But he's an absolute maniac about weighing everything! He weighs his sunglasses, even his shoes. I'm not convinced this is proof of anything; from what I know of professional bike riders they are obsessed with weight, and weighing one's kit is well within the normal range of behaviours exhibited by pro riders. Kevin, they go on to tell me, lives for the bike. He's not interested in money or fame or anything else that comes with success. He just loves riding his bike and he's very serious about it. The car he drives is seven years old, all the money he earns is invested for the long-term by people he trusts. He doesn't have a girlfriend. He trains, he races, he weighs his shoes.

While Joos and Connie tell me about Kevin, Dirk shouts across to a man trudging down through the trees. In his late fifties, he's short and solid, balding, and wears a rather dreary brown jacket. His skin is dark, deeply scored, his eyes are intimidating. He replies to Dirk in Dutch, and they have a brief conversation, laughing at something, probably me. When Dirk returns to us, he nods back to the man. 'Roland Liboton,' he says. In Belgium, they tell me, they have a debate – who was the greatest? Eric de Vlaeminck, Roland Liboton or Sven Nys? Nys has the most wins but Liboton had the style, he made the sport exciting.

The chips seem to have done a good job in soaking up the alcohol, and I feel bad for not having anything to offer in return. Then I remember that my rucksack is full of sugary snacks, among them a box of mince pies. I rustle around and produce the box (Sainsbury's Taste the Difference, no less) and, to general confusion, offer them round. None of my new friends has ever experienced a mince pie, but the reaction is very favourable. I feel I have participated in a significant cultural exchange.

And when Kevin retires? I ask. 'Then this all finishes,' says Joos. Kevin's team doesn't bring young riders up through the ranks, so there isn't anyone else to support. Supporting Kevin gives these people a structure to their winter weekends, it gives them someone to focus on, and it provides many opportunities for travel. Last season they went to the Milton Keynes World Cup and used the event as a good excuse to do a tour of southern England, taking in Oxford and the Cotswolds. They also went to Las Vegas for CrossVegas, and they are more enthusiastic talking about travel than about cyclocross – they are interested in the world, even though the way they speak about it is as if they're from somewhere much further away than the reality. Belgium is at the heart of northern Europe yet I get the sense that anywhere outside Belgium seems exotic to them.

I struggle to believe that Kevin will entirely leave the sport, or that Joos and his crew will never again attend a cyclocross race. But without the focus of someone to support, there won't be the same impetus for them to organise these trips, to spend their money and stand drinking cactus-flavoured genever in a muddy wood. Easier and cheaper to stay at home and watch on television. But nowhere near as much fun. I bid them all goodbye, and stumble away through the undergrowth.

The men's race is heating up. I squeeze through the crowd, under tree branches, over the mud, to a spot where the course loops back on itself, so I can see the leaders three times on the same lap. Pauwels, Van Aert and Van der Poel have escaped the rest and are forging ahead as a trio, not giving each other an inch. This is what the crowd loves: the tension of waiting for someone to make an attack, or a mistake. The different personalities – flamboyant Van der Poel versus the more clinical Van Aert versus the quietly determined Pauwels. As they come into the last lap Pauwels is trying to hang on while the other two attack each other.

It's easy to become accustomed, after enough bike races, to the speed and athleticism of pro riders. But here I have a reality check. The hill I am standing at the bottom of is so steep that it's hard to walk up without holding onto the barriers. A thick rope has been tied around a tree at the top and thrown down the slope to help fans heave themselves up. The surface is slippery gravel. And these three are riding it with such energy and speed. Their leg muscles – brown, defined, the faint shimmer of embrocation – beneath white and red and blue skinsuits, tyres crunching, eyes focused only on what's ahead of them. They're close enough to touch, as my friend Dirk demonstrated, and yet they are in another world. From one side of the barrier to the other is a very long way.

Behind them as the places tick down, through the twenties, British number one Ian Field and Jeremy Powers come through, both smooth but visibly slower, and the time gaps open – into the thirties and the riders with bobbing heads, grunting, snorting, basically acting as any normal person would. If you train hard and dedicate yourself to your sport, you can come to race in Belgium and not be humiliated. But breaking into the top tier is something else. The castle is well defended.

I have a train to catch, so as soon as the race finishes I head back to the press room for one last coffee and to pack up my things. As I do so I watch the live coverage on a television. Behind the podium, waiting to be called up for the presentations, are the three riders. Van der Poel won the race with a stinging attack at the top of the final climb, Van Aert finished second, Pauwels third. As they wait, sipping at their recovery drinks, Van Aert and Van der Poel chat away with each other. They've raced against each other for all of their young careers, and their intense rivalry on the bike doesn't mean they can't have a joke with each other after a race. Meanwhile Pauwels stands awkwardly beside them, smiling shyly, either unable or unwilling to join in the conversation.

I feel for him. As an introvert, I've often experienced the same scenario, that feeling of being unable to participate in some boisterous or animated discussion, the self-consciousness that is then invoked. As you become older you develop strategies for coping, ways to look as if you don't care (which often backfires because people consider you aloof and unapproachable). I can read that in Pauwels's body language – the way he stands with feet apart and one hand on his hip, a strong pose that speaks of his emotional tenacity. By contrast, Van Aert is relaxed, leaning against a wall. A woman in a red jacket, bearing a bouquet of flowers, comes to talk to the trio, presumably about some detail of the prize-giving ceremony. Van Aert and Van der Poel both smile politely and lean towards her, but Pauwels does not move from his rock-solid stance, with the result that the woman talks only to the two younger men.

Stirring music blares from the speakers and the announcer calls out, in French, the third-place rider. No doubt relieved to be out of that awkward situation, Pauwels pushes past the still-talking woman and steps onto the stage with his arms aloft. The crowd erupts into cheering. They love this son of Flanders.

13

Midwinter

I have a very narrow idea of winter. Firstly it's only based on one day of the week, Sunday, as if the other six aren't important in the colder months. And this idea of mine involves a very specific set of activities. There's a long trip out into the harsh weather, either by bike, or on foot. If by bike, the ride should be long and steady and include a café stop where cake is consumed. Ideally I would be wearing colourful thermal kit, a sartorial riposte to the grey weather. Alternatively, a winter's walk sees me ploughing cheerfully along footpaths and bridleways, walking stick in hand, my family chatting away behind me. In this scenario lunch at a country pub, with dark timbered interior and a roaring fire (with a sleeping dog in front of it) is essential. Having embraced the rigours of winter – at least, the modest rigours of a winter in south-east England – I return home and the rest of the day passes in a cosy fug. There are toasted crumpets with jam and endless cups of tea. There is our own fire, lit and fuelled throughout the evening. There's a roast dinner. Possibly even a BBC costume drama.

Growing up in the Oxfordshire countryside, this is indeed what many of our family Sundays looked like, and I remember it as a time of contentment (if it's possible to feel contentment at

12 years old). The passing of time has no doubt erased some of the more scratchy realities of family life, such as the utter boredom of late afternoon as darkness falls and there is nothing on television. (Yes, Morrissey, every day does indeed feel like Sunday.) But this was a happy time that gave me a certain outlook on life, specifically with regards to the natural exterior world and the domestic interior world, and how the two interact.

As an adult, living in the considerably less pastoral world of south London, I used to keep quiet about my vision of the perfect winter's day, thinking it to be weak nostalgia. So I was immensely reassured and grateful to Adam Gopnik for validating, in his excellent book *Winter*, my cosy nostalgia. It seems that not only am I not alone in this conception of winter, it's even possible to place it in a literary context. Gopnik discusses the ways artists and writers have approached winter, showing that the predominant attitude in the seventeenth and eighteenth centuries was negative, seeing winter as a time of brutal conditions and little or no joy. Interestingly, an exception of note was the Dutch and Belgian landscape art of Bruegel and others. Their ice skaters in small villages were the first depictions of winter leisure, but set against the broader context were something of an anomaly. It was only towards the end of the eighteenth century that writers began to see the homely, the cosy, in winter. Gopnik quotes the English poet William Cowper, who wrote in 1783 to a friend, 'I see the winter approaching without much concern, though a passionate lover of fine weather, and the pleasant scenes of summer, but the long evenings have their comforts too, and there is hardly to be found upon earth, I suppose, so snug a creature as an Englishman by the fireside in the winter.'

The apotheosis of this snugness is Christmas, the modern Christmas so influenced by the Victorians, with all its snowy countryside scenes and glittering trees and the bearded old boy in the red jacket. I think I'm not alone in having a very precise picture of what Christmas should entail, down to very specific details, such as which brand of chocolates to eat on Christmas Eve, and I get incredibly grumpy if anything happens to derail that perfect Christmas routine. I know it's daft, but I can't help it. Part of the routine is a Boxing Day walk, which represents a supercharged version of the regular wintry Sunday walk. The weather is invariably grim, but on your return there is a house full of delicious food and drink. There are new books to read by the fire, and new toys for the children to play with.

This winter I've achieved a long-held Christmas ambition – to rent a cottage and celebrate the season with my extended family. It also coincides with my parents' fiftieth wedding anniversary, so there is plenty to celebrate. The cottage is in the village of Camber, on the East Sussex coast, and our Boxing Day walk takes us up onto the high sand dunes that rise behind the sweeping, windswept beach. While the children delight in launching themselves down the dunes, filling their wellies with sand, I take a moment to gaze out across the English Channel. On the other side of the water, Belgian cyclocross is about to embark upon its most intense time of the season, *Kerstperiode*.

It's a pity not to be there, but family is more important, and that's a sentiment entirely in keeping with *Kerstperiode*. For while this is an important week for the racers – both in terms of prestige and earning potential – the significance of *Kerstperiode* lies in the way it reinforces what Belgian cyclocross is all about, that is to say family and community.

Christmas in Belgium is much the same as in Britain, though the main family celebration is on Christmas Eve, and instead of Christmas pudding the meal finishes with *Kerstkronk*, a traditional Yule log smothered in chocolate. Christmas Day sees most Belgians visiting family, exchanging small gifts and indulging in another round of stuffed turkey and *Kerstkronk*. Belgian race organisers know that cyclocross fits perfectly with the Christmas period. Their core audience are not at work, are in a mood to drink and party and see friends, and by Boxing Day probably just a little bit fed up with sitting indoors watching American movies. Because cyclocross in Belgium is seen as entertainment, like the village fair, fans are happy to pay the ticket price, have a drink and some *friets*, see their friends and family and shout for the riders they saw on television the previous weekend. During *Kerstperiode* this social aspect of the races becomes festive, even poignant. Like all blue-collar sports, cyclocross acts as a kind of social glue. It brings people together, gives them a weekend release valve. Over the extended Christmas holiday, with its unique mix of celebration, relaxation and boredom, what better than to meet one's friends in a muddy field and raise a glass together while the nation's chaste heroes plough past. If nothing else it gets you out of the house, and away from that *Kerststronk*.

While the World Championships is the climax of the season, the *Kerstperiode* is arguably the most important week of the winter for racers. With four major races over seven days, plus many other supporting races, there is a lot at stake. A good string of results can significantly boost a rider's campaign in the World Cup or Superprestige series. And there is a great deal of start money and prize money on offer. Good form over the *Kerstperiode* means that you become a favourite for your national championship races, which all take place a week or so after New Year. But the period can be tough. The physical and mental strain of so many races in a short time, along with the usual stress of the time of year (even cyclocross racers have to buy their mum a Christmas present), can mean a rider emerges in the cold light of January exhausted.

For Geoff Proctor's development team, it's probably a good thing that this period is so intense because being in Belgium over Christmas can result in homesickness among the riders. The accelerated cycle of racing and recovery, and all the associated organisation and travelling, keeps the young men and women occupied. Still, in the quieter moments, it's understandable for them to miss their family at this time. For some it will be their first time away from their family over Christmas. Proctor and his staff make sure to foster a team spirit through a celebratory meal and a secret Santa gift-giving, and in their diaries many of the riders, including Gage, mention that they enjoy spending the holiday with their cyclocross friends, but it's easy to read the homesickness between the lines.

Proctor (who has his own children back in Montana) must be glad to get through Christmas Day and back into the routine of a race day on Boxing Day. For this is the first race of *Kerstperiode*, when devoted cyclocross fans take their hangovers to the Zolder motor racing circuit near Hasselt. The course is fast, with a long road section and very little serious mud. This year the race has added intrigue because the World Cup event will be a dress rehearsal for the World Championships, taking place on the same circuit a month later. I watch the race on a live feed, losing all my journalistic objectivity as Katie Compton leads the race for the opening lap and I shout at her to go faster. In the end Sanne Cant manages to pass and drop Katie on the hardest climb of the circuit, but Katie hangs on for second place, and gives a little punch of delight as she crosses the line ahead of Ellen van Looy and a fast-finishing Thalita de Jong. In the junior race Gage takes an encouraging fifth place, while the elite men's race is won by a resurgent Mathieu van der Poel. Wout van Aert can only manage eighth. Twenty-four hours later Gage takes fourth place at the Superprestige in Diegem. Father Christmas, or should I say Saint Niklaas, seems to have given him and Katie the gift every cyclocross racer wants for Christmas – good form.

Within the cyclocross community Diegem is rightly celebrated as a unique race. The town of Diegem is a suburb of Brussels, close enough to Brussels airport that you can see the planes winding their wheels into their undercarriages. The race takes place at night, under spotlights, and the course is a creative combination of suburban streets, small urban parks and scraps of woodland behind the local football ground. It could be dismissed as a glorified criterium but there are several small climbs which make it an unforgiving course, especially because the riders all have the Zolder World Cup still in their legs. Because the course doesn't get very muddy, the racing tends to be fast and frenetic. The atmosphere is the best of any race anywhere in the world. By the time the elite men take to the course in the early evening, the circuit is tightly packed with spectators, most of whom are tightly packed with alcohol.

Two days after Diegem comes the race at Loenhout, a small town close to the Dutch border. Here is a race designed principally for spectators. The course describes a big loop around three football pitches, alongside a dyke, and taking in a large meadow that sits behind a housing estate – an utterly suburban and banal setting. Accordingly the course has no elevation, so the organisers have added several artificial bridges to give the riders a bit of a workout. What Loenhout does have is mud, and huge crowds. There must be drainage issues on this land, for the mud gets so heavy that even flat sections become unrideable. One of the muddiest stretches runs past the beer tent, where a gallery of drunken rogues yell at their favourite riders. It was in Loenhout in 2012 that Sven Nys gave a good example of why he's become such a crowd-pleaser. Nys was having a bad day at the office. After two crashes in the deep mud, and mechanical issues, he was much further down the field than he was used to, and out of contention for the win. On top of which, every time he came through a certain section he was being sprayed with beer by a group of fans. When a plastic glass of beer was thrown at him, Nys jumped off his bike, walked over to the course tapes and said some choice words to the young man who threw the glass. Said glass-thrower began to back away through the crowd so Nys ducked under the tape and pursued him across a muddy paddock. The kid looked to be in a state of shock as Nys delivered a brief lecture on cyclocross etiquette, before walking back to the bike he'd left lying on the ground.

Another famous rider–crowd interaction was when Bart Wellens executed an impressive karate kick on a fan who he claimed had been throwing beer on him – while staying on his bike – in the 2005 Druivencross. The kick, which later earned him a disqualification and a month's ban, reinforced Wellens's reputation as the wild child of Belgian cyclocross, and made the fans love him even more.

The final race of *Kerstperiode* is on New Year's Day, the GP Sven Nys at Baal. Set on the Balenberg hill near Nys's home village of Baal, the race is distinctive because virtually every fan who attends, and probably a few riders too, have a hangover. Getting out in the cold reality of the New Year, with a few inches of mud underfoot and a wincingly sharp wind, is certainly a good way to blow away the cobwebs. A few seem to handle this reality by sticking to coffee, but most simply carry on drinking. By the time the elite men start, the barriers are proving very useful for propping up the sodden and the sozzled.

Kerstperiode is special because it is such a heady distillation of the relationship between the fans and the riders. It is concentrated cyclocross. The heroes come out to perform, their stage being the local fields and parks, and in this natural arena they compete not only for the win but for the favour of the crowds. When I was at Overijse for the Druivencross I had a brief, funny conversation with Renaat Schotte about British wrestling. We reminisced about the days of Big Daddy and Giant Haystacks, when huge hairy men in leotards slammed each other around a ring in some provincial British town. The bouts were televised on Saturday lunchtimes, and enormously popular. Part of the fun was the ridiculous, and often rather camp, fanfare that accompanied some of the wrestlers. Big Daddy, a 26-stone man from Halifax in Yorkshire, whose real name was Shirley Crabtree, made his way into the arena to the tune of 'We are the Champions', wearing a gold-sequined top hat. His arch-enemy, Giant Haystacks, whose murderous expression was as terrifying as his 48-stone bulk, had no such fanfare. He was usually booed from dressing-room to ring. As an eight-year-old the fights enthralled me, but watching them back now it's easy to see that they were fixed. It did not matter. This was entertainment, not sport.

I don't think cyclocross is fixed, but there are parallels one can draw to wrestling. The action takes place in a highly visible arena in front of partisan and paying crowd, there are a relatively small number of competitors for victory, and the racing has a more gladiatorial feel than other parts of cycle sport. It's no accident that Richard Fries regularly uses boxing as an analogy in his announcing. What makes the public respond to the gladiators? Well, there are number of features the riders have to fulfil:

1. Look like a pro. This means wearing immaculate and co-ordinated kit at all times, keeping your legs clean-shaven and keeping your tan topped up (not easy in Belgium in December). One of the principal functions of the support crews for pro cyclocross riders is keeping everything clean.
2. Be relatable. Cyclocross racing is all about doing something extraordinary but understandable. Belgian and Dutch folk are brought up with bicycles omnipresent in their lives as a method of getting around – a dependable if boring mode of

transport. They love cycle racing because they can relate to it, but at the same time what Sven Nys can do on a bike is so far beyond their own experience of cycling that they will pay to see it.
3. Always move about by bike. Spend any time wandering around the team buses at a cross race and you will feel riders brushing past you as they ride through the crowds. Racers always ride their bike, they never walk anywhere if they can ride. They see the bike as an extension of themselves. This is attractive – we all love to see people who are so skilled at something that it becomes a natural, unthinking trait.
4. Have fun. Everyone loves to see bike riders having fun. If you're not racing for a podium spot, you may as well back off the pace, and try to pull off some cool tricks – get some air over a ramp, bunny-hops, that sort of thing.
5. Get covered in mud (not that you have much choice with this one). It makes you look humble, a man or woman of the fields. It's hard to behave too much like a spoilt celebrity when you're covered in mud and cowshit.

Characteristically, Geoff Proctor can add some heavyweight literary foundations here. Writing in his online journal, he evokes the hero-warrior tradition of 'Beowulf'. Against harsh competition, in grim conditions and with the value of glory as high as it is, cyclocross is pure 'Beowulf', he argues. Proctor understands the entertainment value of cyclocross, and the way riders are branded and commodified. But, unlike me, he understands what it is to be an elite rider in Europe. He uses the word 'brio', meaning spirit or vigour. When recruiting for his development camps he's looking for riders with a hint of brio, and when they come to Europe he wants them to pursue that same brio. Whether it's leading a race, clocking a fast lap, or just clearing a gnarly section, the young rider can feel that brio. They can be a hero-warrior worthy of Beowulf. And they need to be, for European racing is more aggressive than American. No one will give you an inch, and if they think they'll get away with it, many European riders will use any means necessary to get into that corner first. Whether you use the metaphor of a battle, a boxing match, or a wrestling bout, the message for any young rider is the same – stay tough or you'll end up in a ditch.

14

The Deep South

The man at Alamo car rental looked at me askew. Really? I really didn't want to upgrade? I mumbled something about only being little, which he almost certainly didn't understand, and he shrugged. 'One born every minute,' he was probably thinking. In the car park, the attendant showed me a line of cars in the economy section. I went for the only one I recognised, a Fiat 500. Having had small European cars since I started driving, I felt immediately at home in its cosy cabin. Then I tried to get the little thing moving.

There is a scene at the end of *Annie Hall* when Woody Allen's character flies out to Los Angeles to try a last-ditch reconciliation with Annie. We see a shot of a wide, sunny road and then Allen comes into view, jerking along in a huge rented car. After failing to persuade Annie to come back to New York with him, Allen gets into his car and executes a disastrous three-point turn, crashing into a parked car then a police car. This is me in rented cars. Hopeless. I used to be ashamed of my utter incompetence, but I no longer care. I'm secure enough in my masculinity to take this setback. I think.

'First time with automatic?' called the young attendant, as I lurched towards him and came to an abrupt halt. I nodded, considered making a joke about limeys, but thought better of it. 'Focus on getting out of the car park,' I told myself. Having successfully achieved this objective I found myself on a road so wide I could barely see the sides. Fortunately there was no other traffic around so I could meander from lane to lane as I wished. I pulled up at a set of traffic lights and consulted my map – I'd declined the GPS with a sneer. The map didn't seem to correspond to the options in front of me, but fortunately my inability to control rented cars is compensated by a good sense of direction, so I guessed which way to point my Italian beast. A car pulled up alongside me. I glanced across to see the driver laughing at me. He was on his own, belly-laughing at the sight of a grown man in a Fiat 500. I took it on the chin. 'I am Euro,' I told myself, whatever that means.

The drive from Charlotte airport to Asheville, North Carolina, took about three hours. After a delayed flight to Newark, a missed connection and tense wait for an alternative connecting flight down to Charlotte, it was a relief to be on the last leg of my journey. I'd expected travel weariness to make this a challenging drive, and had equipped myself with enough sugary snacks to give a cycling team diabetes, but as it turned out I felt OK, even somewhat exhilarated to be driving alone through the American night. Motels, fast food outlets, unfamiliar petrol stations with 1970s colour schemes, it was all strange yet familiar. As if in tribute to my arrival, the local radio station played Euro house music. In the advertising breaks I learned what to do if I was worried about my weight. It didn't involve eating less, because we all know how impossible that is. As the Interstate 40 freeway climbed over the Black Mountain, fog closed in around my little Fiat, and I was grateful for the tail-lights of a huge timber truck just ahead. Out here alone, in the middle of the night, surrounded only by trucks, I felt very far from home.

When I told friends in Britain that I was flying out to Asheville for the weekend to see the US National Cyclocross Championships, many of them told me that between races I should try to check out some country music – after all, isn't that what the place is famous for? 'No, no, *Asheville,* North Carolina,' I replied. 'It's famous for . . . [surreptitious Google search] . . . the Vanderbilts.' 'Oh,' said my friends. 'Right. Good luck.'

The Nationals, as it's universally known, is the biggest event on the domestic US calendar, and its objectives are multilayered. First and foremost it has to crown champions in all 36 categories recognised by USA Cycling. Secondly it aims to be inclusive, with competitors of all generations – and a fun, exciting event to watch. And thirdly it aims to develop and promote the sport in the US and beyond. Achieving all three is quite a tall order.

Cyclocross in America still has something of an inferiority complex about its relationship with European cyclocross, specifically Belgian cyclocross. At this point it's worth reminding ourselves that Belgium hasn't always been the dominant force it is today. In the 1970s Switzerland led the way. Only when Belgium started to take a more professional approach in the 1980s did their strength in depth begin to develop. And the sport's historical roots are French. So we shouldn't take Belgian dominance for granted. The compass can always move.

'They have so many riders, don't they? Of all ages?' said one member of the Kevin Pauwels fanclub, discussing US riders as we stood beside the barriers at the Namur World Cup, drinking shots of cinnamon schnapps. 'But when their riders come over here they're not so good.'

A bit of an oversimplification – Katie Compton has been at the top of the women's sport for years – but arguably true for the men. In order to develop, American cyclocross needs its youngest riders to have heroes who are delivering results at the top of the sport, to be competing with Wout van Aert and Kevin Pauwels. But the scene also needs to grow, become more professional and more visible.

Venues are critical to this development. Part of the reason cyclocross is so popular in Belgium is that the organisers have created a set of iconic venues. Every sport needs venues that hold a power of their own – Old Trafford, Augusta, Wimbledon. These places resonate with the sporting battles they have hosted. When you enter Old Trafford and see the pitch, the hairs on the back of your neck prick up. This is how it feels when you arrive at the Koppenberg, or feel the sand of Koksijde under your wellies.

The consistent factor in all the best cyclocross venues is that they have one memorable feature. Whether it's a famous cobbled climb (Koppenberg), a massive sand dune (Koksijde), or a pit in the middle of a forest (Zonhoven), the identity of a race comes from topography as much as its list of winners.

Asheville, North Carolina, has that too. A town founded on its railroad, Asheville's tobacco warehouses and lumber and textile mills brought considerable economic growth in the 1880s. Railroad baron George Washington Vanderbilt settled in the town at this time and used his riches to build the Biltmore Estate. The centrepiece is a spectacular 250-room mansion but there are also some of the finest gardens in the country, a dairy and winery, and eight thousand acres of meadows and forests. There are hotels, inns, shops and a farm. The estate has stayed in the hands of the Vanderbilt family and today is one of America's finest private houses open to the public.

But for Tim Hopkins, from nearby Hendersonville, the Biltmore Estate looked like more than a slice of history that also happened to sell some decent wine. It looked like a great place to put on a bike race. Hopkins works in the Asheville Parks & Recreation department and has been organising cyclocross races in the area for many years, building a scene, and working tirelessly towards his goal of bringing the US Nationals to Asheville. When a new generation of Vanderbilts took over the administration of the estate, Hopkins saw his chance. This younger generation were more approachable, and could see the commercial benefit of hosting such an event in the usually quiet period just after New Year. On Sunday, late afternoon, as the elite men rolled across the finishing line, Hopkins and his team were celebrating the culmination of almost ten years of work.

Standing with me near the finish line that day was Brook Watts (it's always good to stand with Brook for a while at big events – you learn a great deal about different types of barriers, digital advertising screens, inflatable arches and how big the beer barrels need to be at a World Cup race). One of Brook's claims to fame is that he organised the 1978 national championships in

Austin, Texas, while a student in the city. On that day there were eighteen riders on the start line, all in one race. This week in Asheville there are a total of 1808 riders.

Over a forty-year span cyclocross in the United States has seen a rapid but rather uneven growth. From the start it was a grassroots movement. Racers, organisers and supporters fell in love with the sport and got involved, their primary motivation being to enjoy themselves. Few, if any, saw it as a vehicle to make money, so the atmosphere remained decidedly Do It Yourself. Professionalism has only arrived relatively recently. Those involved in putting on races were amateurs, though that's not to say they were amateurish. Even for national-level events, courses were rough and sometimes rather vague affairs, with a lot of brightly coloured tape and not much else.

This apparent reluctance to professionalise the sport seems rather at odds with my general perception of American sport, which is that everything is sponsored and commodified to within an inch of its life. But, having spent some time with the American cyclocross community, I've come to understand that most of those involved want to retain that counterculture feeling; they like the idea of just pitching up in a truck, offloading the bikes and racing around a park, unencumbered by all the trouble that money brings.

In Europe in the early twentieth century the sport was a way for road racers to keep fit, while embracing the often foul weather of their region. Going to Majorca for three weeks wasn't an option. When a Tour de France star like Charly Gaul came to ride a cross, his fans, starved of seeing cycle racing during the winter months, also came. When fans come, organisers see money to be made. In the United States in the late twentieth century no road racer *needed* to ride cross for winter fitness. If they wished they could simply fly south to get some sun. Those who rode cross chose to do so because it was fun, safe and sociable. To a significant degree that atmosphere is still prevalent today.

*

Saturday morning dawns cold, dry, washed out. I wake early, shower and head to the hotel reception to enquire about a good place to go for breakfast. I've been looking forward with relish to an American breakfast, something involving maple syrup. As the concierge gives me directions, I notice a small sign on his desk. 'Are You Bear Aware? Bears occasionally roam our property. Please do not approach, please tell a member of staff immediately.' Belgium this is not.

In the hotel car park an SUV loaded up with cross bikes is reversing out of its parking space. Inside is a whole family in warm cycling kit, the children in the back already wearing their helmets, though whether this is in anticipation of their race, or due to anxiety about their dad's driving, I can't tell.

At Bruegger's Bagels (Bruegel's Bagels would have been just too perfect) I plough through a pastrami and Swiss cheese on sesame seed bagel, with coffee half and half, and feel thoroughly like a New Yorker. Then jump back into my trusty Fiat, of which I am now in masterful control, and gun it out of town. I'm heading for the Holiday Inn where Katie Compton is staying. The directions she's given me ('It's at the shopping outlets') seem pretty vague, but turn out to be effective. All roads lead to the shopping outlets.

This is the glamour of professional cyclocross racing: a Holiday Inn near the shopping outlets on the edge of town, a cold morning and bad coffee. As I wait in reception for Katie a tall, lean woman walks through. Unmistakably a pro cyclist – dressed casually in jeans and trainers, her build athletic. I recognise her as Georgia Gould, one of the clutch of riders expected to challenge Katie for her title. Gould, one of the country's top mountain bikers, also hails from Colorado, and has been racing against Katie for many years. For her, cyclocross plays second fiddle to mountain biking, whereas for Katie it's the other way round. So Gould has rarely got the better of Katie in a cyclocross race, and never in a national championship. This year looks like as good a chance as she's ever had. Katie's form has been inconsistent, although her second place in Zolder on Boxing Day is promising. But Gould has also been posting strong results, and if there is a sniff of overturning the champion, surely she'll have the hunger to push that bit harder?

Katie and Mark come swinging into reception in their matching red team jackets, and over coffee she updates me on her health and her form. As ever, Katie is good-humoured and modest as she talks. But I get the sense that she is tired too, tired from many years fighting a body which has seemed intent on scuppering all her plans, and tired of all the work involved in maintaining a career as an elite athlete. She is emblematic of the sport in her independence and self-sufficiency. We talk about the young riders of professional road teams who can't work a washing machine because they've gone straight from the care of their parents to the care of the team structure, in which everything is done for you. Cyclocross, even at the highest level, is very different. Between them Katie and Mark organise everything – travel, bikes, vehicles, administration, diet, training, medicine, finances, sponsorship deals. At the start of your career, having that sense of control must be tremendously liberating and satisfying, but when you've been doing it for ten, twelve years . . .

The conversation comes round to the question of retirement. Katie and Mark talk about it constantly, but for the moment, on-the-record, it's a 'don't know'. While Katie seems tired of the life, she also seems excited at the prospect of racing without the pains in her legs. For the first time in her racing career she is in control of her body. It's not going to ambush her. Yet this comes at the age of 37, when for most riders their best years are behind them. She's caught in a paradoxical situation where her body is cured of health problems but ageing, and her mind is excited about the future but also weary from the past. As we end the conversation, I remember seeing Georgia in the corridor and wonder how much rests on tomorrow's race. If Katie loses, will she retire at the end of the season? I ask her if she's nervous. She shakes her head. 'I just go through the same process for every race,' she says. 'I don't think about the result, just about the process, what I'm doing next.' I think I believe her.

I drive back to town and through the formidable entrance gates to the Biltmore Estate. When I first heard where the Nationals were to take place, I imagined them carving a course out of the fine lawns directly in front of the great house. But in reality the estate is so huge that the owners could site the

Nationals in a picturesque valley all of its own. Antler Hill, the part of the estate where the American cyclocross has set up camp, is the farming and wine-growing corner of the estate, and has a wilder feel than the more showy, manicured gardens nearer the house. Alongside the vineyard and winery there's a quaint barn full of tractors, a courtyard of ancient farming machinery, a tavern and, of course, several gift shops. Towering over these modest timber buildings, which look old even if they are not, is a huge modern hotel.

It's an oddly inspired place for a cyclocross race. As well as having great facilities, it's private land, so for USA Cycling it's politically simple. They strike a deal with the owners, and as long as they stick to the contract, there should be no surprises. In 2015 the Nationals took place in Austin, Texas, in a public park, and the local authority officials grew so concerned about damage to the park's trees that they demanded Sunday's events be delayed by a day. Such an occurrence demonstrates just how far American cyclocross has to go. In Belgium, every component involved in putting on a race – landowners, residents, businesses, local government – works together to make it happen. In America there is always the sense that the cyclocross community have to fight to grow, even maintain, their sport.

This venue is symptomatic of the position in the US where promoters don't have the economic model to use whatever land they want. As a venue it's great, but too detached from the town, so the event will never be part of the community. And because the Nationals use a new venue every year – for good reasons to do with spreading the love, and the spreading of economic benefit – they don't become part of a local calendar. In Britain in the eighties the course at Sutton Park in the West Midlands became a regular venue, and grew in status and popularity as a result.

Being something of a cyclocross course obsessive, the first thing I do when I arrive at a new venue is set off for a lap on foot. There's been a lot of comment on social media about the Asheville course being 'Euro', 'Rad' and 'Awesome'. As a cynical Londoner who has witnessed first-hand the precipitous terrors of Namur and the ankle-sucking sand of Koksijde, I'm sceptical. The first thing I see is a group of children, perhaps ten-year-olds, standing astride their bikes at the top of a steep drop, peering anxiously down while an adult talks to them. This I find very encouraging.

The course is indeed very challenging compared to most American courses, and wouldn't be out of place at a Superprestige or World Cup event. It makes the most of the natural features close to the Antler Hill village, taking the riders on a long climbing loop across rutted pastureland, then plunging back down through a steep, tree-root-strewn wood. There are sections of fast grass, boggy grass, tarmac and gravel, a treacherous off-camber feature, and several steep climbs on every lap. The professionals have got a course to race on, worthy of their status. The irony is that while the organisers haven't pandered to the needs of 12-year-old kids, they also haven't arranged separate practice sessions for the different categories. Everyone goes out onto the course together. So I watch, wincing, as world-class professionals try to charge around at race speed, surrounded by little leaguers, rank amateurs and septuagenarians. The democracy and community spirit of American cyclocross is a wonderful thing, but if a ten-year-old falls off in front of a professional in full flight, the result isn't going to be pretty.

Throughout the day there are races for various children's categories, from one to eight years, up to 15 to 16 years. Earlier in the week these children's parents were probably racing in the masters categories. There have also been collegiate championships, a team relay and singlespeed championships. In all, between Monday and Sunday there are fifty-six races, of which forty-seven have championship medals up for the taking. In the press room I visited later in the day, on a table were piled up a huge stack of medals. I considered pocketing one and taking it home for my children, but my conscience was too strong. There are some who feel that the inclusion of so many categories puts too much of a strain on the logistics of organising the Nationals, and detracts from the elite races. I can see an argument for moving the collegiate races to another slot in the schedule, if only to make the atmosphere a little less like a frat party, but I think the children should be able to race in the same event as their heroes. It will inspire and educate them. And if the children are racing, you may as well let their parents race too — no one wants grumpy, jealous parents around.

Gage Hecht's Alpha Bicycle Co. team, who are based in Colorado and focus on juniors riding cyclocross and mountain biking, have around a dozen riders here. They must have got here early in the week because they've pitched their camp in a prime spot within the elite parking. Clearly someone in their management understands the importance of good parking. Invariably, as I wander past, there are four or five riders sitting inside their roomy tent, wearing the bright green team colours and staring at their phones. Their parents are buzzing about, swapping wheels on bikes, mixing up energy drinks and packing warm clothing into rucksacks. Gage introduces me to his father, Bruce, a genial giant in brown overalls. Gage seems more comfortable here, surrounded by family and friends. He's less guarded, and I begin to see the 17-year-old kid, exchanging wisecracks with his teammates, as opposed to the keyed-up athlete representing his country that I witnessed in Koksijde and Namur. Under the good humour, though, there is apprehension. Gage knows that his friend and teammate Spencer Petrov has made gains on him this season, and will feel a win tomorrow to be within his grasp.

Walking through the parking lot, I see BrittLee Bowman, who I haven't seen since she raced at Koppenbergcross in late October. She is naturally busy, she waves at me as she speaks quickly into her mobile, pacing up and down the track beside her team's rented van. Afterwards she does a photo shoot – the photos will go on a cycling magazine's Instagram page. Then she makes another phone call. I get the sense that this weekend is important to BrittLee, but that racing is only a part of its importance. Everyone she knows in the cross world is here in Asheville, and in her world, where social life, sport and business blur, that means a lot of opportunities. Perhaps if she'd been born Dutch at this moment she'd be lying down, resting her legs. But she's an archetypal New Yorker, always on the go. Bike racing at the highest level means accepting boredom into your life, and BrittLee doesn't seem able or willing to do that.

Saturday's racing concludes with two events that perfectly encapsulate the American approach to cyclocross. First up is the

Industry Race, for men and women working within the bike industry. Boasting a large field, and some very flashy equipment (as one would expect), this is probably the most intensely competitive race of the whole week. After all, if you're racing someone from a rival bike manufacturer, you want to give them a good whipping. And if you're racing someone from your own team, you want to give them an even bigger whipping. In the bike industry, while everyone has a good laugh and pretends not to be bothered, you *are* judged on how fit and lean you are. Personal pride is at stake and, given that this race is highly visible, there are some seriously fierce faces on the start line. Sadly, fitness and technical levels don't quite match the psychological drive. The charge off the line is impressive but by lap two many of the riders are so deep in the red that the medical teams are rubbing their hands in glee. With tiredness, as with foolishness, comes technical errors. The crowds gather at one short but very steep descent, with lots of loose gravel at the top, and cheer whenever an overly optimistic sales rep locks up his back wheel and slides heroically downwards. For some there's the cheer of a fluke, for others there's the collective intake of breath when Lycra connects with North Carolina soil.

During the race I get held at a crossing point and start talking to the volunteer guarding it. He's come down from New York, originally intending only to watch, but having organised some events himself back home he knows how helpful a few extra pairs of hands can be for the organisers, so he volunteered. He too is impressed with the course, and impressed with the fact that I've been to several races in Belgium this season. He understands the difference in the types of courses and the racing in Europe, and seems rather in awe of everything 'Euro'. We watch as the industry riders screech and lurch past, and when a gap opens up he pulls back the tape and lets a few of us dash across the course. As I walk away I can't help but wonder whether the American cyclocross community would do better to be a little less in awe of European racing, and focus instead on their own unique values.

The Industry Race is really only a warm-up for the main event of the day, a race that has had a great deal of social-media attention across America. The Donut Race. A new event to the programme for 2016, and channelling some West Coast counterculture, the Donut Race involves doing laps of a smaller circuit, and pulling into the Donut Pits on every lap to consume one or more of the deep-fried delights. The principle is that the more donuts you eat, the more laps go on your score. There is some kind of system to tally up donuts with points but no one seems to understand it, and no one really cares anyway. It's for charity, not a gold medal. However, one rule being taken very seriously by the motley crew who assemble on the start line is that if you throw up, you're disqualified.

The television camera pans slowly across the front row of the grid. There is a man in a Hawaiian shirt and lei garland. There is another man in a lumberjack shirt and hiking boots (it's hard to tell if it's a fancy-dress costume or just his regular clothes – we are in the South, after all). Next to him is a man in a skinsuit, not smiling, perhaps wishing he'd played it a bit more casual. Next to him, grinning from ear to ear, is a pale blue unicorn.

The unicorn does not get a good start, but she doesn't seem too worried, she's still smiling when she arrives at the donut pits for the first time. She knows that this is where everything can change. In the pits every rider comes to a stop and grabs a donut from a tray from one of the race officials who are shaking with laughter. Each rider then must eat the donut before leaving the pits, though this rule is being tested by those who have realised that merely fitting all of the donuts inside your mouth could be construed as finishing the said item. They set off with cheeks full of dough and sugar, but swiftly regret their strategy because just after the pit comes the fairly stiff climb up to the finishing line. By the third lap, with some riders taking two donuts per lap, the cardinal rule about not throwing up looks like it might be invoked. Some of the riders look distinctly pale and queasy. Though she does not win, the unicorn gives a good account of herself – at least she doesn't vomit.

As the Donut Race descends into good-natured chaos, I look across to the nearby elite parking area. Inside her tent, Katie is pounding away on the rollers, keeping the legs loose. This is her career, her livelihood. If she doesn't perform tomorrow her sponsorship deals could be put at risk. She's a long way from donut races.

In my bid to experience all the delights of the smoky Appalachian mountains, I choose poutine, a local speciality, for dinner at the restaurant adjacent to the course, just downstairs from the press room. Poutine is probably the most savoury thing I have ever tasted, being composed of beef, chips, gravy and cheese. When combined with the local beer it seems entirely appropriate for a cyclocross race. The teenage waiter absorbs my feeble jokes about the menu with aplomb then grows enthusiastic when I ask what it's like to have this strange event land in his world.

'It's great, it sure has livened this place up,' he smiles. 'Not our usual crowd.'

Another perspective on an American cross race. This travelling circus has elite athletes, shouty announcers, hipsters and free-thinkers, and some pretty cool vehicles to boot. Easy to take for granted when you're on the inside, but when it lands on you for the first time it must make quite an impact. For a young man working in a heritage attraction where the grey-haired brigade shuffle from bus to café to gift shop, this is a good week. Plus, there are lots of girls in skinsuits.

After my poutine and beer I start to feel sleepy and head back to the hotel. Local time, it's early. In London, it's late. I'm somewhere in the middle, my circadian rhythms totally screwed. After writing up some notes and failing to find anything interesting on the local television stations, I go to bed. With no children, and no need to start early in the morning, I've got ten hours of blissful, unbroken, restorative sleep ahead of me.

Six hours later I'm awake. Very awake. It's four in the morning. Godammit! Never mind, I have work to do.

Fuelled by another of Bruegger's finest, and considerable amounts of coffee, I get up to Antler Hill early. A mist hangs heavy over the surrounding hills. The championship site is starting to come to life. This is the biggest day in the American domestic calendar, the climax of the season. The titles for the junior,

Under-23 and elite categories, across men and women, will be decided today. It's also national championships day in Europe. In Belgium, Holland, France, Britain and a host of other countries the jersey of national champion will be awarded today. The United States championships used to be held in December, which put their calendar completely out of sync with Europe. The decision to move them into line with the major cyclocross nations was a good one, though not straightforward. Because travelling distances can be so huge in America, and there are over a thousand competitors at Nationals, many of whom are of school age, USA Cycling and the organisers have to consider things like travel costs, the timing of exams.

I head down to the elite village, where most of the trucks and tents are still shuttered. Gage, though, is already on the rollers, wrapped up snugly against the early-morning chill, spinning out a silent rhythm, staring into space. Is he visualising victory, as we are told successful athletes do? Is he thinking about his rivals? Or is he merely listening to his body, trying to sense whether his power will open up today, or freeze? He does not see me, and I know better than to intrude. I nod hello to Bruce, and carry on walking. Ridiculously, given he is only 17, Gage is in much the same position as Katie. Both have won multiple titles without a break (Katie comes into the weekend with eleven consecutive titles to her name, Gage has four titles across various age groups) so there is an expectation that they will win again. Being an outright favourite heaps on pressure. When, a little later, I poke my head into Katie's tent to wish her good luck, she is sitting on a camp chair, curled up in her puffa jacket, looking at her phone.

Nearby Mark is working on her bikes. Other than the wind flapping at the tent door where I stand, the only sound is the constant low bustle of Mark's work. He is silent, scientific, controlled as he moves around the baby blue Trek suspended in the air. That he is wearing blue plastic gloves only reinforces the idea that he's performing surgery on this confection of carbon and aluminium. I wonder whether hearing him at work is reassuring to Katie at this stage of the day.

'Starting to feel nervous now,' she says, forcing a smile that ends up more of a grimace. 'All part of the process, I guess.'

Gage too looks nervous, as he rolls to the start line, though with cyclocross it's easy to confuse a nervous rider simply with a cold rider. As defending champion he is in the centre of the front row of the grid. He's surrounded by the riders with whom he trains and races on the USA squad – Spencer Petrov, Denzel Stephenson, Eric Brunner, Evan Clouse and Cameron Beard. As we've seen, in cross a good start is essential. Mess it up and you'll get bogged down in all the traffic of riders who should be far behind you. There are many aspects to getting a good start, but the first, and probably the most important, is getting your foot into the pedal. Every rider starts with one foot on the floor and the other clipped into their pedal. When the light goes green, or the whistle is blown, the rider uses the clipped-in foot to push forward and create momentum, then on the same revolution brings the other foot up onto its pedal and clicks in. Then you're free to sprint like a maniac towards the first corner. If you can't find the connection between foot and pedal, if you don't click in, you're left floundering, trying to wriggle the shoe into the right position while all around you the rest of the field come thundering by.

This is what happens to Gage in his championship race. I've walked a little way up the start–finish straight, hoping to see him lead the charge up this first little climb. But instead he gets swamped and is in the middle of the pack, jostling for position with some kids who are probably surprised to see him there. Fortunately the first corner is wide enough that the group get around it without too much of a compression. Still, as Eric Brunner flies into an early lead, Gage is a long way back.

It's mid-morning and the crowd is building steadily. It's incredibly noisy, mainly due to the number of cowbells around the course. Up on Heckle Hill – a steep climb and off-camber descent, so-named to try to encourage heckling from the spectators – the atmosphere is overwhelmingly positive. Disappointingly so. I'd been looking forward to hearing some trademark American dissent. Perhaps at the Nationals it's not quite the done thing.

To compensate for the lack of heckling, the organisers have laid on a brilliant duo of announcers, Richard Fries and Joe Jefferson. Standing on a truck overlooking the finish line, each with a microphone in hand, the pair work as a team, handing off to each other and responding to each other's commentary. Fries is a stalwart of the American cyclocross scene, a race organiser, former marketing man and professional racer. He's a punchy announcer with a whole cupboard full of useful images, analogies and superlatives. My personal favourite from the weekend comes towards the end of a race, when he shouts out, 'THE FAT LADY MIGHT NOT BE SINGING BUT THE BIG GIRL IS AT THE PIANO!'

Eric Brunner leads the race for the first lap. Watching him race is a little strange for someone old enough to remember the eighties, because Brunner's team, Boulder Junior Cycling, are sponsored by 7-Eleven and wear an almost identical kit to the trailblazing team that was home to Andy Hampsten, Davis Phinney, Raul Alcala and many other great riders. Long before Brunner was born, the same green, white and red jersey was causing a stir in the Tour de France. Undoubtedly someone in the Boulder Junior Cycling management has a taste for nostalgia, or thinks the jersey will bring his kids good karma.

Into lap two and Brunner needs more than good karma. Spencer Petrov and Denzel Stephenson are closing him down, with Gage there too. His start may have been sticky but on this course, with plenty of climbing, sticky mud and a long headwind section towards the finish, Gage's strength has shone through. He bides his time then, on lap two, he attacks on Heckle Hill. As they see the defending champion come to the front of the race for the first time the crowd lift their volume, the cowbells ring and a man dressed as a Viking waves his Flemish lion flag as frantically as he can. At the top of the hill, which they are all running, Gage has a small gap. He drops the bike from his shoulder, skips back onto it, clipping into his pedals (this time) in one fluid movement and plunges down the slippery descent. After the descent there is a long section of gravel track, then a steep drop-off and another long section of grass. Petrov knows this is the moment the race could be won. In Europe this season he and Gage have been exchanging positions – on some courses Petrov comes out top, on others it's Gage. Petrov's confidence is surging, and he comes into this race believing he can beat Gage, but knowing that to do so he has to get everything right on the day. He puts in a huge effort to try to get back to Gage's wheel, but Gage too knows the importance of getting clear at this moment. By the end of the lap, Gage has 19 seconds on Petrov, who is pushing himself deep into the red, and being pursued by teammates Brunner and Stephenson. Petrov, growing tired, makes a mistake on a slippery off-camber section and slides out, allowing his chasers to close the gap further. Stephenson, coming strong towards the end of the race, passes him and takes off in solo pursuit of Gage. As they take the long technical descent through the woods, he looks to be closing Gage down, but it proves just beyond him. Gage wins by just three seconds, and the look on his face is one of overwhelming relief. For Petrov a race that could have been his ends in disaster. Close to the finish Brunner makes a pass and relegates Petrov to fourth. If he'd closed down that attack by Gage he would have had a chance of gold, but he ended up with nothing.

For Katie the women's race turns out to be a battle of nerves rather than the physical punch and counter-punch we saw in the juniors'. Usually Katie is a relatively slow starter. She takes half a lap or so before her engine gets going. So it's something of a surprise to see her sprinting up the start straight at the front of the race, and going into the first corner in second place. After a few short-lived attacks on the opening lap, Katie and Georgia Gould get clear of the chasing pack, and the narrative of the race begins to develop. For three laps Katie and Georgia ride together, swapping turns on the front, pulling away from the rest. The women are friends and sometimes train together, but this co-operation is tense; there is a National title up for grabs, and both know that expending too much energy in the middle of the race might be costly. On some sections of the course Georgia is stronger, and she can test Katie. On other sections it is the other way round. The crowd watch the pair progress, waiting for a mistake or an attack, the situation growing more tense as the lap numbers count down.

The decisive moment comes on the part of the course furthest from the finishing straight, where there are few spectators and no static cameras, so it is witnessed by hardly anyone. After a long climb up the side of a cow pasture, along narrow mud paths, the pair turn sharp left and drop into a narrow, twisting descent through a wood, with tree-roots and rocks. The crowd there is huge, vociferous and by now fairly drunk. Gould leads down the descent, but as the path opens out into a fast but slippery descent across another meadow, she bobbles and has to unclip her foot to correct herself. Katie knows this is as good an opportunity as she'll get. Instinctively she attacks and gets a small gap. Fortunately for her the next section is the long slog into a headwind towards the finishing line – one of the sections in which she has been stronger than Georgia during the race – and she is able to extend that small gap. When she races through the bell with one lap to go she has a handful of seconds. She wins the race by 22.

Later, I see her as everyone hangs about in the warmth of the Antler Hill tavern, waiting for the awards ceremonies to start. She is back in her red puffa jacket, beanie hat on, her eyes a little pink from tiredness and the dry wind. I congratulate her then tell her I always knew she had the situation under control. She just smiles, rolls her eyes, and says, 'I don't know about that.' Having spoken to her throughout the preceding months, and come to understand a little of the anxieties that plague professional cyclists, I feel like I can understand something of what she is feeling right now – that blend of exhaustion and relief. From outside elite sport, we imagine victory makes an athlete happy. It seems a straightforward equation. Yet when victory is expected, perhaps the best an experienced athlete can hope for is to feel satisfied.

My journey back to London starts with an early flight from Charlotte to Newark. As I get settled in my seat, a tall young man in a baseball cap sits down in front of me. It's Gage. He's wearing his team sweatshirt and cap – ever the professional – and seems the seasoned traveller. We say hello, compare trips home, he has school the next day, and then both fall asleep. It's an exhausting business. When he wakes up on the descent to Newark he gets his phone out and plays a game – Bike Race. He seems quite good.

15

Climbing the Mountain

Back in Britain, in the soul-sapping hinterland known as the Heathrow Express, I stare bleary-eyed at my phone, looking for the results of the British championships. Nikki Harris won the women's race, mountain biker Liam Killeen took a surprise victory in the men's race. In the juniors Dan Tulett finished fourth, a result I know he won't be happy with. His younger brother Ben won the Under-16s. This year the event featured the new Under-23 women's category, as the World Championships will too. The winner of the British championship was Evie Richards, not a name I'd heard of before, though a quick bit of Google research tells me that she took a silver medal in the Junior Women Cross-Country Mountain Bike World Championships in Andorra a few months earlier. Her victory yesterday at the British cyclocross championship was by a margin of nearly two minutes and her lap times were similar to the top three riders in the elite women's category. Impressive stuff.

Over the next few days, as I absorb pictures and videos of the championships, I almost begin to regret choosing to go to America rather than Shrewsbury Sports Village. It doesn't sound a very glamorous place, but in cyclocross terms it had glamour in abundance. That is to say, it had mud in abundance. A week of heavy rain made the ground waterlogged, then the supporting races churned it into the kind of quagmire that has ardent cyclocross fans taking to Twitter in excitement. While the Belgian championships took place on a fast and mainly dry circuit, and the Americans slipped and slid over a greasy top surface, the British competitors heaved their bikes through glutinous mud so deep it went over the riders' rims. Most of the course could be ridden, but it made for brutal and very physical racing.

As I watch clips of young riders struggling to keep their bikes moving forward through the thick mud, I think of the feelings I had standing in Campbell Park, Milton Keynes, watching the world's best riders compete in the first World Cup outside continental Europe. I was happy, overwhelmingly so, but my happiness was tinged with regret. For it was in Campbell Park that I rode my last cyclocross race.

In late January 1989 I was about to turn 16. I'd learned that the English Schools Cycling Association's (ESCA) cyclocross championships were to be held in Milton Keynes, and asked my parents if they'd take me to spectate. It wasn't the most rock 'n' roll way to turn 16, but I was a dedicated racing cyclist. Perhaps thinking that the subtext of my request was that I really wanted to ride the championships, my father phoned the organiser and secured me a last-minute place on the starting grid. I made a show of being annoyed, but really I was glad of his enterprise; my imagination began to build scenarios in which I ran out a surprise but worthy winner of the title race. Rational thought would have tempered this sort of daydreaming – I was never anywhere near good enough to challenge for the win at national level – but when has rational thought ever been something embraced by 15-year-old boys?

Much like the British championships in Shrewsbury, the mud that day in 1989 was shoe-suckingly thick. I have only two memories of the race. The first is of coming to a grinding halt on an uphill section, my tyres seemingly glued to the floor, my lungs about to burst from the effort of just getting that far, then remembering that this was the point I was supposed to leap athletically from my bike and leg it to the top of the hill (it was really no more than a grassy knoll). The second memory is of a flatter but very muddy section further round the course. Several riders were passing me, including younger girls. In my heart I knew I wasn't good enough to be challenging for the win, but I also knew that, generally speaking, I was stronger than a 13-year-old girl. It was at that point that I looked down. An entire spadeful of mud had collected in my brakes and was preventing my wheels turning. My race was over. I got off my bike and dragged the bloody thing, which was heavy to start with, but now carried as much weight again in Bedfordshire earth, back to the car park. Needless to say I was in a fairly substantial sulk on the journey home.

The reason my wheels weren't turning when other competitors' were, was that I didn't have a cyclocross bike. I had a modified road bike with caliper rather than cantilever brakes. With the resulting minimal clearance, mud built up quickly between the brakes, forks and wheel and brought me to a stop. Until then my makeshift cross bike hadn't caused me any problems, but until then I hadn't ridden in such muddy conditions.

The ESCA race was one of the last of that season, so my mind was soon back to all matters tarmac. It was my final year racing as an Under-16 on the road. That autumn I did not return to cyclocross racing.

My parents had spent a great deal of time and money on my brief racing career, and I honestly don't think it occurred to my father that there might be a valid reason why cyclocross bikes were different from road bikes. His mentality was always to make do and mend, from modify an existing bike rather than buy something new. In his mind I was a growing lad taking part in a pretty odd branch of cycle racing. It wouldn't last, so even if there was a good reason to have a cross bike, it wasn't going to be worth the investment. He was right, though my decision to give up was precisely because I didn't have the right machine.

*

The Tuletts live in a picturesque village near Sevenoaks in Kent. It's an area I'm familiar with because it's within easy reach by bike from my house. Indeed, one of my regular riding routes passes their front door. The village sits in a river valley, with the North Downs rising on either side. When I visit them at home one evening, I'm surprised to find their address is a tiny cottage on the principal road through the village. Knowing they have three children (Dan, Ben and their younger sister Amy), plus surely a lot of cycling equipment, I'd expected something a bit bigger.

I ring the doorbell but instead of the door, a side-gate opens and Dan welcomes me in. And as he shows me through to the kitchen I realise that the cottage is rather like the Tardis – considerably bigger on the inside than the outside. It's like any other family house, except for the proliferation of bicycles. There seem to be bikes in every room. Dan is sponsored by Specialized so naturally that brand dominates. Every bike, I notice, is immaculate and leaned carefully against a wall or another bike. We have a cup of tea and talk about Dan's season so far, how disappointed he's been with the results, and whether there's some underlying physical problem. Dan's father, Allister, has been involved in the bike racing game for many years, and has been around top-level racing enough to know that it takes more than a love of the sport to make it. Now he has his own plumbing business, which gives him not only enough income to support the family and his sons' racing, but a degree of freedom to travel to races. The plan is for Dan to turn professional, Allister tells me, but if Dan's legs don't pay dividends he'll be learning the plumbing trade. Dan looks less than impressed at this prospect.

Before this season Dan's career plan seemed to be on track. Last year he won the Nieuwelingen (Under-16s) race at Koppenbergcross, a performance that grabbed the attention of the big Belgian teams. A few weeks later at the Milton Keynes World Cup he and Allister were courted by Niels Albert. Dan could come and race full-time in Belgium, he'd be looked after and paid well. The attention was flattering but premature; Dan was 15 years old. He was clearly talented, but Allister knew that throwing his son into the hotbed of European cyclocross at such a young age would be counterproductive. No matter how mature a young man Dan was, making the cultural and linguistic adjustment would be tough. It would also narrow Dan's career options.

Like the newly crowned Under-23 national champion Evie Richards, Dan is a member of the British Cycling Olympic

Development Academy, and favours mountain biking over cross. When he talks of turning professional, it's as a cross-country mountain bike racer. He has a British Cycling coach, support from the British arm of Specialized, and is studying at his local college. Allister has invested in a motorhome so that the family can travel abroad to races without the hassle of finding local accommodation (when British Cycling organise a hotel for the riders, Allister sleeps outside in the motorhome). Everything has been set up to give Dan and his brother Ben the best chances of success, at home and abroad. After a cup of tea, the Tuletts show me round the rest of their property.

Behind the cottage is a large, new-looking barn. The ground floor is a fitness studio where the boys can ride the indoor trainer (as Ben is doing now – stripped down to an undervest, headphones on, zoned out) or do their core exercises and stretching. Upstairs is a home cinema. Across the garden is a workshop for working on the bikes. Back in the cottage Allister shows me the boys' bedrooms, which look like any other teenage boys' rooms, apart from the Wout van Aert poster, the framed national champion's jersey and the array of helmets stacked on top of a wardrobe. Finally, I am ushered up a ladder into a loft space, filled with rows of bikes and wheels, underneath which are big bags full of race clothing and the various miscellany that goes with running a team of two. I haven't been counting, but there must be at least twenty-five bikes on the property.

This is what it takes to propel a young rider towards a professional career. The whole family has to commit to it, to the investment of time and money, to the emotional support. Critically, the parents must also know when to take a step back and let the experts run things. Allister is an experienced race mechanic, so is heavily involved in preparing Dan and Ben's bikes, but he's not a coach, so he leaves training and nutrition to others. This, of course, is the advantage of having the boys in the Development Academy. I'm struck too, by what a collaborative effort it is. Around Dan there are three or four people directly managing his career, but a whole host of others on the periphery. Like any team project, communication is important. When I saw Allister at Koksijde he was on the phone to Simon, Dan's coach. Back at home Dan and Simon talk regularly by phone and email. This is nothing out of the ordinary for an athlete at an elite level, but it does reinforce what I already suspected – that bright young talents don't just appear from nowhere. They are recognised early and developed by professional teams, with the support of family members.

Would I, as a parent, make the kind of commitment Allister and Katherine Tulett have made? I like to think so, but it's hard to say with any measure of certainty. If one of my children shows promise at cycling, I would worry that I'm living the cliché of a pushy parent pursuing their own failed dreams through their children. Perhaps pushy parents are something of a myth? After all, when a child shows talent at sport, it's only natural to encourage them, and before you know it you're sucked into a system that leads to deep investments, both emotional and financial. Yet, for all my neuroses, it would be nice to have a rainbow jersey in the house.

After my somewhat petulant decision to retire from cyclocross at the age of 15, I continued racing on the road. Roger Hammond, meanwhile, dominated the junior ranks both on the road and in the mud. In 1992, two days after his 18th birthday, he was on the

British team at the World Cyclocross Championships in Roundhay Park, Leeds. It was the second time the event had been staged in the UK, the first being the Crystal Palace championships when Erik de Vlaeminck won his last title.

My father and I drove up to Leeds and stayed in a nearby Youth Hostel for the weekend. The weather was cold and dry and the course was a testing one, with lots of elevation change, including a long flight of steps, some adverse cambers and a technical section through a wood. Indeed, the course was so challenging that a section had to be changed on the eve of the first race, after team managers had complained to the UCI about how dangerous it was. Several riders had crashed heavily in training on an icy descent. Arriving early, we spotted Roger cleaning his bike in the pits with a pressure washer, went over and wished him luck. My father would certainly have tried to engage him in a much longer conversation had I not dragged him away. 'Roger's got to get ready,' I hissed.

An hour later Roger crossed the line as the new Junior World Cyclocross Champion. I was stunned but elated. That someone I knew could become a World champion seemed astonishing. I wasn't in the slightest bit jealous because I knew Roger's quality – I'd seen it at first hand on the school playing fields of Buckinghamshire. We weren't close friends but he'd always been friendly to me, sometimes giving me advice before a race. I don't remember anything of the actual race in Leeds, only that he won by a comfortable margin. The moment that has stayed with me, however, is the presentation of the rainbow jersey. The Union Jack was raised, the national anthem played, and tears pricked my eyes. I couldn't believe what I was seeing.

The men's professional race, later in the day, was expected to be a tussle between reigning champion Radomír Šimůnek and Danny de Bie. However, neither even finished on the podium and the race was won in convincing style by Mike Kluge of Germany. Kluge was a flamboyant character (you would have to be to wear a fluorescent pink and yellow helmet and sunglasses for a cyclocross race in 1992) who loved the social side of the sport, loved the media, and whose principal challenge was avoiding boredom. In 1985 he won the Amateur World Championships and was propelled into the public eye. He looked set for a meteoric career, but everything changed at the 1988 World Championships in Hägendorf, Switzerland. The course there ran through cornfields that had been frozen throughout the winter. But in the week before the event the temperature lifted, rain fell, and the fields were turned into so much mud that riding was impossible. In protest at what he thought were ridiculous conditions, Kluge spent a whole lap walking with his bike upside down on his shoulder. In reciprocal protest the crowd spat at him and the German federation gave him a stern telling-off.

A few months later Kluge was passed over for selection for the Seoul Olympics road team. As one of the best road riders in the country, he expected to get a ride, and thought that his Hägendorf antics had influenced the decision. Most riders in this scenario would have turned professional straight away, but Kluge was so disillusioned with cycling that he went for a much more fun option. He moved to California and went surfing.

16

If the Shoes Fit

Beauty and ugliness. Perhaps that's why I love cyclocross so much. On the side of beauty we have the joy of riding your bike, community, friendship, humour and the human spirit's bravery in the face of adversity. On the opposing team there is money, cheating and cynicism. Beauty and ugliness are never far from each other. They need each other, for without ugliness how can we appreciate beauty?

Unlike road racing, which slowly fades into the autumn, or soccer, which pushes its supposedly climactic games into the incongruous setting of summer, the cyclocross season ends with a very clear finale. The rhythm of the season has been the same for many years, and though it may have a few tweaks now and then, its pattern is both reassuring and exciting. After the national championships in early January the build-up towards the World Championships starts. The Worlds is the most important event of the season. No other single event comes close to the status of winning the rainbow jersey. In road racing there are the yellow and pink jerseys of the Tour de France and Giro d'Italia respectively, as well as a host of single-day Monument races, all of which most riders would happily win instead of a World Championship. In cyclocross there is only the rainbow jersey, and it is exalted. To win it is to go down in the annals of the sport.

It's the last week of January. It has been raining. A lot. Across the cycling media – social and otherwise – speculation about the World Championships has been developing to a fever pitch. The form of every rider is scrutinised. Photographers are sent into dark forests in Belgium to try to find riders training. The soil composition of the Brabant region is discussed. The last race of the World Cup, at Hoogerheide in the Netherlands, turns out to be an unreliable guide to who is on form because a combination of heavy rain and construction work has turned the course, normally fairly fast, into a quagmire. Mathieu van der Poel wins his fourth consecutive World Cup, reinforcing his status as favourite for the World title. For Van der Poel there is the added pressure that his father organises the Hoogerheide race. Van Aert takes second and Pauwels third, in a replica of the result at Namur. In the women's race Sophie de Boer takes a popular home victory ahead of the newly crowned Dutch champion Thalita de Jong. De Jong, who lives close to the course, just holds off Nikki Harris and Caroline Mani.

The cyclocross season may be relatively short but its intensity is exhausting. To win a World Championship you need to be in the form of your life, both physically and mentally. Because it's impossible to stay at the peak of your form from October through to the end of January, most riders aim to either take a break during December, as Van Aert did by going to Majorca instead of riding Druivencross, or simply alter their training plans to allow for a slight dip in form, as Sanne Cant did. The demands of the season-long Superprestige and World Cup competitions mean that no cyclocross professional can prepare exclusively for the Worlds. Sponsors want their riders visible week in, week out. Cant, like Nys and all the other elite men, sees herself as a full-time cyclocross professional, and as such her targets are season-long. But in the women's side of the sport there have been riders capable of switching from the road to cyclocross and winning a World Championship with relatively little preparation, the most notable being wunderkinds Marianne Vos and Pauline Ferrand-Prévot. In the past both women have joined the cyclocross fray mid-season, then come to the Worlds with fresh legs and won. In Tábor in the Czech Republic last year, Cant lost to Ferrand-Prévot, then was bitterly critical of part-timers swooping in and taking advantage of her tiredness. She later retracted the comments. I have some sympathy with this view, but ultimately when a rainbow jersey is up for grabs, the only right approach is the winning approach. No one is forced to ride all season long.

By the time the Worlds arrive, there is a sense that some of the best riders are at the edge of their physical and mental capacity, on great form but only a hair's breadth away from complete exhaustion. Media hype, plus pressure from sponsors and national teams, only intensifies the pressure of the World Championships. And this year, with the event being held at Zolder, the Belgian team have another dimension of pressure.

As I sit in my rented car in the queue for the Eurotunnel, I check the weather forecast on my phone for the forty-second time. Heavy rain, light rain, heavy rain, light rain. One of my friends has a weather app that gives him much more optimistic forecasts. Having previously scorned it, I now wish I'd downloaded it too. I try to console myself that this is classic cross weather. I don't manage to wholly convince myself.

Between Antwerp, the capital of Flanders, and Liège, the prominent Walloon city, runs the Albert Canal. Built during the 1930s, the canal's intended use for industry was delayed by the Second World War, during which it functioned as a key defence line. In 1940 the German crossing of the canal signified the end of Belgian freedom. In 1944, first the Canadian then British then US forces crossed it on the way to liberating the Netherlands and Luxembourg before invading Germany. After the war it reverted to its original function of carrying goods between Antwerp and Liège. Today its broad waters are still ploughed by laden barges, but along some of the more picturesque sections you will also see cycle paths, picnic areas, cafés and recreational boating.

This spot, where I sit in my car facing the canal, is not one of those picturesque sections. Far from it. Running parallel to the canal is the A13 motorway, and along the motorway runs a strip of industrial estates. This is the engine of modern Flemish industry. While in centuries past the cities of Ghent and Bruges were home to the textile mills that powered Flanders' affluence, now this unlovely sprawl of factories, warehouses and truck depots is the beating heart. Some of the biggest brands in Belgium cycling are based here – Ridley has its factory here, and Golazo, organisers of many major cyclocross events, have their headquarters nearby. In the midst of it all, fitting right into the drab aesthetic, is the Zolder motor racing circuit. In motor racing terms, this is a place of past glories. The Belgian Grand Prix was held here during the seventies and early eighties, but ended in tragedy when Gilles Villeneuve was killed, thrown from his Ferrari when it crashed during qualifying for the 1982 event. Villeneuve's death prompted the FIA to move the Belgian Grand Prix to the safer Spa-Francorchamps circuit – now also home to the witchy cyclocross race – and Zolder switched its focus to Gran Turismo, Touring Car and Formula 3 racing. Sensibly, the venue has diversified into cycling events, hosting two editions of the World Road Championships, three editions of the Cyclocross World Championships and one edition of the BMX World Championships. As host of the regular Boxing Day World Cup cyclocross, Zolder has a special place in the affections of the Belgian cyclocross community.

The road I have driven down is a dead end. To keep going forward would mean a plunge into the grey waters of the Albert Canal. On the opposite bank is a wall of pine trees, behind which, somewhere, is the hallowed ground upon which five rainbow jerseys are to be decided. However, my first objective is to find the place where I can get my accreditation. I need that all-important lanyard. Not only is it essential for my self-esteem, it gets me into that warm, dry press room where the coffee and rolls are. The information sheets I have printed out tell me to go to something called 'Truckstop'. I turn the car around and retrace my steps, peering at each factory gate in turn. Ah, there it is – a small supermarket called Truckstop. I park and get out of the car. A sign on the door points to the side of the building, so I head that way. But the concrete track takes me to the rear of the supermarket, where there is only a huge, scruffy hangar full of tractors and trucks, some piles of tyres, assorted unidentifiable machinery. No lighting, rain dripping through the metal roof. This can't be right. I begin to feel rather nervous. Is this some kind of set-up? Am I about to be robbed, kidnapped, thrown in the canal?

To my relief, a group of people come wandering in with umbrellas and wellies, looking equally confused. Together we figure out that to get to the official accreditation office for the UCI World Cyclocross Championships we have to go *through* the scary truck storage facility, up some stairs and into an office above the supermarket. Cyclocross may not be the most naturally glamorous sport but sometimes its governing bodies don't really help its image.

Suitably lanyarded, I drive out of this godforsaken industrial estate, along the motorway for one junction, and follow signs that take me over the canal and into the forest. It's early but there are many spectators already lining the sides of the road that enters the circuit through a giant black tyre. As I head for the team trucks, a man walking alongside me nods hello and tells me in English it's going to be a great weekend. We exchange comments about the racing and the weather and then, as we stride past one of three huge party tents, I make a rather crass remark about him leaving his wife at home, which I instantly regret. He tells me his wife died last year, aged 53. This year, partly in response, he is taking time off work and travelling around Europe in a campervan, going to see as many of cycling's big races as he can fit in. 'Life's too short,' he says. Saddened, humbled, I wish him well and we part ways. If sport is nothing but escapism, if it has no higher meaning but helps people get through their lives, that's good enough for me.

Because it uses the circuit's facilities, the start and finish straight at Zolder is surrounded by a jumble of brutally ugly buildings and high mesh fences. Everything has a kind of eighties styling, from the architecture to the signage and murals. It's difficult to imagine any of it looked good even when it was newly built and freshly painted. Coming here for the Worlds is a rather cynical and lazy move. Yes, it has a course everyone knows and respects, and it has the facilities to cope with a huge number of spectators – the organisers are hoping for 70,000. But isn't it also just perpetuating the Belgian protectionism around cyclocross, keeping the money circling within a small community who have come to see it as *their* sport? The only weapon the UCI possesses to help them expand the sport is the awarding of the World Cup races and the World Championships. However, the UCI also see the World Championships as something of a cash cow: they charge such a hefty fee to the race organisers that putting on the event becomes commercially difficult unless you can be sure to bring in significant revenue through ticket sales, sponsorship and by selling TV rights. In Belgium and Holland this model is proven, so the UCI know they can always secure their fee by awarding the Worlds to one of those two countries. There have been excursions to France, Germany, Italy and Switzerland, plus one notable transatlantic trip to Louisville, Kentucky. But if the UCI genuinely wish to globalise the sport they should revise their fee structure to encourage newer nations into the party.

I peer out of the hood of my rain jacket, through dripping glasses, and try to get my bearings. The team trucks are grouped by country and mostly shut. As usual the mechanics are outside working, taking shelter under awnings and tents where possible, but there are very few riders to be seen. This will be the story of my weekend – the rain and the pressure of the event conspiring to keep the riders shut in behind closed campervan doors. The Belgian team have constructed a fence around their vehicles. I can't blame them, but it does change the atmosphere. Typically, the American team are the most open and welcoming. Along with several other media types, I loiter between the trucks, watch preparations and say hello to everyone I know. Bruce Hecht has come over to watch his son. He must be a reassuring presence for Gage, though Bruce knows to stand back and let the team managers, mechanics and helpers get on with their job. Having finished fifth in the World Cup race here on Boxing Day, and fourth at Hoogerheide last week, Gage knows he has the form and the experience to get a medal today.

By the time I get to the British camp, Dan Tulett is already on the rollers warming up. By his standards it has been a disappointing season. To finish outside the medals at the national championships then be down in 26th place at the Hoogerheide World Cup falls a long way short of Dan's expectations. The cause of this loss of form is a mystery to Dan and his coaches. A good result at this race could redeem his poor season, but it's a hope rather than a justifiable expectation. Still, as he warms up he looks as supple as ever, turning the pedals smoothly. The four other British riders are powering away too, going through the same officially approved British Cycling warm-up routine. Among them is Thomas Pidcock, a talented road rider who has come to cyclocross this season for the first time. An eighth place in the European championships in November booked his spot on the team for Zolder, but the pressure here at the Worlds is another level again.

In heavy rain, and with a strong wind driving across the circuit, the best juniors in the world line up for the race they've been building towards for months, if not years. They know that the television cameras are rolling, that the whole cyclocross community across the world is tuned into live feeds and social media updates, that the most influential managers and sponsors are watching. A good result today could be the start of a lucrative career, or, to look at it another way, a good result today will be the culmination of months of preparation. These are young men whose school friends will be out drinking while they are getting an early night, who get up early and train in the dark before college, who have to carefully measure everything they eat. Today could make all those sacrifices worthwhile. Gage is front and centre on the grid, a perfect starting position. Dan is in the middle of the pack, but Pidcock, by virtue of being relatively new to the sport, is back on the sixth row. On a fast course like Zolder, this is a big disadvantage.

At the last moment, the rain jackets are taken off and thrown to team helpers, skinsuit zips fiddled with, cheeks puffed out, fingers waggled. Gradually the crowd of officials in front of the grid dissolves until there is only one man left holding the white tape across the road. When he winds the tape back between his hands, then jumps through a slim gap in the barriers, there is nothing but tarmac in front of the riders. The traffic lights go red, then green.

Being a strong road rider, the fast tailwind road section that opens the race should suit Gage, but from the start he gets swamped by other riders, and when the field charge into the first slippery off-road corners he's outside the top ten. A trio of French riders speed away, towing with them Jens Dekker, winner in

Namur, with Spencer Petrov the leading American. Watching on the big screen, I keep expecting to see Gage's form come charging up from behind, but the television director has a habit of cutting away after the first ten riders clear a section, and Gage never comes into the picture. By the second lap Dekker is alone in the lead, Petrov has slipped into the mid-teens, and Gage is nowhere to be seen. This, I suppose, is what bike racing is like when you know someone in the race. It can be just a little gut-wrenching. I knew, for all his casualness and his big-picture view of the world, this was the big target of Gage's season, he wanted to win here in Zolder.

By the end of the third lap Dekker is extending his lead over two French riders, with Jappe Jaspers chasing not far behind. Then comes a gaggle of riders in twos and threes. Petrov is there in twelfth, Hecht not far behind in fifteenth, with Pidcock on his wheel. Hecht puts his head down and piles on the hurt in an effort to get up to his teammate's back wheel. Pidcock is the main beneficiary. On the last lap, after 35 minutes of racing, the medal positions are all but decided. But the minor placings are still in contention, with a group of five, including Pidcock but not Gage, racing for fourth place. Towards the end of the lap a Swiss rider attacks going into a technical off-camber climb. Pidcock works his way past two other riders then sets off in pursuit. After the off-camber climb there is a huge bridge that has been specially constructed for the event. It is new to the course, and its length and gradient make it an instrument of torture for the riders. Pidcock, a diminutive figure in his red, white and blue skinsuit, turns himself inside out on that bridge. His elbows thrust out, slender legs pumping the pedals, his face contorted in pain, he can sniff a possible fourth-place finish. On the first lap he crashed three times and came through the finish line for the first time in thirty-second place, so to finish in the top five will be a remarkable feat. As they drop down a series of gloopy sandy drops, where many riders have already crashed into the inflatables at the bottom, it looks like Pidcock might just get his man. But at the finish the Swiss rider still has a gap. Pidcock takes fifth. Half a minute later Gage comes through in twelfth. Dan Tulett finishes in twenty-first place.

It was a smooth, controlled performance by Dekker, who did not look threatened by those chasing him. Having won the European championships and the World Cup, Dekker was the favourite, and he was able to absorb the pressure, adapt to the horrible weather conditions and dominate the race. For the Dutch it is a great start to the Worlds, while the Belgians only got one rider into the top ten, Jappe Jaspers in seventh. On home soil, with the strength in depth of Belgian racing, this is an abysmal start, and the national coach Danny de Bie will know how uncharitable the Belgian press can be about underperformance of the national team at the Worlds.

It's soon to get a whole lot worse.

As Gage, Dan and all the other juniors disappear to their campers to get changed, have a recovery meal and, for some, lick their wounds, the rain begins to fall more heavily than it has done all morning. Spectators take cover underneath trees, hotdog van awnings and inside the party tents. The sudden influx of people puts the bar staff under pressure, and as the Europop bangs out, groups of friends gather in the gloom, their wellies bouncing on the temporary flooring, plastic pint glasses held safely out in front of them. There are leprechauns, Vikings and cowboys, plus many women wearing pink feather boas, and a group of three lads in grey overalls and flat caps. Is this 1950s worker look perhaps an ironic social comment on the gentrification of cyclocross in Belgium? Probably not.

Deciding that it would be unbecoming of a professional sports writer to buy a drink and start dancing to 'Sweet Caroline', I head instead for the media room. Within seconds of walking in the fug of radiators and overheating photographers causes my glasses to mist over. The catering today is excellent: four different types of roll, coffee, crisps and soup. In a corridor lined with photographs of long-forgotten motor racing drivers, I bump into Balint. He is wearing the yellow fisherman's trousers, held up with sturdy braces, which have become something of his trademark, and he's in a despondent state. Rain has got into all his cameras, and though he was able to retrieve his shots of the junior race, he's got very little working equipment with which to shoot the next race. For a professional photographer who specialises in cross, the Worlds weekend is the most lucrative of the year, so camera failure is a disaster. He's considering driving back to the UK to get more cameras. I give him my sympathies, and head back to my laptop, feeling thankful for being a writer.

Replenished, and marginally drier than when I walked in, I head back out for the next race, the women's Under-23s. This will be a little piece of history in the making, for this is the first running of a World Championship in this category, and is a progressive step towards gender equality in the sport. Unfortunately there have been too few other steps. Forty-three riders from nineteen nations are on the start grid, getting pummelled by the rain, which is a bigger field than the women's elite race, and shows the strength in depth at this age group.

One absurdity is that the new, and first, women's Under-23 World champion will never get to wear her rainbow jersey in a race because there are no other events on the calendar which run a separate race for Under-23 women. When she rides a senior women's elite race she won't be able to wear the rainbow stripes because she's not racing in the category in which she won them. But running this race is important because it gives young female riders something to aim for, a bridge between the junior categories and the tough world of senior elite racing.

Because it's a new event, and these riders have never raced against each other without the company of senior women, the commentators are having a difficult job picking out a favourite. On the front row, looking very nervous and very motivated (two related, but different things) is Ellen Noble. After a dominant victory in the national championships in Asheville, a string of creditable World Cup performances, and a solid training block in Sittard, she has to be among the contenders for gold. Britain's Hannah Payton is also on the front row of the grid. And, as you would expect, so is European champion Femke van den Driessche. Also the Belgian champion, Van den Driessche has had something of a breakthrough season, first impressing with that strong ride on the Koppenbergcross when she motored away from her more illustrious rivals on the first of the cobbled climbs. Today, she is in the blue skinsuit of her national team, and inscrutable behind dark sunglasses, an interesting choice given the thoroughly dismal conditions. Looking further back into the grid I can see Evie Richards, the British champion. This is her first cyclocross race outside Britain – quite the baptism of fire.

The announcers try to excite the crowd over the PA system. It's good to hear Richard Fries here, doing commentary duty. To have an English announcer alongside the usual laconic Flemish announcer seems a progressive move on the part of the organisers. The pair are not really a cohesive partnership though: every time he speaks the Flemish announcer sounds like he's discussing a new boiler with his plumber, such is his level of excitement (he's probably done fifty World Championships before). As if he feels he needs to overcompensate Fries goes into full fight mode. If this is a boiler we're discussing IT'S THE ROCKY BALBOA OF BOILERS, IT ROLLS WITH THE PUNCHES AND IT COMES BACK FOR MORE!

Red light, green light. The sprint away from the line is fierce, led by an Italian rider with Ellen Noble in close attendance. Hannah Payton gets a good start but Femke van den Driessche falls back into the group, then gets impeded at the first corner and has to jump off her bike. During the first lap, the Italian Chiarra Teocchi ploughs on alone through the many deepening puddles of brown water, with Noble and a host of other riders chasing. Evie Richards, starting from the third row, works her way to this front group. Then comes a moment which makes the hairs stand up on the back of my neck. The flyover bridges are constructed of scaffolding, with a timber road covered in a kind of grabby black felt. There are three such bridges per lap: the first is a true up and over, the second a long steep climb that leads straight into another long steep climb, and the third is a smooth descent into the finishing straight. On the first, Richards comes to the bottom of the climb at the back of the group, but in the course of only ten pedal strokes she powers past two riders in front of her. This was not a race-winning move, and many spectators will have missed it, but you can be sure those just behind Richards won't have failed to notice the strength of her acceleration.

One of the most interesting features of the Zolder course is a switchback climb that looks relatively straightforward, but is actually technically very challenging, and often plays a role in deciding races here. The riders approach the climb on a flat mud path then swing left into a steep 180-degree left turn, where there are two possible lines. The inside line is shorter and therefore easier but deposits you on a low line across the next section, an adverse camber climb, giving you more work to do. The outside line around the turn puts you on a high line across the camber, and you have less climbing to do. At the end of the adverse camber section is another steep turn, this time going right, onto a tarmac road. Often you will see two riders take different lines through this section and come back together at the end, their choices apparently having made no difference to their position. The difference comes when the surface is slippery, making the high line very tricky to get up without putting a foot down – to do so you need to hit it hard and expend more energy than someone who takes the inside line. Being in a group adds to the complexity here, because if you're behind someone who makes the wrong decision, or is indecisive, you're likely to get baulked and lose momentum.

Past the pits and into the approach to this famous switchback climb, Noble loses momentum on a relatively easy section and slips back five places in a matter of seconds. Meanwhile Richards has manoeuvred herself into a position which gives her a clear run into the climb. While many of her rivals come to a grinding halt on that first 180-degree turn, Richards uses her combination of sheer natural power and mountain biking technical skill to ride around it, take the low line across the camber then charge up around the second corner. As Teocchi hits the long flyover climb, the British girl is not far behind, and leaving everyone else gasping in her wake.

Anyone who has done some road racing will know that going over the top of a hill is a good time to attack, because everyone who has gone into the red eases up, and if you have some reserves of energy it's a good time to use them. Richards catches Teocchi and immediately sweeps past her. It's a wise strategy because it means she hits the series of horribly rutted and wet and steep descents in the lead, with no one to put her off her line. Here her mountain biking skills are in evidence again — while other riders are forced into panicky corrections to avoid hitting the barriers, Richards picks a smooth line, keeps full control of her bike and takes a couple of seconds out of her pursuers in the process. Onwards she charges, with Noble and Van den Driessche looking pained at the wrong end of the top ten.

Just like Jens Dekker in the junior men's race, Richards pulls steadily away from those behind her, always looking in control of her bike and her effort. Once or twice she takes a visibly slower line through a relatively straightforward section, showing her inexperience, but it doesn't make much of a difference. As the race goes on I find myself peering at the big digital screen, then at her when she passes, to try to get a better look at her bike. It's a Trek in a red, white and blue colour scheme, and it looks familiar, though I can't figure out why without getting a better look. Confident of seeing the first British gold medal at the Worlds since Roger Hammond's win in Leeds in 1992, I rush down to the home straight to get as near as possible to Richards's moment of triumph. I get there after she has gone through the bell, but can watch her progress on one of the big screens. The British contingent, which is much bigger than at any of the other races I've been to during the season, have very sensibly set up camp in the grandstand by the finishing line. There they can see the finish, the podium and the big screen. And stay dry. When it comes to rain, the British have the best strategies.

I, however, am getting wet. I don't care; this unexpected performance has lifted me. If before I had approached this Worlds weekend in a rather analytical manner, now my heart is engaged as well as my head. There's a part of me that decries being partisan or patriotic, but there's another part, much stronger, that says, 'Give in to it. Cheer for the Brits!' As I watch Richards progress into the second half of the course, with all its climbing and descending, a rider passes me, running down the finishing straight, her bike beside her. It's Femke van den Driessche. She's had a mechanical problem, and it must be something with her gears if she cannot even ride her bike down the tarmac finishing straight. 'Poor girl,' I think. 'From favourite to nowhere.' It's a long run to the pits, and even if she gets another bike and carries on, it will only be for the sake of pride.

*

Twenty minutes before I saw Van den Driessche running down the finishing straight, Allister Tulett was standing in the pits, where he was helping out with bike changes for the British team. Next to the British section was the Belgian section, including Van den Driessche's crew. Tulett watched, perplexed, as a group of UCI officials came marching down the pit lane and approached Van den Driessche's crew. One of the officials produced a tablet computer, took hold of one of Van den Driessche's spare bikes, bent down and began scanning the bike's seat tube. The officials then seized the bike and took it away for further inspection.

One can only imagine the panic that must have set in at that moment. While Evie Richards was celebrating her brilliant victory, Van den Driessche's crew must have known what the UCI would find inside that spare bike – a Vivax Assist motor connected to the drivetrain and operated by a small button hidden underneath her bar tape. The motor is capable of producing 110 watts of power, weighs 4lbs and costs $3000. The UCI's new magnetic resonance testing techniques, also employed at events earlier in the year, had snared its first motor.

After years of rumours, and a fair amount of scoffing, motor doping had been exposed in cycling. And in the most unexpected place. The rumours and speculation of previous years had centred on the professional road men. Some had pointed to Fabian Cancellara's relentless speed over the Paris–Roubaix cobbles. Or the incident in the 2014 Vuelta a España when Ryder Hesjedal crashed and the pedals on his bike seemed to keep turning as it lay on the road. No evidence was provided to back up the claims, and the rumours seemed to fade away, but with their history of chemical doping, the men's road disciplines were always first to be under suspicion. For the first culprit of mechanical doping to be a young Belgian cyclocross rider, a woman, and a woman riding in a new category, took everyone by surprise. As news of the suspected motor got out on social media, the cycling world expressed its shock and disbelief. But many of those at Zolder were less than surprised. Van den Driessche's brother, Niels, was serving a two-year suspension for a more traditional form of doping. And then came the surreal story that Niels and his father, Peter, were in trouble with the police for the equally heinous crime of parrot theft.

In February 2015, two men entered the De Gouldamandine pet shop in Varsenare and warmly greeted the owner, Patricia Inghelbrecht. The two men, one in his twenties, the other much older, took their time looking around the shop, studying the rare birds kept in cages. Inghelbrecht grew suspicious of them and made sure to watch carefully the black spots in her CCTV coverage. Another customer demanded her attention, and while she was busy the two men reached into a cage, removed two parakeets and put them into a bag. They then left the shop, bidding her farewell as they did so. It was brazen parrot theft. It was also pretty stupid parrot theft because Inghelbrecht's CCTV had clear footage of the two thieves which, when posted on Facebook, led her and the police to the culprits. This combination of criminal activity and rank stupidity was on display again at Zolder.

With the technological fraud (a wonderful phrase coined by the UCI) uncovered, cycling journalists cast their minds back to the Koppenbergcross in November where Van den Driessche had finished second. Specifically, they pointed to the first ascent of the Koppenberg when Van den Driessche rode away from the best riders in the world. The video of that moment, with the benefit of hindsight, is eye-poppingly scandalous. Later in the race, again on the cobbled climb of the Koppenberg, the camera shows Van den Driessche having trouble with a gear change. She stops pedalling, missing two strokes, but her bike keeps moving forwards. Every cyclist knows that to miss two pedal strokes on a steep gradient like that means the bike will very quickly come to a dead stop.

Nikki Harris's husband, the Irish professional Matt Brammeier, had been helping in the pits that day and told journalists that there was a 'weird' atmosphere around the Van den Driessche crew and that they were all equipped with walkie-talkie radios and earpieces, something rarely seen at cross events.

Once the UCI had confirmed the presence of the motor in Van den Driessche's spare bike, her family put out a statement claiming that they had no knowledge of it. Their story went along the lines of: we sold one of Femke's bikes to a friend, who brought it to Zolder and joined Femke and Niels on one of her course reconnaissance sessions. He left it leaning against the team truck in the parking area, before a team mechanic must have mistaken it for one of Femke's bikes, cleaned it up and brought it into the pits. This implausible story was not a particularly wise line of defence for Femke because UCI regulations state that the mere presence of a motorised bike in the pits is illegal, irrespective of how it gets there. Perhaps the Van den Driessches, knowing they'd been caught red-handed, were just trying to save the reputation of their daughter. They must have known that the UCI would make an example of Femke, and that the Belgian federation would withdraw all support for them.

A few days after the Worlds, Femke appeared on Sporza to give her version of events. The interview, which was pre-recorded, took place at her house. Sitting at a dining table, in a dimly lit room, Femke has her blonde hair pulled back into a tight ponytail. Her hands, on the table, fidget with each other. Her dark eyes unwaveringly focus on the off-screen interviewer who asks interrogative but not unreasonable questions. At times she stumbles over her words and, towards the end, breaks down in tears. She repeats the story about the friend owning the bike, and claims to not be a cheat. She acknowledges that this could spell the end of her racing career, and says that she has no appetite for racing anyway. The interview has a staged quality to it. Van den Driessche looks like she has been coached, both in what to say and how to sit. Beside her at the table is her father, a bulky, bald-headed man in a thick grey jumper. He is silent initially, but then begins to join in, and at one point when Femke starts answering a question in faltering tones he speaks over her. She goes quiet, he puts his point across with understated force.

Before the advent of social media, this interview would have been carefully scrutinised and responded to by the written press. In 2016 this response comes far too late. Femke and her family have already been tried and found guilty by social media. But if television can no longer respond as quickly as Twitter, it can still produce the depth of sporting analysis that we need. The Van den Driessche interview holds a kind of morbid fascination because we love to watch liars exposed, and try to worm their way out of their lies. Ultimately the truth of what happened will probably never be known because once the UCI began formal proceedings against Van den Driessche she announced that she wasn't going to defend herself (her reason being the cost of doing so) and that she was retiring from the sport with immediate effect. The UCI continued with their proceedings and banned her for six years.

The interview is also interesting in so much as it tells us about the family dynamic that may have caused the whole affair. While there were hysterical (and possibly misquoted) reactions from some former riders – calling for life bans – most journalists and commentators noted that this form of doping could not be achieved by a 19-year-old girl with no assistance. In order to procure, set up and maintain a motorised bike, Van den Driessche would have needed help from her support crew. Indeed, given her family history, it seems likely she was pressured into it.

Writing in a Dutch newspaper, former professional Marijn de Vries expressed her sadness at the affair, but reserved her anger for those around the rider, rather than Van den Driessche herself. De Vries noted that she had witnessed many examples of children pressured to race when they didn't want to, of Flemish girls who only kept going because 'they didn't want to disappoint their dads'. She described seeing 'children forced to ride the rollers before a race, even in the pouring rain', and how she felt physically sick when she saw how the girls 'shuffled around with their parents, head bowed, after every race'.

Whatever the truth of the Van den Driessche case, it does expose the darker side of the sport. Where there is money, there is pressure to perform. This can be stressful enough within the professional structure of a big road team, but when your support team is your family, the possibilities for destructive behaviour are multiplied. If we assume that Femke's father was the architect of her downfall (this is unproven, merely a hypothesis) what does that say about his motivation? Presumably, it must have been financial. He can have derived no pride from seeing his daughter win races on a motorised bike. It's possible he derived some kind of absurd pride in having cheated the whole world of cyclocross. Either way, the best interests of his daughter were not central.

*

So much for the ugliness. Let's get back to the beauty. I'm standing with the British fans (none of whom, I should note, are dressed up in fancy-dress) in the grandstand. The third- and second-placed riders are announced and take their positions on the podium. Then comes the moment. The announcer calls out, '*La nouvelle champion du monde, Evie Richards.*' Those words, said in French, have an incredible frisson for me. They take me back to the World Road Championships in Plouay, France, in 2000. There, my father and I saw Nicole Cooke storm to her first rainbow jersey, the junior road race. She attacked with a few kilometres remaining and held a small lead as she came off the last small descent into the long, grinding uphill finishing straight. When we realised that she was in the lead, my father launched himself at the barriers and yelled, 'COME ON, NICOLE', at the top of his voice, shattering the eardrums of a nearby French lady, who seemed only mildly interested that there was a bike race going on. I can still hear the announcer's voice, '*La nouvelle champion du monde, Nicoooole Cooooke . . .*'

Here in Zolder, amidst the grim industrial landscape, with the Belgian team imploding unbeknownst to us yet, Evie Richards is pulling on her dazzling white jersey with its coloured bands. She accepts her gold medal, which catches the spotlights above the stage and shines out of the gloom as if illuminated, and we have a great big singalong to the national anthem. Among the crowd, somewhere, are Richards's mum and dad. In their campers, as they prepare for the elite women's race, Nikki Harris and Helen Wyman can hear the national anthem – though whether it inspires or intimidates them is hard to guess. After the jersey presentation comes the obligatory jersey signing. Richards is ushered to a table and given a black marker pen to autograph a stack of fresh rainbow jerseys. 'But I haven't got a signature,' she exclaims. She does a pretty good job of improvising. The camera focuses on her bright red fingernails, one of which is painted with a Union Jack.

'That girl,' Allister Tulett tells me later, 'is so strong she could win races on a penny-farthing.' With a cyclocross World Championship and a silver medal at the mountain bike World Championships, Richards has career options. Despite the lingering sexism in cyclocross, she could earn good money if she committed to riding a full European season. The combination of team salary, prize money and start money could add up to a tidy sum, and the physical commitment wouldn't, at her age, harm her ability to ride a full international mountain bike season. The important thing is the support structure she creates around herself – the team, the coach, the sponsor – and where she bases herself. Living in a foreign country with no knowledge of the language, away from the parental home, at 20 years of age, can be a lonely and disorienting experience if handled badly. For Richards, as for Gage Hecht and Dan Tulett, long-term career goals have to be kept in mind. That means staying within the shelter offered by their national federations.

The rain shows no sign of relenting. Neither does the Europop; nor does the mountain of potato lozenges being plunged into hot oil. Walking across the circuit I bump into Joos and Connie from the Kevin Pauwels fanclub. We exchange jokes about the Britishness of the weather, and I enquire as to Kevin's form. He thinks he can get a medal, they say, but of course he wants gold. They tell me that the course will drain overnight and be faster tomorrow, then we bid farewell so they can set off to find a spot up on the hill.

My nerves are beginning to tighten, as the women slowly ride their bikes through to the start line. To keep warm they ride up and down the finishing straight. I'm standing at the barriers near where the final flyover bridge hits the tarmac, a place where plenty of riders have slid off in years past. Katie Compton comes pedalling towards me, well wrapped up in waterproof jacket and trousers. I shout, 'Good luck,' to her, but if she hears me she doesn't react. She looks focused, as you'd expect, but I wonder what those eyes are hiding. Does she believe this will be her day? Or is she trying to suppress doubt? She claims to be 'over' the fact that she has never won the World Championship, but she's not very convincing when she says it. I want her to win today. I feel her sadness at this gap in her otherwise exceptional record, and I sense that it's a sadness that will bite for the rest of her life. With no Marianne Vos or Pauline Ferrand-Prévot, and on a course Katie likes, this could be the final credible chance of her career.

On the start line there are no smiles, no little waves for the camera. Not even the perennially chipper Eva Lechner is smiling today. As at the US national championships, Katie gets a good start. Coming off the tarmac she's in fifth place. She's done the hard work to get into this advantageous position, but on the first corner she makes an unforced error. She brakes too hard on her front wheel, the bike slides out from under her and she falls to the ground. Quickly, instinctively, she's back up and running. Her bike doesn't seem to be damaged. An innocuous fall, but in the first corner of a World Championship race it's a terrible mistake. By the time she's regained her momentum the leaders are far away, and there are twenty riders ahead of her. If she was the strongest rider in the race she would be able to pick off those twenty riders one by one, getting back to the front within two laps. But today she doesn't have that kind of zip. Every time I see the leading riders come into sight I crane my neck to see if she is coming up from behind, and every time I am disappointed.

For this race I've decided to position myself on the hardest climb of the course, and stay there. It goes up in two stages. Firstly there is a very steep bank of deep, wet sand. The riders come into the bottom of the bank at speed, dismount and carry their bikes up on their shoulders. To call it a 'run-up' would be inaccurate because it's so steep, and the ground underfoot so soft that it's more akin to climbing – and, indeed, many stick close to the side of the course in order to use the fencing to haul themselves up with their spare hand. The ground then flattens out for about 20 metres before climbing again, this time up through pine trees on a muddy but firm surface. It is possible to ride this section but you have to be feeling strong, and in the right gear. I wedge myself into the crowd just past the top of the sandy bank, and even manage to get a hand on the safety fencing.

And it's here that my wishful thinking for Katie becomes tempered by reality. The visceral intimacy of cyclocross means that nothing can be hidden. When a rider comes past where I am standing I can see everything because they are going slowly, and only inches away. I can see the strings of snot hanging from their nose, the shapes of their muscles beneath sodden skinsuits, the clumps of mud stuck in their gears, the sand clinging to their socks. Katie comes up the hill, and though she's still in control (her technique is second nature to her, she would never completely fall apart), I can see that she has given up. To say her mind is on other things would be daft, given the intense concentration required in a cyclocross race, but perhaps she is slightly going through the motions. This is the end of her season, perhaps the end of her career.

At the front of the race, a tight battle is unfolding between Nikki Harris, Caroline Mani and Eva Lechner. Harris rides clear but never gets a significant gap, and when she falters on the complicated switchback, the group ride back up to her. Sanne Cant is hanging in there but doesn't look comfortable. She's not able to dictate the pace of the race, as she has done so many times through this past season. Then, from nowhere, an orange figure comes gliding up to the back of the group. It's Thalita de Jong, the young in-form rider from the Netherlands. The large mass of Dutch fans gathered underneath the big screen close to the finish cheer, blow their air-horns and wave their flags.

I clamber down the hill, almost landing on my backside as my boots slip through the sandy gloopy mess beside the course, and rush back towards the screen. There I bump into Brook Watts and his wife. Brook is watching the race unfold with a look of astonished joy on his face. When the inevitable attack from De Jong comes, he shouts, 'THALITA! THALITA!' I ask if he knows her personally (such is the warmth of his enthusiasm for her ride). Silly question, Brook knows everyone. We watch the action on the big screen then run to the barriers to see the riders come through. The track here is flat but so waterlogged that sprays of water sluice up from the riders' wheels, soaking our feet. Thalita flies past. She looks good on a bike – tall, lean and powerful. The endurance and speed she's gained from a successful summer of road racing, together with her late start to the cross season, give her the edge. Cant and Mani are chasing but they look tired from a race-long battle at the front. De Jong's surge from the back is unstoppable.

As the leading riders leap off their bikes to tackle the sandy bank for one last time, a young woman walks towards Brook, his wife and me. She's short, bundled into a warm jacket, with a woolly hat covering most of her blonde hair. She has a vague, shy smile on her face as Brook throws his hands up in the air and rushes over to shake her hand. Evie thanks him for his congratulations, and, still pressing her hand, Brook makes sure to reinforce what a historic event she has taken part in. Then he asks to see her jersey. Evie unzips her black jacket and there, underneath, as bright as it looked on the podium, is the rainbow jersey. On top of it is her gold medal. I am so dumbstruck by this technicolour dreamcoat hidden beneath an ordinary winter jacket that I can barely mumble my congratulations. Brook, ever the marketing man, invites Evie to ride CrossVegas. Britain's new World champion then ambles off. She's in her own dazed world of happiness and thoroughly deserves it. While she might have natural talent in abundance, no one gets to pull on that jersey without a lot of hard work. Around the circuit, team managers from all over the world are doing calculations on their iPhones to work out how much they can afford to offer her.

De Jong wins, taking the Netherlands' second win of the day. On Belgian soil. The silver medal goes to a jubilant Caroline Mani. Sportswriters like to write about 'breakthrough' seasons, to the point where the term has become a cliché. Breaking through what, exactly? For Mani many years of hard work, improving results and steady progression has paid off this season. She has proven herself as one of the top five riders in the world. On her bright blue Raleigh with pink handlebars, she cuts a distinctive figure in any race. With Mani you know she's laying it all out there, and fans respond to that. Her counterpart, with regards to her riding style, is the veteran French pro Thomas Voeckler.

But if De Jong and Mani are overjoyed, for Sanne Cant a bronze medal is a disaster. As soon as she crosses the line her face becomes staring and sullen. She offers no excuses. The result wasn't close – even if you discount De Jong, who started the season late and came to the Worlds fresher as a result, you can't discount Mani, who has ridden a full season. Cant was not on a good day, it's as simple as that. Before the race she told an interviewer that she couldn't imagine training any harder for a race, so to lose that race, having been dominant all season, must be heartbreaking. There is another cliché in sport that the worst position to finish in a championship is fourth. Not for Cant. Third is the worst position, because it means she has to go on the podium with De Jong and Mani – she has to stand beside De Jong as she receives her rainbow jersey; she has to listen to the Dutch national anthem while thinking about what the Belgian newspapers will make of her performance.

As the three medallists prepare themselves backstage for the presentations a television camera crew catches Cant breaking down in tears. *This* is heartbreaking. She sobs uncontrollably. A man who knows her takes her in his arms. Behind him Richard Fries is watching, and he looks visibly shocked at Cant's tears. Fries knows cyclocross inside out, yet I sense in that moment he learns a little more about what it means to be the world's best rider, and to lose a home World Championships. We all do.

Exhausted, thrilled, and wet (so wet even the Euros in my wallet were sodden), I retire to the soulless, corporate hotel I'd booked a few miles up the road. There, lying on my bed, I watch the social media storm whip up around Van den Driessche. By midnight Twitter has her arrested, tried and thrown into the UCI dungeons. If Sanne Cant had worried about being the shame of Belgium, she needn't.

On a more positive, if still rather poignant, note, Katie Compton sends a tweet saying that at least one of her bikes has won a World Championships, even if she never has. Of course – that red, white and blue Trek that Evie Richards was riding was one of Katie's old bikes, complete with a stars and stripes colour scheme and KFC logo. Richards got it through a connection at Trek, and was rightly proud to ride it.

The next day is, you guessed it, grey and wet. Fans, media, teams, beer-sellers and *friet*-handlers arrive at Zolder early for the biggest day of the season. Since last summer the anticipation has been building for this day, specifically for the elite men's race and the showdown between Wout van Aert and Mathieu van der Poel. The season hasn't quite delivered a definitive battle between the two. Van Aert won all the early races while Van der Poel was out of action due to injury. Once he was back up to speed, Van der Poel began to win races, his first being the Druivencross at Overijse (the race with the racist Father Christmas) in early December and he has maintained that form all through January. The Belgian fans are hopeful of a Van Aert win, but fearful of their man's Dutch nemesis.

Having not won any of Saturday's races, and seen their nation dragged into the gutter of motorised doping, the Belgians are desperate for some success. The first opportunity comes in the Under-23 race on Sunday morning, a category in which Belgium has been dominant throughout the season, thanks to Eli Iserbyt and Quinten Hermans. For Iserbyt, like Sanne Cant, anything but a gold medal will constitute failure. With two laps to go, however, Iserbyt's chances are looking decidedly slim, and the local fans are hushed. A Czech rider, Adam Toupalík, not well known on the Belgian and Dutch circuit, is leading the race from Iserbyt and Hermans. True to Joos's and Connie's prediction the course has drained overnight, and the deep muddy puddles we saw the women splash through yesterday have disappeared, though there are still some pretty nasty ruts. Cheered on by a small but very vocal contingent of Czech supporters, Toupalík drops down the descents towards the finish line and powers down the finishing straight. He has one lap to go before he claims a World Championship.

With 100 metres to go he sits up, takes his hands off the handlebars and punches the air. The crowd gesture frantically at him to keep going, but he misinterprets their hand movements and responds by giving the universal gesture of trying to whip a crowd up. Meanwhile the bell is ringing, the lap board over the finish line says one to go, and Iserbyt and Hermans are storming up, hardly able to believe their luck. Only when they fly past him does Toupalík realise his rookie error. He sprints hard, but has lost their back wheel and is on his own. At the pits, which follow the finishing straight, his crew run out of their pit and lean over the barrier, yelling at him. Whether it's their chastisement (it's hard to imagine they would be sympathising with his predicament) or sheer adrenaline, Toupalík goes into overdrive. Every Belgian is shouting like crazy for Iserbyt, everyone else is shouting like crazy for the hapless Czech. Incredibly, Toupalík makes it across to the leaders, takes a minute or two to recover then puts in an attack. But Iserbyt has been schooled in the same professional world as Van Aert and Van der Poel – many think him their heir apparent. He isn't fazed by any of these events, and is confident that his final sprint will win him the rainbow jersey. It does.

As we all start trying to process what we've just seen, the elite men are beginning to appear for their warm-ups. With a lengthy gap between the Under-23s and the elite race, the crowd have time to get *friets* and beer and then go for a wander around the team trucks to see who they can spot and shout at.

I head back to the American encampment and stand watching the team warming up. The elite men look more professional, pound the rollers harder, and have more photographers around them. And yet the atmosphere is subtly different now. Where the United States team had realistic medal chances in every other event, no one expects any of the American men to be on the podium for the elite men's race. The best of the team, Jeremy Powers, could get a top ten if he is on a fantastic day, though top twenty is a more realistic objective. Geoff Proctor is still buzzing about, as he has been all day, but his role here is more limited because these senior riders aren't under his guidance and care. BrittLee Bowman is there too, supporting her boyfriend Stephen Hyde. Tucked into a hooded raincoat and stamping her feet to stop them getting too cold, we talk about our plans for the summer, the road racing team she manages in New York, cycling photography and websites. She's excited and happy to be here at the Worlds, but at the same time she takes it all in her stride. Throughout this season so many people have emphasised the separation between Europe and America, the cultural differences, so much so that the presence of BrittLee here in Zolder is something of a shock, as if she belongs in a different part of the story. But, of course, it's only a flight. If you have the confidence to say, 'I'm coming over,' who's going to stop you? As we talk she occasionally glances over to where Stephen is warming up. In the next two hours, if he has a good ride, his career could take a leap to another level, which could mean a European team, possibly a move to Belgium. It's hard to imagine BrittLee existing for very long this far out of New York's orbit.

Away from the intensity of the men's warm-up the younger riders, most of whom raced yesterday, are simply enjoying the atmosphere, and being free of racing commitments. Gage, back in jeans and trainers, stands at the tape, offering his rider cards to passers-by. Beside him are Allison and Hannah Arensman, twin sisters from North Carolina, who raced in the Under-23 women's event. They are also handing out rider cards and getting a higher hit rate than poor Gage. For some reason, young American girls with bright white smiles seem to appeal to drunk older Belgian men. They tease Gage, as you would an older brother, and I sense a warmth between the three of them that isn't flirtation (though it could be I'm just getting too old to pick up on such nuances) but is the kind of friendship forged between young people who have been through an adventure together.

I expect Gage to be profoundly disappointed with his performance yesterday, given his ambition to be on the podium, but he's surprisingly philosophical about it. In part this is because Gage is a naturally upbeat person, and in part because he has other ambitions running concurrently with his cyclocross career. But it's also a factor of taking a professional attitude towards his sport. By the time you get to World Championship level, even as a junior, most riders understand what it means to be a full-time, professional athlete. There is a time for throwing the furniture around in a rage, or going off in a massive sulk, but you get that out of your system and then you analyse, correct, improve; look ahead to the next goal, not continually back at the last failure. For

Gage's father Bruce, who is standing nearby, enjoying the atmosphere of his first World Championships, the fact that Eli Iserbyt has won the Under-23 race is reassuring, because Eli at 17 was in a similar place to where Gage is now. The Hechts know how Gage compares to Iserbyt and can use him as a benchmark.

There is plenty of time for that, though. Tomorrow morning there will be a lot of packing of kit and bikes and wheels, and then the beginning of a long journey back to Parker, Colorado. Eventually, thoughts will turn to the road season. Before that there are essays to write for school, and more hours in the cockpit. Gage heads off into the crowds with the Arensman sisters to find a spot to watch the men's race. With the huge crowd, and the general chaos of a World Championships, I sense it's the last time I will see him for a while, probably until the following season. Watching his tall frame bob through the sea of woolly hats, hoods and umbrellas, I feel a little sad that we didn't connect more, that our relationship was always encumbered by the rider–journalist dynamic. Seeing Gage in a relaxed, jokey mood with the two girls makes me realise that he was always a little on his guard with me. But that is understandable. After all, I'm twenty-five years older than him, and from a very different background. And I'm a writer, so he was arguably sensible to immediately be on his guard.

'ELITE MEN REPORT TO STAGING! ELITE MEN REPORT TO STAGING!' Richard Fries's trademark call pulses out into the still-gloomy afternoon. Every American in the venue, familiar with this method of corralling riders, smiles. Everyone else frowns. What is 'staging'? Does he mean 'come to the start'? Who is this guy they've got?

By mid-afternoon Zolder has the feel of an old-fashioned British rock festival: an all-white, mostly male crowd drinking strong beer with no attempt to be hip, counterculture or in any way mystic. Looking down I see thousands of wellies, broken plastic beer glasses and *friets* cones pressed into the mud. Groups of young men are staggering out of the beer tents, several sitting on the muddy grass with their heads in their hands. I see one lad vomiting onto the ground between his knees while his mate calmly carries on drinking beside him. Close to me a group of Wout van Aert supporters break into song and begin jumping up and down. The atmosphere has become more raucous and more tense. Drunk teenagers barge through the crowd. Rival fanclubs are exchanging insults which are, for the moment, good-natured. And over it all is the ear-splittingly loud music from the PA system, only interrupted by the announcers cutting in to shout about something or other.

The rain isn't as heavy as the previous day, but the length of time standing out in it has given me a chill I can't shake off. 'How I love cyclocross,' I think. 'How I can't wait for the summer and the Tour de France. Sitting on a grass verge in the Ardèche, eating bread and cheese and drinking a beer – that's the way to watch bike racing.'

The race is close for the first few laps, with more riders at the front than most had expected. For a short while Sven Nys takes the lead, to huge eruptions of noise from around the course. By the fourth of eight laps Van Aert, Van der Poel, Van der Haar and Pauwels are all in contention, with several other riders not far behind.

Then comes the moment that changes the race. Coming into the off-camber switchback section, Van der Poel is in front of Van Aert. The Dutchman tries to take the higher outside line but loses momentum, tries to cut across to the lower line, but can't avoid having to dismount. As he does so he closes the door on Van Aert, who has been going for the lower inside line, and the two become tangled. Van der Poel's right foot has swung back over his saddle and lodged itself into the spokes of Van Aert's wheel. Time seems to slow down. The crowd I'm standing with, watching one of the big digital screens near the finish, watches in silent astonishment, mouths agape. Van der Poel tries to pull his foot out of his rival's wheel but it's firmly wedged in. Initially they're calm, in that manner of professional bike riders, but when the foot doesn't come out and the two favourites for the World Championship realise their opponents are riding away from them, the body language becomes more panicky. Van Aert gives his wheel a fair old whack and the foot comes out.

Ever the opportunist, Lars van der Haar attacks as soon as the incident happens. Van der Poel and Van Aert give chase but within half a lap it's clear that the incident has affected them very differently. Van der Poel makes more unforced mistakes and seems to become disheartened; Van Aert, in contrast, is riding on adrenaline. It is as if his entanglement with Van der Poel has woken him up. Knowing he has three full laps to close the gap to Van der Haar he pushes hard but controls his effort. However, to the Belgian fans this is suddenly a heroic and desperate fight for the pride of their nation.

When Van der Haar comes into sight, some sections of the crowd – by now very drunk – spit at him and flick beer into his face. A few seconds later they lean over the fencing and shake their fists and roar at Van Aert to go faster. As Van Aert makes the inevitable connection to Van der Haar's back wheel, Richard Fries is shouting, 'HE'S BACK! HE'S BACK,' and the crowd let out a huge collective cry of relief.

The race isn't over, but the psychological advantage is with Van Aert. Coming into the final climb, the sandy bank combo, Van der Haar is in the lead, but he makes the rookie error of not changing down onto the little ring. So when he jumps back on his bike to ride up the second part of the climb, he's hopelessly overgeared and unable to match Van Aert's speed. That's it. Belgium's star becomes Belgium's superstar. Elated, with the crowd going absolutely berserk, Van Aert crosses the line with his arms aloft and collapses into the arms of his support crew. After all the media speculation and the resulting pressure, Van Aert has delivered on his potential. And he's done so on home soil, twenty-four hours after the Van den Driessche scandal engulfed Belgian cycling. Distraught, Van der Haar rolls across the line for a silver medal. The course suited him, and he knows that the Van Aert–Van der Poel entanglement presented him with a golden opportunity. For Van der Haar this is a disaster. Demonstrating that there is no room for sentiment in pro cyclocross, Pauwels makes a late surge to snatch a bronze medal from Sven Nys. But Nys, riding his last World Championships, doesn't seem too worried. He applauds the fans as he comes down the finishing straight, and when he sees his coaching staff waiting for him just after the line he is overcome with emotion.

For the American squad, the race has been another reality check. Stephen Hyde is the best finisher, in twenty-third place.

Jeremy Powers missed his pedal on the start line, hit the first few corners at the back of the race, and never recovered, finally finishing thirty-fourth. Whereas Hyde's career is still in its ascendancy, Powers, aged 32, knows that time is running out for him to prove that his star status in America can translate to Europe. In his post-race interviews the sadness in his normally upbeat voice is heartbreaking, and endearing.

The rain gets heavier again as the fans head either to the exits or the party tents, the mechanics wash bikes and begin packing up the campers, and the riders sip on their recovery drinks. The Belgian national anthem plays, the television interviews will go on for some time, but for most a quick escape is the objective. Back at my rented car, another little Fiat, I unpeel sodden layers, throw my muddy boots into the trunk and join the long line of cars queuing to get out.

Tearing along the motorway past Brussels, trying to make my Eurotunnel connection, scenes from the weekend play across my mind. I'm only awake due to copious amounts of sugar and caffeine, too exhausted to think straight, but in time I'll come to realise that these Cyclocross World Championships were one of the most intense sporting experiences of my life.

17

A Lifetime

Femke van den Driessche's motor, of course, was the story of the World Championships. It overshadowed all the other races and performances. In Britain it made the national newspapers, and you could sense the glee of some reporters: 'Look, cycling has sunk even lower . . .'

But for me those two days in Zolder were a fitting climax to the season. They were raw and visceral and tense. There was to be no fairytale ending for Katie Compton or Gage Hecht and no redemption for Dan Tulett, who was later diagnosed with viral fatigue. The weather was horrible and the landscape ghastly. But therein lies the essence of cyclocross: it's not supposed to be picturesque and easy. It's brutally hard. It's about a connection to the land, and it's unforgiving. Most importantly, it's dramatic.

There are many who want to globalise cross. Some see market opportunities, dollar signs. But most of those who want to globalise the sport are doing so for altruistic reasons – to give more people a chance to enjoy it. If the tentative expansion that we see now to countries such as Japan, Australia and China continues, will it be to the detriment of the sport? There will always be those who say it was better in De Vlaeminck's day, when men were men and all the biggest races took place within an hour's drive of Antwerp. And there are many fans of cross now who view it much like an underground music scene – it's cool, until everyone else finds out about it. But if cross is to thrive it must expand. Like a child growing up, it must be allowed to find its own way. To their credit, the UCI understand that and are trying to help cross grow.

In political terms, Zolder was a curious event because it looked like it was going to be an expression of the power of Belgian cross, and came close to being a disaster. The controversy around Van den Driessche, together with Dutch and British success on the first day, could be construed as a once-dominant nation trying desperately to hang onto its status in the face of newer, faster competition. Little wonder the crowd were so vocal when Van Aert escaped from Van der Haar on the final lap of the elite men's race. Van Aert was rescuing the nation's pride. In years to come, will we look back at that race in Zolder and see it as the swansong of Belgian cyclocross? It's hard to imagine so now, but in ten, fifteen, twenty years, will we see American men winning regularly in Belgium? As races like CrossVegas and Jingle Cross grow in status, they will be taken more seriously by European teams, and new generations of American kids will be inspired to ride cross bikes. Shifting cyclocross away from Belgium would be like turning a container ship, but perhaps the wheel is already turning.

Back in London, for the last time this season, I'm unpacking a rucksack full of sodden clothes, half-eaten snacks, media accreditation, Euros and phone chargers – the usual detritus of going to watch bike racing in Europe. Van Aert's clothing sponsor is designing his new rainbow skinsuit, and Evie Richards is still slowly floating down to planet Earth. There are a few more races for the professionals based in Europe, but they have a more relaxed atmosphere. In cross racing, the time to prove your value is December and January. February is too late. This is the time for awards ceremonies, parties and cringe-inducing television specials. For the British and American riders the Worlds are the last race of the season. The next few weeks are dedicated to recuperation. Thoughts turn to road racing, mountain biking, holidays, family.

A week after the end of the cyclocross season, on a Friday afternoon, I receive a text from my brother-in-law asking what time we should meet tomorrow. Not having the faintest idea what he's talking about, I reply with a confused face emoji. I've recently learned how to use emojis and like to employ them at every opportunity. Thirty seconds later I remember I'm supposed to be going to see Brentford play, with my brother-in-law and my father. My mum got my father the tickets for his birthday, back in January, and delegated the accompaniment to us. I groan inwardly; it's been a stressful week at work, I've got a head cold that makes me feel like a stuffed toy, and the forecast is for heavy rain. But, of course, I should go.

The next day, still feeling sick, and after an eventful night in which both my children ended up in our bed, I feel even more grumpy about it. I head for the train station, where there's a man in a booth who sells very strong coffee. As my train rumbles along through Lewisham and New Cross the rain begins to fall.

Soccer might be a moneyed game compared to cycling, but the glamour of the Premier League doesn't translate to lower-league Griffin Park on a wet Saturday in February. As we queue for a cup of tea, rainwater drips from the steel girders over our heads, pooling on the concrete floor. The gents toilets are down in the category of toilets where you don't want to touch anything, not even the wash basins, and it's best to hold your breath. There is beer for sale, but most people are drinking tea or Bovril, a meat-based solution that tastes of the 1950s. A vinyl poster on the wall next to the food concession menu catches my eye, and makes me think of cyclocross. It reads:

> It's not just a stadium – it's our home
> It's not just a kit – it's our skin
> We're not only 11 – we're thousands
> We're not just a crowd – we're family
> It's not just 90 minutes – it's a lifetime
> It's not just fun – it's our passion
> It's not just a game – it's our life

We settle in our seats and watch the teams warming up. The sound system is playing 'Rat Race' by The Specials, a band whose songs evoke for me the atmosphere of London streets before money poured into the capital, when everything was a bit more scruffy, when taxis wouldn't go south of the river, and bored kids kicked a ball around in empty streets. I was only six when the song was released, but I watched a lot of *The Sweeney*, the detective show set in London in the 1970s, when I was growing up. My brother-in-law disturbs my reverie by telling me about the meal he'd recently had a Michelin-starred pub. Whitebait to start, then some excellent duck.

Here lies the joy of modern sport. Social class still exists, of course, but when we walk into a sporting arena, whether it's a soccer ground, an ice hockey stadium or a cyclocross course, it is suspended. We are all the same. For an hour, or maybe even only for a few minutes, we forget everything else in our lives, and together we live out the drama in front of us. In Zolder I stood in front of a screen with five or six thousand others, and when we watched Mathieu van der Poel desperately trying to wrestle his shoe out of Wout van Aert's wheel we were all utterly absorbed in that moment. Half an hour later the crowd began to disperse, to go back to their lives, to work worries and difficult love affairs and the happy mundanity of the school run, restaurant meals, household chores, internet shopping and all the rest of life. Every facet of human existence is present at a sporting event like Zolder; within that crowd were all the universal truths of humanity – love, despair, hope, fear, greed, charity. The joy of sport lies in its capacity to allow us to turn off all that noise. We can truly exist only in the present, and that escapism is exhilarating.

In the first half Brentford are dismal. The visitors, Derby County, seem to have fielded a team of brutes who can simply barge the Bees off the ball and then punt it upfield. Sitting behind us is a chap who feels as frustrated as we do, but is happy to voice it to the players at quite a volume. 'Oh, that was fucking poor, Brentford . . . Oh come on, he brushed you off like a fucking feather.'

Astonishingly, Brentford limp to half-time with a clean sheet. After the break, they come out fighting, score a great goal and suddenly we're singing. From 80-year-olds with walking sticks to the seven-year-old boy sitting behind us. The rapture doesn't last for long. The singing subsides as Brentford repeatedly give away possession, and before long we're all shouting advice at the players. In football grounds *everyone* thinks they know what to do better than the professionals playing the game. It's not something you see at a cyclocross race. You don't get fans shouting at Kevin Pauwels to dismount earlier on a run-up, or exhorting him to use a different gear on the sandy sections. There is at least some respect for the professionals. Brentford cannot hang onto their slender lead and with ten minutes to go Derby equalise. They then score twice more and the home fans fall silent.

Walking back through the cold, damp streets towards the train station, I feel tired again. Not in a miserable way, just tired of winter. It's hard to believe that spring sunshine is on its way. I want that sunshine to come and warm my bones, I'm more than ready for it. I want to sit on a grass verge somewhere in France, with the crickets chirruping around me and heat radiating from the tarmac as a cavalcade of motorbikes sweeps slowly past, clearing the path for a glimmering, chatting peloton. And then I want summer to fade into September. That precious time of year when we begin hunting for clues that autumn is on its way – the shortening days, the early morning chill. When three words will yet again reinvigorate my jaded but deep love for cycling. Cross is coming.

Acknowledgements

I am hugely grateful to many people who have provided me with insight, friendship and coffee throughout the writing of this book: Elle Anderson, Charlotte Atyeo, Geraldine Bergeron, Joos Beyers, Martijn Boot, Derek Bouchard-Hall, BrittLee Bowman, Simon Burney, Louis Chenaille, Ben Clark, Ian Cleverly, Nick Craig, Katie Compton, Brecht Decaluwé, Danny Delchambre, Dirk Delchambre, Nico Dick, Gabby Durrin, Jeremy Durrin, Dan Ellmore, Charlotte Elton, Ian Field, Colin Garnham, Jenny Govaerts, Halcyon Books, Balint Hamvas, Nikki Harris, Gage Hecht, Bruce Hecht, Molly Hurford, Christophe Impens, Eli Iserbyt, Marshall Kappel, Luc Lamon, Shane Lawton, Chris Layhe, Mark Legg, Vincent Luyendijk, Robert Macfarlane, Michael Mayer, Noë Nachtergaele, Ken and Maureen Nichols, Ellen Noble, Connie Pauwels, Spencer Petrov, Jeremy Powers, Geoff Proctor, Karen Ramakers, Jonas Renders, Nicky Renders, Evie Richards, Brad Roe, Roebijn Schijf, Renaat Schotte, Dan Seaton, Gordon Siers, James Spackman, Allister Tulett, Dan Tulett, Ben Tulett, Katherine Tulett, Peter van den Abeele, Lars van der Haar, Gert van Goolen, Corné van Kessel, Ellen van Looy, Christine Vardaros, Rene Vermeiren, Brook Watts, Michel Wuyts, Helen Wyman, Stef Wyman, Jim Yeatman.

Index

Ace Racing Team   119
Albert, Niels   99, 146, 218
Albert Canal, Belgium   226
Alpha Bicycle Co. team   201–2
Amstel Gold Race   48
Anthony, Crystal   51
Antonneau, Katie   51
Arensman, Allison and Hannah   255
Asheville, North Carolina   193–4, 198–213
   Biltmore Estate   194, 198–9
   Donut Race   204–5
   Industry Race   202–3
Asper-Gavere, Belgium   95, 131, 148
Atkins, John   66
Auer, Kris   78–9

Bagshot Scramble   31
Baker, David   119, 120
BCCA (British Cyclocross Association)   63
Beard, Cameron   208
Belgian Cycling Union   41
Belgian Grand Prix   226–7
Berden, Ben   101
Biltmore Estate, Asheville   194, 198–9
Blue Lagoon Challenge, Iceland   5–6
Boels–Dolmans team   169
Boulder Junior Cycling   210
Bowman, BrittLee   79–81
   Asheville   202
   Koppenbergcross   76–8, 80–2
   Zolder   255–6

Bpost Bank Trofee (GVA Trofee, DVV Trofee) series   41, 42: *see also* Koppenbergcross
Brammeier, Matt   242
British Cycling   86
British Cycling Mountain Biking Academy   104
British Cycling Olympic Development Academy   218–19
British Cyclocross Association (BCCA)   63
British cyclocross championship   214–15
Bruegel, Pieter, the Elder   70, 73–4, 180
Brunner, Eric   208, 209, 210, 211
Burney, Simon   119, 123

Campbell Park, Milton Keynes   215–16
Cant, Sanne   107, 224–5
   CrossVegas   20, 21
   Druivencross   153–5
   GP Mario de Clercq   43
   Koppenbergcross   80
   Namur   169
   World Championships, Zolder   249, 250, 251–2
   Zolder   184, 249, 250, 251–2
Catford Paperchase   31
Caubergcross   48–51
Chabanov, Dan   56
Chany, Pierre   60–1
Charm City Cross   78
Christmas   137–8, 181–4, 186
Christophe, Eugène   31

INDEX

Clouse, Evan 208
Col du Tourmalet incidents 30–1
Compton, Katie 4, 5–6, 46–8, 134, 169, 197–8
   Asheville, North Carolina 207–8, 211–13
   Caubergcross 50, 51
   CrossVegas 18–19, 20–1
   Druivencross 139
   Gran Prix, Gloucester, Massachusetts 26, 27–8
   health issues 6, 18, 47
   Koksijde 97, 105–6, 107–8
   Manitou Springs Incline 132–3
   Namur 168
   World Championships, Zolder 247, 248, 249, 252–3
   Zolder 184, 247, 248, 249, 252–3
Compton, Mark 6, 19, 105, 132, 168–9, 197–8, 208
Conscience, Hendrik 71
Cooke, Nicole 245
Cowper, William 180
Critérium International de Cross-Country Cyclo-Pédestre 32
CrossVegas 14, 15–24
   first World Cup race 18–20
   sponsorship for 15
   as World Cup race 16–17
Cycling Weekly 31, 121–2, 124
cyclocross
   in America 56–9, 192–3, 195–6, 199, 200–1, 202–4
   and Beowulf 188–9
   characters on podium 156–7, 159–60
   design features 33–4, 128–9
   in Flanders 150
   functional threshold and 26–7
   hierarchies 165–6
   origins 29–32
   race format 13–14, 19–20
   rider expectations 187–8
   teams and 27
   techniques 32, 136
   television coverage 42, 44, 145–8
   in UK 61–3, 118–19, 199–200
   unpaid helpers 141–2, 165
Cyclocross de Montmartre 2–3, 32, 60
Cyclocross Development Race Camp 86

de Bie, Danny 222, 233
de Boer, Sophie 224
de Clercq, Mario 112–13, 161, 162
de Jong, Thalita 224
   Koppenbergcross 80
   Namur 169
   World Championships, Zolder 249, 250, 251
   Zolder 184, 249, 250, 251
De Leeuw van Vlaanderen (Conscience) 71
de Vlaeminck, Erik 65–7, 68–9, 100, 101, 102, 155
   Druivencross 139
   World Cyclocross Championships 65, 66–7
de Vlaeminck, Roger 66, 68
de Vries, Marijn 244
Dekker, Jens 166, 167, 231–2, 233
Denuwelaere, Jan 83–4, 85
Desert Breeze Park Soccer Complex 17–18
Development Cross Camp 89
di Tano, Vito 122
Diegem, Brussels 184–5
Dirk (fan club member) 170–2
Dodge, Cam 56
Donut Race, Asheville 204–5
doping 1, 161–3
   mechanical doping 240–4, 262
Douce, Steve 120

271

INDEX

Druivencross   67, 138–9, 152–6, 186
Dufraisse, André   61
DVV Trofee (Bpost Bank Trofee, GVA Trofee) series   41, 42

Eneco Tour   12
English Schools Cycling Association (ESCA)   215–16
equality campaign   42, 78–9
EuroCrossCamp   88, 91–2

Fennelly, Beth Ann   91
Ferrand-Prévot, Pauline   225
Field, Ian   177
Fight Between Carnival and Lent, The (Bruegel the Elder)   73
Flanders   70–1
Flemish nationalism   71–2
football   10–12, 264–5, 266–7
Freiburg, Germany   86
French Cycling Union   30
Fries, Richard   187, 209, 236, 252, 257, 260
Frischknecht, Peter   68
Froome, Chris   1

Gadret, John   65
Gaul, Charly   64
Gazet van Antwerpen Trofee   149
Géminiani, Raphaël   64
gender equality   42, 78–9, 100, 234–5
Gevaert, Etienne   40–1
Gilchrist, Sandy   123
Gloucester, Massachusetts   24–6, 27–8
Godefroot, Walter   71
Golazo   159, 173
Gopnik, Adam   46, 180
Gould, Georgia   197
   Asheville, North Carolina   211–12
   CrossVegas   20–1
Gould, Tim   119, 120

Gousseau, Daniel   30
GP Mario de Clercq, Ronse   42, 43–4
GP Sven Nys, Baal   186
GP Twenty20: 78, 79, 80: *see also* Koppenbergcross
Gran Prix, Gloucester, Massachusetts   26, 27–8
Grandstand (BBC sports programme)   120
Gravesend, Kent   115–17, 125–30, 131–2
   course design   128–9
   Cyclopark   115
   Under-10s race   116
   Under-12s race   116–17
Grealish, Chris   15
Groenendaal, Richard   45, 101–2
Grundig World Cup series   58
GVA Trofee (Bpost Bank Trofee, DVV Trofee) series   41, 42

Halfords International   120
Hammond, Roger   117, 220–1
Hamvas, Balint   74–5, 76, 94, 234
Harris, Nikki   151, 224
   Asper-Gavere Superprestige   131
   British championships   214
   Druivencross   153, 154, 155
   Koppenbergcross   80, 81
   Namur   169, 170
   Spa-Francorchamps   159, 160
   unpaid helper   141–2
   World Championships, Zolder   249
Hasselt, Belgium   34
Havlíková, Pavla   43, 107
Hecht, Bruce   202, 230, 257
Hecht, Gage   89, 90–1, 102–3, 201–2, 213, 230
   Asheville, North Carolina   207, 208–9, 210–11

INDEX

Koksijde, Belgium 97–9
Namur 164, 165, 166–7
Superprestige in Diegem 184
Zolder circuit 184, 231, 232, 233, 255, 257
Hemingway, Ernest 46
Hermans, Quinten 253, 254
Herygers, Paul 101–2, 148
Hill, Richard 52, 53–4
Hinault, Bernard 65
Hoban, Paddy 64
Hopkins, Tim 194
Hopper, Edward 24–25
House Industries–Richard Sachs team 79
Hunters in the Snow (Bruegel the Elder) 70
Hurford, Molly 56
Hyde, Stephen 79, 160
    World Championships, Zolder 255–6, 260

Iceland 5–6
Incredibly Cross series, London 58
Industry Race, Asheville 202–3
Interbike trade show, Las Vegas 15
Iserbyt, Eli 143, 253, 254
Izegem, Belgium 7–8, 86, 88

Jaarmarktcross course 34
Jackson, Alan 63
JAM Fund development squad 106
Jaspers, Jappe 166, 167, 232, 233
Jebb, Rob 39
Jefferies, Richard 35
Jefferson, Joe 209
Jim (friend) 127–8, 129–30, 131–2
Jingle Cross, Iowa 160
Julian (video producer) 154, 155
Junger, Sebastian 25

Junior Women Cross-Country Mountain Bike World Championships, Andorra 214
Junior World Cyclocross Championship 122

Kerstperiode 181–4, 186
Killeen, Liam 214
Kluge, Mike 222
Koksijde, Belgium 94–114, 148
    Koksijde course 95, 97–8
Koppenberg, Belgium 75
Koppenbergcross 33–4, 60, 74, 75–9, 80–5
    Nieuwelingen (Under-16s) 104, 218
    see also GP Twenty20

Landbouwkrediet 90
Landuyt, José 161
Lapize, Octave 30–31
Last Show, The (Belgian TV show) 146
Lechner, Eva 20, 21, 51, 170
    World Championships, Zolder 248, 249
Liboton, Roland 100, 138–9
Loenhout, Belgium 34, 185
London Cross League 115
Longo, Renato 63, 64
Lucca, Italy 86

McConnell, Mark 53
Macfarlane, Robert 35
Madiot, Marc 65
Mandalay Bay Convention Center, Paradise, Nevada 15
Mani, Caroline 170, 224
    World Championships, Zolder 249, 250, 251
Manitou Springs Incline 132–3
Marshall, Stuart 122–4
Martini International 64

INDEX

mechanical doping 240–4, 262
Meeussen, Tom 144
Miller, Amanda 49–50, 51
Moby-Dick (Melville) 25
motocross 172–3
mountain biking 57–8, 86, 118
Munich, Germany 96, 102, 148
Museeuw, Johan 161

Namur, Belgium 158–9, 163–7, 168–70, 176–8
Nash, Kateřina 20–1
Nichols, Ken and Maureen 62
Nicky (van Kessel's girlfriend) 144–5, 156
Nighthawks (Hopper) 24
Noble, Ellen 106–7, 235, 237–8
Nys, Sven 8, 44–6, 51, 77, 145, 162–3
    Caubergcross 50
    CrossVegas 21–2
    and doping 162
    Druivencross 139, 152–3
    and equality campaign 42
    GP Mario de Clercq, Ronse 44
    Koksijde 101, 110–14
    Koppenbergcross 83–4
    The Last Show 146
    Loenhout, Belgium 185
    training 135
    Under-23 category, Munich 102
    World Championships 148–50, 258, 260
    Zolder 258, 260
Nys, Thibaut 163

Olympic Games 14, 58, 96
Ortenblad, Tobin 55
Oubron, Robert 32
Overijse, Belgium 139–45, 148, 150–7
    Overijse course 34
    unpaid helpers 140–3

Paris terrorist attack 95–6
parrot theft 241
Pauwels, Kevin 112–13, 146–7, 174–6
    CrossVegas 23
    fan club 170–2, 173–6
    GP Mario de Clercq, Ronse 43
    Hoogerheide race 224
    Namur 176–8
    possible autism 174–5
    World Championships, Zolder 258, 260
Payton, Hannah 235
Pélissier, Francis 32
Pendrel, Catharine 20
Perfect Storm, The (film) 25
Petrov, Spencer 89, 166, 202, 232
    Asheville, North Carolina 208, 210–11
Pidcock, Thomas 230, 231, 232–3
Pikes Peak International Hill Climb 132–3
Powers, Jeremy 106, 135, 160, 177
    CrossVegas 22–3
    World Championships, Zolder 255, 261
Proctor, Geoff 88–90, 91–2, 164, 166, 183
    online journal 188–9
    Zolder 255

Rabobank team 45
Ramakers, Karen 140, 142–3, 144
Rawnsley, John 37, 38
Repack downhill race 57
Richards, Evie 214, 246–7
    World Championships, Zolder 236, 237, 238, 239, 245, 246, 250–1, 252–3
Robic, Jean 3, 32, 60
Rondeaux, Roger 61
Ronse, Belgium 42, 43–4

INDEX

Rough-Stuff Fellowship 37
Roundhay Park, Leeds 220–2
Royal Belgian Football
    Association 150
Ruddervoorde, Belgium 34

Saar Protectorate 61
Saccolongo, Italy 122
Sachs, Richard 79
Salmon, Fred 119, 120
Santa Cruz, California 54–5
Schotte, Briek 71
Schotte, Renaat 44, 45, 151–2, 154
Sellink, Manfred 73–4
7-Eleven 14, 210
Shaw, George 122, 124
Shrewsbury Sports Village,
    Shropshire 214–15
Šimůnek, Radomír 222
Sittard, Netherlands 86–7
Smirnoff Scramble 120
Spa-Francorchamps, Belgium 159, 160
sponsorship 6–7, 15, 55–6
Sporza (Belgian broadcaster) 42, 44, 146–7, 148, 149, 151–2
Stage Fort Park, Gloucester,
    Massachusetts 25–6
steeplechase 29
Stephenson, Denzel 208, 210, 211
Štybar, Zdeněk 146
SuperCup series 58
Superprestige Pernod International 41
Superprestige series 40–1, 42
    Asper-Gavere 131
    Diegem 184
    Zonhoven 52–3, 54
Surf City All-Hallows Costume
    Cyclocross 54–5
Surf City series 54–5
Switzerland 40, 41, 99–100

't Zand, Alphen-Chaam 134
Telenet–Fidea team 17, 140–5
Teocchi, Chiarra 236, 238
terrorist attacks 95–6
Three Peaks Cyclocross race 37–9
Toronto Star 46
Ťoupalík, Adam 253, 254
Tour de France 1, 12, 30–1
Tour de Trump 14
Tour DuPont 14
Tour of Alberta 17
Tour of Flanders 72, 75
Tour of Texas 14
training: group sessions 134–5
trou du diable, Critérium International
    de Cross-Country Cyclo-
    Pédestre 32
Tulett, Allister 104, 218, 219–20, 246
    World Championships,
    Zolder 239–40
Tulett, Ben 214, 219–20
Tulett, Dan 104, 105, 134, 217–20
    British championships 214
    World Championships 230, 233, 262
    Zolder 233, 262

UCI (Union Cycliste
    Internationale) 12, 263
    Eneco Tour 12
    and mechanical doping 240, 242, 243–4
    and mountain biking 57–8
    rules 13–14, 122, 128–9, 242
    World Championships 60, 61, 229
    World Cup 16, 229
USA Cycling 86–7, 88, 96–7
USA Cycling Cyclocross Development
    Race Camp 86

INDEX

Valkenburg, Holland 48–50, 51
van Aert, Wout 17, 99, 111–12, 113, 253
   Caubergcross 50
   CrossVegas 22, 23–4
   GP Mario de Clercq, Ronse 43–4
   Hoogerheide race 224
   kit 53
   Koppenbergcross 83
   Namur 176–8
   World Championships, Zolder 258–60
   Zolder motor racing circuit 184
van Damme, Albert 66, 67–8
van den Driessche, Femke
   Koppenbergcross 80, 81, 241–2
   mechanical doping 240–5, 262
   World Championships, Zolder 235, 238, 239, 240–1, 242–5
van den Driessche, Niels 241
van den Driessche, Peter 241, 243, 245
van der Haar, Lars 17, 21, 23, 43, 50–1, 135
   World Championships, Zolder 258, 259–60
van der Linden, Wesley 45, 46
van der Poel, Mathieu 22, 50, 99, 111, 253
   Namur 176–7
   World Championships, Zolder 258–9
   World Cup 224
   Zolder 184, 258–9
van Kessel, Corné 144–5, 156
van Looy, Ellen 80, 151, 184
van Paassen, Sanne 131, 160
Van Roy, Willy 152
van Wijnendaele, Karel 71–2
Vanderbilt, George Washington 193–4
Vanthourenhout, Michael 22
Verschueren, Jolien 80–1, 153, 172

Vervecken, Erwin 159, 173
Villeneuve, Gilles 226–7
Vos, Marianne 225

Watson, Kevin 37
Watts, Brook 14–16, 20, 194–5, 250–1
Wellens, Bart 143, 145, 146, 148–50, 186
Wellens en Wee (TV show) 143, 146
Wolfshohl, Rolf 63–4, 67
World Cyclocross Championships 60–7, 148–50
   Koksijde 100
   men's Under-23: 253–4
   Roundhay Park 220–2
   in UK 66–7
   women's Under-23: 234–5
   Zolder 225–61
World Road Championships 48
Wouters, Kris 140
Wreghitt, Chris 120, 122
wrestling 186–7
Wyman, Helen
   Druivencross 153
   and gender equality campaign 42, 78
   Koppenbergcross 76, 80, 81
   Spa-Francorchamps 159, 160

Young, Chris 120

Zolder, Belgium
   Boxing Day World Cup cyclocross 227
   World Cup 183–4, 227
   World Cyclocross Championships 225–61
   Zolder course 183–4, 226–9
Zürich-Waid event 120
Zweifel, Albert 99–100